ENVIRONMENTAL POLITICS AND INSTITUTIONAL CHANGE

RESHAPING AUSTRALIAN INSTITUTIONS

Series editors: John Braithwaite and Geoffrey Brennan, Research School of Social Sciences, Australian National Univeristy.

Published in association with the Research School of Social Sciences, Australian National University.

This program of publications arises from the School's initiative in sponsoring a fundamental rethinking of Australia's key institutions before the centenary of Federation in 2001.

Published in this program will be the work of scholars from the Australian National University and elsewhere who are researching and writing on the institutions of the nation. The scope of the program includes the institutions of public governance, intergovernmental relations, Aboriginal Australia, gender, population, the environment, the economy, business, the labour market, the welfare state, the city, education, the media, criminal justice and the Consitution.

Brian Galligan *A Federal Republic*
Patrick Troy (ed.) *Australian Cities*
Ian Marsh *Beyond the Two Party System*

ENVIRONMENTAL POLITICS AND INSTITUTIONAL CHANGE

ELIM PAPADAKIS
Department of Sociology,
University of New England

Published by the Press Syndicate of the University of Cambridge
The Pitt Building, Trumpington Street, Cambridge CB2 1RP, UK
40 West 20th Street, New York, NY 10011–4211, USA
10 Stamford Road, Oakleigh, Melbourne 3166, Australia

First published 1996

Printed in Australia by Brown Prior Anderson

National Library of Australia cataloguing-in-publication data

Papadakis, Elim.
Environmental politics and institutional change.
Bibliography.
Includes index.
1. Environmental policy – Australia. 2. Environmentalism – Australia.
3. Australia – Politics and government. I. Title.
(Series: Reshaping Australian institutions).
363.700994

Library of Congress cataloguing-in-publication data

Papadakis, Elim.
Environmental politics and institutional change/Elim Papadakis.
p. cm. – (Reshaping Australian institutions)
Includes bibliographical references and index.
1. Organizational change. 2. Environmental policy – Political aspects.
3. Political science. I. Title. II. Series.
HD58.8.P35 1996
658.4'06–dc20 96–15629

A catalogue record for this book is available from the British Library.

ISBN 0 521 55407 1 Hardback

For
Nicos Emmanuel Papadakis

Contents

Part IV The Media, Agenda Setting and Public Opinion

Part V Conclusion

Tables and Figures

Tables

Figures

Preface and Acknowledgements

This book reflects a continuing interest in environmental politics that was stimulated some time ago when, as a student at the University of Hamburg, I was captivated by the rise of new social movements that challenged the development of nuclear power in Germany. As I argue in this book, there are strong parallels between the concerns of environmentalists in Europe, in North America and in Australia. There are also definite similarities in the responses emanating from established political institutions. Although much of the empirical detail in this work is derived from Australia, links are made with patterns of political change in other countries. Above all, the work is located in intellectual traditions and challenges to these traditions that have emanated from and apply to many different contexts. This will become obvious as the reader works through the text.

What does need to be made transparent in the preface is the contribution by certain friends, colleagues and acquaintances. Anya Moore, apart from being a true companion, made numerous constructive comments on the entire manuscript. John Braithwaite, Peter Corrigan and Ian Marsh provided encouragement and detailed commentary on many aspects of the work. Conversations with and work by Ian McAllister, Clive Bean, Jan Pakulski, John Warhurst, Eric Livingston, Graham Maddox, Uma Pandey, Leslie Sklair, Barry Hindess and Bob Jackson have all been most helpful. A large portion of the data on public opinion is from the Australian Election Surveys in which Ian McAllister, Roger Jones, David Gow, David Denemark and Anthony Mughan have all played a key role. Gillian Evans and Jennifer Rindfleish both rendered fine research assistance. Gina Butler redefined standards of excellence for administrative assistance, and she was ably supported by Jodie Attenborough.

My children put the whole enterprise into perspective. As the book was in the final stages, my daughter attached a notice to the fridge door to the effect that the book was going well and that I was 'trying very hard to end it'. She also added that: 'Elizabeth Papadakis has been hard at work in school but she is now having a nice holiday at home with no work.' The Australian Research Council and the University of New England provided funds and infrastructure. The dedication is to someone who has always taken a great interest in my endeavours.

The author and publishers would like to thank the following for permission to quote copyright material:

De Gruyter & Co. Scientifica Publishers for extracts from *Political Theory and the Welfare State,* 1990, by Niklas Luhmann.

Sage Publications for extracts from 'Intersystemic Discourse and Co-ordinated Dissent: A Critique of Luhmann's Concept of Ecological Communication', 1994, by Max Miller in *Theory, Culture and Society,* volume 11, pp. 101–21.

Blackwell Publishers and Polity Press for extracts from *Ecological Communication,* 1989, by Niklas Luhmann.

Princeton University Press for extracts from *Making Democracy Work. Civic Traditions in Modern Italy,* 1993, by Robert D. Pitnam.

Columbia University Press for extracts from *Essays on Self-Reference* by Niklas Luhmann. Copyright © 1990 by Columbia University Press. Reprinted with permission of the publisher.

Penguin Books Ltd. for extracts from *Water Logic* by Edward de Bono (Viking, 1993) copyright © McQuaig Group Inc, 1993 and from *I Am Right You Are Wrong* by Edward de Bono (Viking, 1990) Copyright © Mica Management Resources Inc, 1990. Reproduced by permission of the publisher.

Abbreviations

ASEAN	Association of South-East Asian Nations
ACF	Australian Conservation Foundation
AES	Australian Election Survey
ALP	Australian Labor Party
CFCs	chlorofluorocarbons
CSIRO	Commonwealth Scientific and Industrial Research Organisation
ESD	ecologically sustainable development
EIS	Environmental Impact Study
IAEA	International Atomic Energy Agency
UNSCCUR	United Nations Scientific Conference on the Conservation and Utilization of Resources

PART I

Introduction

CHAPTER 1

Innovation and Tradition

This book uses the challenges posed by environmental issues to explore and test speculations about institutional change, and about the character and effectiveness of the political system as a whole. In other words, it focuses on the particular issue of whether or not political institutions and organisations can contribute to addressing concerns about the deterioration of the environment, and on the broader issue of whether or not these institutions are capable of dealing with all manner of challenges. This is not to underestimate the complexity of matters: in some instances political institutions and organisations may play a constructive role and in others a less than helpful one in dealing with environmental and other concerns. Hence an important consideration in this book will be to identify some of the obstacles that prevent effective policy-making. These obstacles may include the varying levels of power (say, between government, industrial and business interests, labour organisations, the bureaucracy and the legislature), the different interests (for instance, of labour unions and environmental groups) and the distinct logics of action (for example, of the political system, the economy and the legal system).

Another consideration will be to explore the possibilities for overcoming these obstacles and for achieving political consensus. The notion of consensus is closely tied to the notion of dialogue or, in the words of writers like Habermas, to the notion of conversation or rational communication. Habermas (1981a) has focused on what promotes and hinders communication, and has drawn the distinction between instrumental and communicative rationality. Whereas instrumental rationality implies attempts by social actors to measure as precisely as possible the costs to themselves of taking a particular course of action, the concept of communicative rationality emphasises the possibilities for mutual understanding between social actors. Hence an important theme of the book will be to reflect on how political and other institutions and organisations engage in some form of dialogue and how effective policies emerge out of this process. Consensus and dialogue will be treated, along with trust and goodwill, as key principles underlying any attempt to deal effectively with the challenges facing contemporary societies.[1]

As regards the arrangement of the book, this chapter describes the main themes and defines terminology, while chapter 2 looks at the rise of the environmental movement. Chapter 3 provides the framework for the discussion, and ends with an overview of subsequent chapters. In anticipation of the remainder of the book, this part will therefore expand briefly on the concepts of effectiveness and dialogue, on the notions of innovation and tradition and their relevance to the study of institutional change and on the notion of institutions.

The introduction of the concept of effectiveness immediately raises the question: effective from whose point of view? From the point of view of an individual or of a collectivity?[2] In other words, does the introduction of the concept of effectiveness presuppose a 'subjectivist' or an 'objectivist' analysis of interest? Or, more generally, does the analysis presuppose the existence of a 'social system' with well-developed interests? The notion of a social system is widely used in the social sciences to refer to the connection between the interrelated parts that may constitute a society or the components of a society. In the past this notion has been linked to a theory of society that posits a tendency towards a balance or equilibrium between the interrelated parts. Still, a focus purely on the social system invites ridicule from those who question the notion of an equilibrium between the interrelated parts, particularly in the approach by the sociologist Talcott Parsons which was most influential in the 1950s and 1960s. The main criticism of this approach was that it excluded the notion of conflict from attempts to explain social change. Other objections were: the notion of equilibrium in society was based on conservative beliefs, the theory did not adequately explain what was taking place in society, the arguments were circular and the approach failed to specify the connection between two potentially contradictory claims, namely, the possibility for individuals to influence and bring about decisive changes in society and the many constraints on individual human behaviour. In the words of an English-speaking friend and colleague of mine, despite the introduction by writers like Habermas and Luhmann of the notion of conflict into models of social change based on systems theory and their ability to address some of these objections, 'most English-speakers take out their trusty anti-Talcott Parsons shoulder-mounted ever-ready scatter-bazooka when they sniff "systems" '. My intention is neither to defend Habermas or Luhmann nor to provoke an adversarial slanging match with the proponents of subjectivism or those of objectivism. By effectiveness I mean the capacity of political institutions and organisations to attract support for policies, and then to implement policies over which there is broad consensus.[3]

The notion of dialogue, or to be more precise, of *constructive dialogue*, is pivotal both to describing the process of the effective implementation of policies and to prescribing a distinct approach. In other words, the notion of constructive dialogue can be used to describe empirical instances and can serve as an ideal type in the manner suggested by Weber (1904). Constructive dialogue refers to a dialogue in which both parties are looking for solutions that will benefit both sides, where parties attempt to develop an empathetic understanding of divergent viewpoints or of divergent goals and where this understanding involves goodwill, the willingness to listen and discretion (Handler 1988).[4] If a political or bureaucratic system is not open to constructive dialogue and to exploring new ideas, it is more likely than not to develop arrogance or complacency or both. It more easily adopts a bureaucratic mind-set: in other words, it responds to new challenges or ideas with statements like 'we have always done things this way' or 'we've never done it this way' or 'this sets a precedent'.

There is, according to many social scientists and bureaucrats, an inevitable contradiction between the bureaucracy as something that puts into practice the policies legitimately decided upon by a government in a democratic system and as something that exists to perpetuate itself. Weber reflected this pessimistic view. My own approach is less to deny that there are grounds for being pessimistic (hence the focus on the obstacles to effective policy-making) than to draw attention to the terrain that lies outside Weberian pessimism (hence the focus on the possibilities for effective policy-making).

Some will argue that dialogue, even if coupled with trust and goodwill, will not necessarily overcome the many impediments to effective policy-making. This is certainly the case if the dialogue takes place among people who lack competence – the necessary technical skills, for instance, in economic management or in understanding the dangers posed to the environment. There will also be disagreements over definitions of competence or of what constitutes an impediment to effective policy-making. It could even be argued that attempts to introduce new ideas or innovations serve as a distraction from dealing with problems in tried and tested ways. Although some thought will be given to these arguments, the principal focus in this book will be on whether established traditions and institutional practices (though not necessarily some of the principles that underlie them) do or do not represent a formidable barrier to addressing new challenges.

This leads us directly to the notions of innovation and tradition. Political thinkers have acknowledged that the survival or prosperity of a modern society depends both on innovation and on tradition. In his *Autobiography*, John Stuart Mill wrote that: 'No great improvements in the lot of mankind are possible, until a great change takes place in the fundamental constitution of their modes of thought.' By contrast, David Hume recognised that we draw assurance from precedents and past practices, and from beliefs, customs and ways of thinking that have been passed on to us. 'Custom', he wrote, is 'the great guide of human life'.

This book shows how both innovation and tradition can provide a basis for effective political action over the long haul, especially if they are based on principles like trust and goodwill. Tradition can represent principles that have stood the test of time and doctrines that have been passed on from generation to generation. Although some traditions, like an adversarial approach to politics, have stood the test of time, they are not always appropriate for dealing with new challenges (see below). However, in rejecting or questioning certain traditions or doctrines, there is always the danger of throwing out the baby with the bathwater. In other words, in challenging a certain tradition one may inadvertently be rejecting or turning a blind eye to principles that inform us of the motives and, above all, the consequences of human action.

Much the same can be said about innovation. Innovation will be treated as useful and important in so far as it represents an effective response to new challenges. Innovation is defined in the *Oxford English Dictionary* as the introduction of a new thing, the alteration of something established, a new practice or method, and even a (political) revolution. I regard innovation as an idea or practice 'perceived to be new by the relevant individual or group' (Hawkins et al. 1980: 192, based on Robertson 1967). Innovation may be based on strong underlying principles that lead to an improved understanding of the consequences of human action. On the other hand, it can represent a dogmatic and ineffective response to new challenges.

This brings us to the other central theme of this book, namely how established political institutions and organisations deal with new challenges. What do we mean by institutions and organisations? North (1990) has drawn a clear distinction between them. Institutions represent the 'rules of the game' or 'the humanly devised constraints that shape human interaction'; their role is to reduce uncertainty in human interactions. Organisations and their development are influenced by the institutional framework. In the sphere of politics, organisations include political parties, regulatory agencies, and the different houses of parliament. These political organisations can of course influence the institutional framework.

To a large degree, I will adopt this distinction between political organisations and institutions (see also chapter 4).[5] I will also emphasise the interplay between them: 'Both what organisations come into existence and how they evolve are fundamentally influenced by the institutional framework. In turn they influence how the institutional framework evolves' (North 1990: 5). Established political organisations are usually better placed than new ones both to take advantage of and to influence the institutional framework. This point is crucial when we consider the possibilities for institutional change and for innovation.

All this suggests that tensions are likely to arise when political institutions bearing the imprint of the past try to address some of the problems of the future. Past practices often provide a useful guide to what does and does not work. However, they can also present a serious obstacle to addressing problems in appropriate ways. The experience of the early 1990s suggests three things. First, the pace of change means that old policies and structures may be rendered useless. Second, there are many spheres in which some of the ways of seeing and doing things that have been handed down to us continue to lead us in certain directions despite the need for change. Third, some of the principles that underlie traditional practices may still be helpful in addressing new problems.

Our political system can be shown to be exemplary in both respects, in other words, in its capacity for adaptation and in its stubborn attachment to ways of thinking that prevent us from exploring new ways of seeing and doing things. Among the policies and structures that formed part of the foundations of the Australian polity in the early part of this century, the following have come under severe challenge or become redundant: the White Australia policy, the system of industrial relations (for instance, the shift from the imposition of employment conditions and wages from the centre to a less centralised system of conciliation), and the use of tariffs to protect local industries. In areas like environmental protection, perceptions have changed radically about the possibilities and character of economic development.

Several variables have been used to try to explain these changes. One of the most widely cited is the phenomenon loosely described as 'globalisation' or 'the global system'. This has become synonymous with economic forces that make it difficult, if not impossible, for governments to adopt a purely national focus. Another explanation lies in the proliferation of political movements and interest groups seeking to represent the diverse expectations of citizens. Another explication, often associated with the rise of new political movements, is that there has been a shift in values and a redefinition of what constitutes prosperity and well-being. For example, the 'postmaterialist' values espoused by many environmentalists (in other words the focus on a sense of belonging, on self-expression and on the quality of life) are perceived as part of a challenge to the ideologies that were associated with the great transformation of the nineteenth century, including the industrial revolution.[6] This serves to illustrate that 'empirical questions', like the impact of economic development on the environment or on democracy, reflect more than anything the values we place on certain lifestyles or forms of government.

These values change over time. The question then arises whether or not a system of government which once reflected certain values has become absolute or unduly restrictive. Political scientists may then choose to enter upon new situations in a variety of ways (which represent either an innovative or a traditional approach). They can attempt to justify existing institutions. They can describe how they operate in practice. They may even develop new concepts which allow us to view systems of government in different ways and to design improved ways of doing things.

For the practitioners of politics, the tendency is to combine innovation and tradition. Their endeavours in this regard often represent a superficial response to shifts in values or, occasionally, a deliberate attempt to draw on powerful principles that govern human action. Schemes of the 1990s to 'modernise' the Australian polity by promoting the concept of a republic straddle both: the traditional theme is the creation of a distinct national identity which dates back to the late nineteenth century, and the new one is the desire to become serious players both in the international, particularly Asian, economy and in the international political community. It is uncertain whether these efforts will succeed in drawing on principles that will result in beneficial changes for most members of society.

Schemes like those of the republican movement to make the best of both tradition and innovation alert us to the tensions that can arise when political institutions bearing the imprint of the past try to shape the future. Of course, like other political movements, the republican movement has the potential to 'unite' a variety of principles. Similarly, there are possibilities for finding common ground between the expectations of economic development and environmental protection. The question still remains whether or not our political system can free itself of some of the fetters of tradition, which include not only legislation enacted a century ago but ways of thinking that have prevailed for millennia. To illustrate the issue, I will discuss the adversarial approach adopted in political debates and in the social sciences, since this has an impact on policy-making in the area of environmental protection and on many other issues.

Adversarial Politics and Pragmatism

Political debates often reflect the limitations of our thinking about issues. For example, in debates about the welfare state, if you are not a wholehearted supporter of government intervention, you are often labelled an economic rationalist and an unthinking enthusiast for the free market (or a traitor to the cause: see Stretton 1992). Options like the introduction of mechanisms for greater consumer voice in the delivery of services are thereby excluded from debate (Papadakis and Taylor-Gooby 1987). Similarly, statements in favour of economic development are often read as an attack on the principle of environmental protection. No attempt is made to explicate how economic rationality can complement environmental protection (through the introduction of ownership rights, price mechanisms, tax incentives, tradeable emission rights and enforcement incentives). Much of this is linked to our use of binary codes, in this case 'environment' versus 'development', to process complex information (see the discussion of the work by Luhmann in chapters 4 and 5). Social and political theorists are often served poorly by traditional ways of conceptualising social systems and by traditional forms of logic (notably the use of adversarial logic and of rigid dichotomies and categories) when trying to grasp new situations.

This stirs up several issues about traditional ways of thinking. For instance, although we have inherited from the ancient Greeks approaches and forms of reasoning which have undoubtedly stood the test of time, we have also inherited from them ways of thinking which may be unhelpful in dealing with the complex problems confronting modern societies.[7] Take the adversarial approach to political debate developed and articulated by Socrates and Plato. Although this approach appears to be useful in controlling the behaviour of those with political power and in finding fault with their actions, it may present serious obstacles to working towards solutions (De Bono 1994).

The adversarial approach is used to great effect by the mass media. It is also a useful device to promote ineffectiveness. The adversarial approach emerges in various guises. It can involve the exchange of personal abuse among parliamentarians. This is usually reported in the evening news, as a headline item. Another tactic is to focus on the mistakes of a political opponent. This is widely accepted as part of a system of checks and balances and internal control. There is some resistance by people to the first tactic, the resort by politicians to personal abuse, though it is worth noting that exposure to that kind of exchange is bound to rub off on viewers (for instance by promoting cynical attitudes not only towards politicians but towards any debates about politics). One could perhaps dismiss this kind of exchange, not take it seriously and regard it as (perverse) entertainment. Still, the other manifestation of adversarialism, the focus on finding fault, is generally accepted as legitimate and worthwhile.

The benefits of this 'critical' approach to debating politics have to be balanced against the costs. The critical or adversarial approach can be useful in alerting us to the pitfalls of adopting a particular policy or line of argument.

- An exclusively adversarial approach can undermine attempts to learn about the real state of affairs because politicians fear that information will be used against them by their opponents. The adversarial system operates, after all, on the clear-cut division between friend and enemy.
- Adversarialism stirs up intolerance by detracting from attempts to understand differences in opinion. Promoting constructive dialogue and resolving differences between apparently conflicting choices become secondary.
- The adversarial approach operates in terms of rigid and absolute dichotomies: if a

particular policy is 'right' then another must be 'wrong'; if you are for the market you must be against the state; if you are for development you must be against environmental protection; and so on. This way of thinking, which often involves claims to represent 'the truth', means that more imaginative and constructive policies are ruled out of political debate. Political issues tend to be presented in terms of exclusive choices.

- Any insights into the policy process, any policy proposals, any imaginative alternatives are valued, in the first instance, less for their contribution to improving social conditions, than for their contribution to the denigration of political rivals.
- Finally, the adversarial approach leads to the mapping of particular standpoints onto actors so that they come to 'embody' these positions.[8] To defend a position thus becomes the same as defending oneself or a particular side or a particular constituency. This diminishes the likelihood that someone will change their mind as a consequence of argument and debate. To change one's mind becomes a sign of weakness, or even an indication that one lacks principles. All this is not to advocate the outright rejection of adversarialism, but to draw attention to its limitations.

Where adversarialism prevails, attempts at constructive dialogue may be viewed with distrust. After all, there appears to be a discrepancy between acrimonious exchanges on the floor of the House of Representatives and deals which are struck in committee rooms between opponents representing apparently irreconcilable demands. Adversarialism appears thereby to give dialogue and the pragmatic resolution of differences a bad name.[9] Yet it is worth differentiating between the concepts of adversarialism and pragmatism, even if we are led to identify them with one another in the existing political system.

There is a widespread suspicion of pragmatic behaviour, and it is often contrasted with idealism. The following account of the challenge by Alexander Downer for the leadership of the Liberal Party of Australia in 1994 reflects the understandable concern about pragmatism. John Hewson, the ousted leader, is portrayed as the energetic and hapless 'idealist'.

> Politics is not a blood-sport, John Hewson claimed in the middle of his final traumatic week as Liberal leader. He knows better now. It is also a grubby, nasty, unpleasant business. Having watched the political process up close for the best part of 30 years, I find it extraordinary that anyone finds the idea of a political career attractive. . . .
>
> Downer is what Hewson could not be. A politician, pure and simple. As pragmatic as they come, with few illusions, aware that you have to soil your hands to succeed in politics, and ready and willing to do so (Laurie Oakes, in *The Bulletin* 31 May 1994: 17).

Still, there are some drawbacks. Pragmatism and idealism (or action based on principles) appear to be incompatible. The idea that pragmatism (in politics or any other sphere of activity) conflicts with action based on principles is both understandable and difficult to sustain. It is understandable because pragmatism is often regarded as action based on the absence of principles and on the notion that the end justifies the means.

Despite this concern, pragmatism need not necessarily be based on the absence of principles:

> There is a justified fear of pragmatism because it seems to seek to operate without principles. This is nonsense because the principles can be just as much part of the pragmatism as are the circumstances. One strong reason for a dislike of pragmatism is the fear that 'the ends may come to justify the means'. In other words, if the end is worthwhile then the means of achieving that end are justified. Since different people and different bodies will have different notions of worthwhile ends, the result would be chaos and barbarity. Interestingly the very reason we reject this notion of the end justifying the means, is a pure example of pragmatism . . . We are concerned with what it 'will lead to' (De Bono 1993: 13–14).

The notion of pragmatism is particularly important in understanding how political institutions and organisations adapt to change. Political institutions are deeply influenced by past practices. Yet they are often struggling to address new issues. There need not be a conflict between principles and pragmatism in meeting new challenges, especially if we understand pragmatism as a concern about the *consequences* of human action. This insight is crucial to understanding the potential for political institutions and organisations to address issues like environmental protection.

CHAPTER 2

Stimulus and Response: The Rise of Environmentalism

Since the nineteenth century, there has been growing disquiet about the consequences of human action on the natural environment. The emergence of mass social movements, political parties and interest groups focusing primarily on environmental issues is a fairly recent phenomenon, and it provides empirical instances of the means by which politics deals with the consequences of human action. It allows us to explore the significance of theories of social change and of adaptation by political institutions. It creates opportunities to assess how our political system works in practice, and whether or not governments can deal effectively with new challenges. It enables us to consider the possibilities for innovation even though we still carry a great deal of baggage handed down to us. It suggests that we can draw on well-established principles in order to try to improve the quality of life. In sum, environmental politics serves as a stimulus for innovative institutional responses.

Environmental Politics

The new movements and political organisations represent one of the most significant sources of political change in advanced industrial societies for the following reasons. They reflect shifts in values and perceptions (like the endorsement of 'quality of life' and 'postmaterialist' values associated with concern about the environment, peace and nuclear disarmament: Inglehart 1990). Support for groups attempting to represent these new concerns rose steadily throughout the advanced, industrialised world in the 1980s, particularly among the young and those with tertiary education (Curtice 1989; Müller-Rommel 1989; Poguntke 1989; Papadakis 1993). The shift in values was accompanied by a loosening of the connection between political conflicts and the old social divisions based on class, and the erosion of support for the major parties based on these divisions (see Dalton 1988).

Paradoxically, the emergence of new movements and political organisations echoes the expectation by a growing number of people that political institutions and organisations, notably those that evolved during the formation of the welfare state in the nineteenth century, remain heavily involved in regulating the behaviour of powerful groups in society and in shaping the social behaviour of all individuals. For instance, in Australia the majority of people expect the federal government (and to a far lesser degree, the state governments) to assume a major role in encouraging industries which help to protect the environment, in educating people, and in setting standards (see ANOP 1991: 26).

Why do people still turn to established political organisations? The answer lies partly in the inability of new political movements to present a viable alternative form of government, and partly in the inertia of established institutional practices and traditions, particularly those associated with the electoral system, the media, and the connections between industry and the bureaucracy and government. The answer can also be found in the ability of established political organisations to adapt to shifts in values. Although the new green parties have been elected into parliaments all over the world, they remain minor parties.

Yet a transformation has occurred *within* the major parties. They have been receptive to the ideas of environmentalists. Although this response has often been superficial, there has been a deeper response, one that acknowledges shifts in values and shows a willingness to enact new policies, to appoint to positions of influence supporters and leaders of new political movements and, perhaps most importantly, to focus attention on the principles that underlie political decisions. All these responses have contributed to maintaining expectations that government can be, or at least ought to be, in a position to meet new challenges.

Institutional Change

Are these expectations of political institutions misplaced? Many politicians, notably those who favour 'market solutions' to problems, have argued for a reduction in government activity. To a degree, they appear to share the concerns of intellectuals about the effectiveness of government regulation (see Wilson 1980; Mitnick 1980; Breyer 1982), about the failure of the state to secure legitimacy (Habermas 1976; Jänicke 1990; Luhmann 1990a), and about the destructive effects of regulation on social life (Habermas 1981a). Some writers have argued strongly for a 'new positive role' for government which would be based on a culture of collaboration rather than an adversarial one (see Marsh 1995: 8). Though this study also focuses on the possibilities for collaboration or dialogue, it does not necessarily privilege political institutions and organisations. By focusing on political institutions and organisations, I am not suggesting that they will necessarily be the driving force behind social and economic change. Rather, I am probing the expectation – both of the majority of citizens and of many academics and commentators – that government is or ought to be the central force that can bring about change. I am also interested in the argument that government ought not to be a central force, and in exploring the claim that government is not or cannot be a central force.

The stimulus provided by new political movements and the response by established organisations to these challenges raise several other issues. First, how responsive have our political organisations been to environmental concerns? In addressing this question, I will consider arguments about how organisations deal with new challenges during periods of rapid social and economic change. Second, in so far as political organisations have been responsive, how much further are they likely to go? In tackling this question, I will consider the factors that promote or inhibit policy outcomes (like improvements in environmental protection, and new forms of compromise between economic and environmental objectives such as sustainable development). Third, are there ways in which organisations could become more responsive? For instance, how can we reshape political institutions to ensure the effective implementation of policies?

In considering these questions about the responsiveness of institutions, I should draw attention to the following developments:

- The environment has been on the political agenda for over two decades.
- Concern about environmental issues has become deep-rooted over this period and is reflected both in opinion polls and in the behaviour of established political parties.
- In response to threats to their electoral bases and to shifts in values, the established parties have demonstrated immense flexibility in their approach to new issues (Papadakis 1989; 1993).
- Although environmental problems now occupy a central position in political debates in most countries, some commentators have emphasised 'that so far no policy on any societal level has been effective in stopping the trend of progressive deterioration' (M. K. Tolba, 1989, Director of the United Nations Environment Programme, cited by Miller 1994: 102).
- The last point is an over-generalisation (which does not take into account improvements in certain spheres and, at any rate, involves complex calculations and arguments about how you measure total environmental 'deterioration'), but it draws attention to the problem of institutional responsiveness to environmental concerns. It also helps to direct attention to two arguments. One is that any attempt by established organisations to adopt the green agenda involves an exercise in cynical politics. The other is that the agendas of established parties and of a truly green politics are irreconcilable (see Goodin 1992).
- Finally, and this represents a contrasting perspective, there has recently been a dramatic shift in focus by national governments, business and other groups to try to achieve environmental *and* economic goals. This shift has been guided by new concepts like sustainable development (World Commission on Environment and Development 1990; von Weizsäcker 1994; Schmidheiny 1992). It also reflects an interest by political parties, interest groups and social movements in constructive dialogue.

Dialogue or Cynical Politics?

Despite the prominence of environmental issues on the political agenda, people have questioned the sincerity and ability of established political organisations in taking up concerns about the environment (see Goodin 1992: 12–13). Criticism of established organisations is founded on notions of a fundamental conflict between principles and pragmatism, and it recommends that the former should prevail. Sceptics still argue that attempts by established organisations, including business and industry, to rescue the environment, represent a superficial embrace. They point to the failure by governments, like the Australian one, to take the initiative on issues like the emission of greenhouse gases and the neglect by political parties to adopt ecologically sustainable management.

This book presents a less exclusive account. It acknowledges that business and political elites have been slow and reluctant to embrace environmentalism. It tries to understand why they have been ineffective in trying to address some environmental concerns. It also demonstrates that environmentalists, by influencing perceptions, are bringing about changes in institutional practices and in values and behaviour. Far from being superficial, the approach by some business and political elites to environmental protection has become so comprehensive that it is now unconventional not to be green.

This is not to suggest that environmental protection will inevitably prevail over economic development. Multinational companies will take advantage of the differences in regulations between nation-states (Sklair 1994a; 1994b). Businesses will exploit the loopholes in legislation in order to maintain profits. Tensions will remain between environmental and other goals – including concerns about profits, markets and competition, as well as social justice, population policy, and other definitions of the quality of life. Still, there are many examples and new proposals to reconcile these goals (World Commission on Environment and Development 1990; Elkington and Burke 1987; Simonis 1989; Buchholz et al. 1992; Schmidheiny 1992; von Weizsäcker 1994). Governments, partly under pressure from their own citizens, are aware of the need for new regulations and agreements between nation-states to protect the environment. Despite the problems of coordination (between politics and business, between environmental concerns and economic interests), all sectors of society are addressing environmental problems.

Concern about the environment is more than a passing fashion. It is associated with shifts in values and a preoccupation with the quality of life in the home and in the workplace. The definition of quality of life goes beyond the enduring concerns about security of employment, food and shelter. Interest in the quality of life impinges on the symbiotic relationship between formal employment and the informal sector (the home, the family and other social networks). Questions are raised about the location and character of employment (a job that offers the possibility of self-realisation, safe work conditions, a workplace free of fear and harassment, and a reduction of commuting time and the concept of telecommuting), about a more flexible approach to working hours, about the relation of work to family and other commitments, and about new arrangements for monitoring actual work performance. Pressure for reform in the workplace is occurring in parallel with changes in our perceptions of family life, relationships between spouses, and the raising of children. Although some of these issues are not directly related to the interest in environmental protection, they reflect concerns raised by environmentalists about the quality of life. These quality-of-life issues may give rise to new social movements and lead to further radical shifts in the agenda of established parties and interest groups. Above all, the preoccupation with the quality of life reflects the doubts about some of the definitions, categories and dichotomies that have been used to describe human behaviour over the past century.

Concerns with economic survival—the so-called traditional economic issues of unemployment, prices, inflation and taxation—all continue to play a significant and fundamental role in politics. Yet a growing number of people conceive economic and other issues in terms of improving the quality of life. Issues like the health system, education and care for the aged are deemed important not purely for the sake of survival, but in the context of improvements in the quality of life. This view does not accept the dichotomy posited by traditional social reformers between the market and the state, or between the economic and the social; it extends the definition of quality of life beyond basic needs for survival. Environmentalism, along with concerns about the quality of health care, of employment and of education, all serve to remind us of this shift in priorities as certain needs have been met for growing sections of the population.[10]

The rise in environmentalism is linked to much more than the obvious signs of deterioration in the physical environment. It is associated with changes in the social structure, with efforts to adapt to technological change, and with rising levels of education. Among the most significant factors contributing to the spread and durability of environmental values is the instruction of children in the classroom. In a national opinion survey, 69 per cent of 14–20-year-old students at high school mentioned the classroom as a source of information about the environment. Television news and current affairs was mentioned by only 46 per cent, and other sources by a far smaller number (ANOP 1991: 115, table 15.1). Among all 14–20-year-olds, the classroom was mentioned about as frequently as television news and current affairs (50 and 52 per cent respectively). More significantly, 84 per cent of those at high school rated education institutions as credible sources of information (ANOP 1991: 119, table 17.1). Although many children will grow to experience tensions between environmental and other values, they are likely to be highly sensitive to environmental concerns.

The environmental movement forms an integral part of attempts to reconceptualise and design policies on many issues: economic growth, the measurement of wealth and of GNP, the relations between wealthy and poor countries, energy and material resources, transport, agriculture, biological diversity, making polluters and consumers pay more realistic costs for environmental damage, taxation, the relationship between farm and country, and international relations. Despite many setbacks, reformers within government and business are attempting to address in a constructive manner the tensions between economic and environmental goals. There are efforts at all levels of society to implement measures for environmental protection and to explore opportunities for combining environmental protection with gains in economic efficiency and commercial exploitation.

Established organisations and most citizens have generally responded slowly to shifts in values. A minority among the political elites have promoted environmental values since the 1960s. A few businesses, including some of the most powerful ones, realised that these values represented more than a fleeting trend. Still, the process of change was haphazard. Environmental protection was regarded by most governments and by business as a nuisance. It represented a challenge to the paradigm of economic growth and profits, and a source of disruption to plans that had been elaborately laid out. In the Federal Republic of Germany, prior to the emergence of a social movement opposed to the development of nuclear energy, the Nuclear Research Centre in Jülich drew up plans, in 1975, for the construction of 350 nuclear power stations by the year 2000; yet, within a few years, following pressure by environmental groups, these plans were scaled down by a factor of ten—to only 33 power stations by the year 2000 (Papadakis 1984: 102).

Some businesses responded flexibly to the new challenges. By 1980 most of the major corporations involved in the nuclear energy industry in Germany had diversified into developing solar energy (see Papadakis 1984: 108). Some corporations are now playing a leading role in addressing environmental problems, and forming coalitions with environmental groups. In certain respects, business can be made more accountable than government. Though governments can be elected out of office every three or four years, businesses cannot afford to wait that long when facing consumer boycotts of their products if they do not respond to changing preferences and values. Moreover, businesses may not have as many opportunities as governments to argue that they are trying to reconcile conflicting goals and values. McEachern (1991, chapter 6) provides a useful account of both the limits of, and the possibilities for, action by Australian business. He draws on a wide range of neo-Marxist literature, on the influential arguments about corporatism, and on the work of pluralists like Lindblom (1977), to remind us of the privileges enjoyed by business both in and over the political process.

Like governments, environmental groups cannot afford to ignore the influence of business. Groups like Friends of the Earth, though critical of development, play a key role in negotiating with business groups in centres of political influence like Washington (Parker 1991). The notion of sustainable development has been used to forge close links between economic and environmental concerns by governments and by business and environmental groups. For some, however, the notion of sustainable development represents a new form of 'environmental managerialism' (see Redclift 1987; Martinez-Alier 1990), in other words, the introduction of 'environmental and resource management considerations, generally in a cost-benefit formulation, into the national and subnational planning methodologies originally formulated to help Third World states increase their ability to rationalise and control their economies' (Buttel 1992: 19).

Though some environmentalists are troubled by the fact that businesses that have contributed to environmental destruction are now involved in planning for environmental protection, organisations like the private non-profit body Earthwatch regard business as the most capable in meeting the challenges ahead: 'The sheer velocity of change will put a lot of pressure on government agencies so they cannot cope. Business will have an increasing role because it is more adaptive. Major companies, attentive to their own total quality management, are already retraining their staff to be better resource managers' (Brian Rosborough, President of Earthwatch, *The Australian* 6 April 1994). Apart from responding to public demands for cleaner air and water, business has a vested interest in heeding the warnings of environmentalists about sustainability. Business is also in a position to exploit opportunities for addressing major environmental problems that have become apparent in East

European countries following the collapse of communism. In Asia, where economic growth is likely to accelerate over the coming years, businesses could profit if they collaborated with governments, on the premise that environmental protection is necessary both for profitability and for the long-term survival of communities.

Development agencies like the World Bank and the Asian Development Bank have also come to play a significant role, notably through linking aid to environmental protection and resource management (*The Australian* 6 April 1994: 29). Although tensions have arisen between the interests of developing nations and the new coalition of business and environmental groups in the Western world (see Buttel 1992: 20), Asian governments are applying the concept of better resource management and environmental protection. Again, there are sound economic, social and political reasons for adopting these concepts. For instance, there may be huge profits in developing new technologies for environmental protection. There is evidence that even in countries that have only recently begun to follow the path of rapid industrialisation, there is significant concern about environmental protection. Take the Chipko movement, comprising mainly women in Indian villages, which protested against the logging of trees; in 1980 it extracted a significant concession from the government, namely a ban for fifteen years on green felling in the Himalayan forests of Uttar Pradesh. Like other Asian countries, India has experienced environmental disasters, as in the city of Bhopal in 1984, when poison gas released from the Union Carbide pesticide plant killed at least 2500 people immediately and afflicted about 100 000 people with permanent and severe disabilities. Finally, the same Western nations that have contributed to the export of dangerous chemical plants to Asian countries are also insisting on more rigorous environmental standards in international fora, as in the agreements to protect the ozone layer.

The preceding account may give the impression that flexible responses by governments and by business will secure an accommodation between conflicting goals. Though significant changes have occurred recently, the question remains whether or not established political parties and other organisations have responded appropriately to new challenges, or are even capable of doing so.

CHAPTER 3

Framing the Analysis

One of the central arguments in this book is that the spread of environmental values is founded on successful attempts to adopt and promote new concepts. I am using the term *concept* in both a general and a specific sense. In a general sense, it refers to an idea or theoretical construct (for instance, the notion of 'the limits to economic growth'). In a specific sense, it refers to a procedure (for instance, the practice of 'ecologically sustainable development').[11]

By focusing on conceptual innovations (and on changes in perceptions and behaviour that have followed from them), I intend to explore:

- how environmentalism has come to play a more prominent role on the political agenda;
- why the response by established elites has, for long periods of time, been slow, protracted and uncoordinated and, at others, rapid and on a large scale; and
- how established political organisations may, in future, be better able to deal with issues raised by social movements, pressure groups and other concerned citizens.

The previous chapters foreshadowed some of the obstacles and possibilities for political institutions and organisations in meeting new challenges. These obstacles and possibilities will be discussed in more detail in the following chapters. Before exploring these further, I will outline some of the speculations that will guide the empirical analysis of environmental politics and institutional change. The overall scheme is presented in Figure 3.1, which depicts a hypothesised sequence of how certain groups shape the policy agenda and public opinion. The rationale for this scheme will be developed more fully in later chapters. For instance, part II focuses on the influence of political institutions, social movements, political elites and expert communities on social change, part III on the ways in which political parties adapt to and shape the policy agenda, and part IV on competing accounts of the role of the mass media and public opinion in these processes.

It is important to emphasise that the model presented in figure 3.1 serves as a heuristic device. It is not an attempt to prejudge the questions raised so far and in subsequent chapters (and I have deliberately placed a bracket around the arrows).

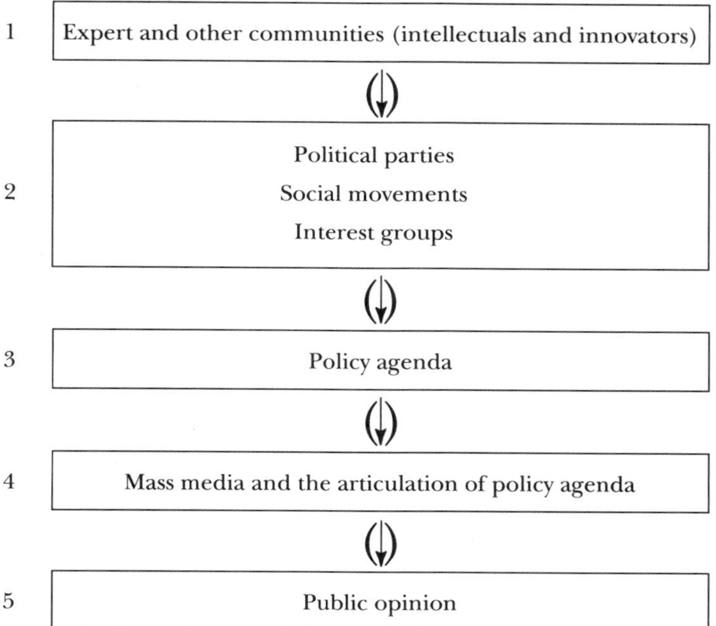

Figure 3.1 Hypothetical sequence of the shaping of the policy agenda and public opinion by certain groups

Beginning with the first row, the role of expert and other communities, the focus is on how new concepts are formulated and how, if the opportunity arises, an issue can become politically significant. The opportunities are of course determined, as noted earlier, by institutions and by the prevailing rules of the game. Although figure 3.1 does not refer directly to institutions, it is understood that they play a crucial role in shaping the process whereby certain groups influence the policy agenda and public opinion.

Figure 3.1 focuses primarily on political organisations and other actors that might influence and reshape institutional practices (in other words, on the dynamism of these organisations and actors). For instance, opportunities for changing institutional practices are created not only by expert communities but also by political organisations that take up the new concepts that emerge from these communities. In other words, if political parties or social movements or interest groups see new concepts generated by expert and other communities as having value, they attempt to place them on the political agenda and claim them as their own.

This leads us to the second row: political parties, social movements and interest groups all contribute to setting the agenda for politics and to reshaping institutions. Again, their opportunities are constrained by institutions. However, political organisations can all, in different ways, set the policy agenda (row three). The media (in the fourth row) are a crucial instrument for political organisations seeking to set the agenda. Information from the media is crucial in framing and forming public opinion (in the fifth row).

Public opinion, which in this analysis is placed at the end of the causal chain, is not usually proactive but rather reactive. Yet, as I argue in chapter 15, depending on the circumstances and on how one defines it, public opinion may either be open to manipulation or represent the considered judgement of policy issues. In the latter case, public opinion can play a vital role in bringing about shifts in policy direction. This serves to draw attention to two key features of figure 3.1. First, as I have already suggested, it represents *speculations* rather than a precise account of how matters actually work; the arrows could, after consideration of the evidence, travel in different directions. Second, as I shall elaborate below, the diagram displays to the reader the overall structure of the book.

The reader should not be misled by the simplicity of the diagram. Just as public opinion may exert considerable pressure on political parties, social movements are sometimes not only quicker off the mark than established organisations in taking up new ideas, they are themselves innovators. On other occasions, political parties pre-empt an initiative being embraced by social movements. There are situations in which political parties have been so slow in accommodating shifts in outlook that new political parties have been formed to articulate some of the concerns of environmentalists, including the so-called 'new politics' parties.

In reporting on environmental issues, the media do not necessarily rely on one source. They draw on the expertise of scientists and the arguments of intellectuals as well as on information provided by established parties, by governments and by social movements.

Finally, the way in which new concepts become politically significant will vary according to particular contexts. There is no predicting when, how and where they will assume significance. Again, it is worth reiterating that, provided new concepts can be formulated and political organisations grasp the opportunity to promote these concepts, an issue that has smouldered in the background of political debate for long periods of time (for decades or even centuries) can rapidly become politically significant.

Although this represents a simplified account of the way in which policy and opinion are shaped, it serves as a useful tool for organising the remainder of this book which, to a large degree, follows the sequence presented in figure 3.1. However, rather than begin by focusing on expert communities and the question of the origins of ideas about the environment, part II will pick up some of the key questions raised in the preceding chapters, notably the possibilities for political institutions to bring about social change.

Chapter 4 tackles the questions raised by many writers about the 'centrality' of political institutions in effecting social change, and about the concepts used in political analysis. Chapter 5 deals with the challenge posed by writers like Luhmann about the circularity of political communication, and suggests that dialogue and rational communication are feasible and can lead to desirable outcomes. Chapter 6 also takes up the challenge of how political institutions can become more responsive to new issues by focusing on the role and significance of social movements, and by considering how they can disrupt the established processes of communication and induce innovation and social change. Chapter 7 develops arguments about evolution and design or creativity, showing how the environmental movement exemplifies the processes of evolution and innovation. In examining innovation and the introduction of new concepts, close attention is paid to the role of elites and expert communities as well as social movements.

The themes of evolution and innovation also run through parts III and IV. In part III (chapters 8 to 12) attention is directed towards established political parties and their response to environmental problems. These chapters present a detailed analysis of the platforms and policy speeches of the major Australian political parties over several decades. Part IV considers the role of the media in articulating issues and policies. In particular, chapter 13 discusses the role of the media in setting the political agenda and in reporting environmental issues over several decades. The analysis focuses on the sources of information for the media and the intensity of coverage. Chapter 14 considers the kinds of stereotypes which are reaffirmed in media coverage. Chapters 15 and 16 examine the role and pattern of public opinion in environmental politics. Key themes arising in these chapters include the ambivalence in public opinion, the consistency of attitudes about environmental issues, and changes over time. The analysis focuses on issues like uranium mining and nuclear energy, forests, conservation, mining, sustainable development and pollution.

The final part of the book (chapter 17) summarises some of the reasons for being both pessimistic and optimistic about the possibilities for politics to respond to challenges and for the political system to be effective. It outlines some of the ways in which established political organisations and institutions can embrace new issues, adopt new ideas and discoveries, articulate political issues, and influence public opinion. In sum, this chapter revisits arguments about whether our political structures have been rendered otiose and whether our political institutions can address new challenges. Although recognising the limitations to introducing effective reforms, this chapter concludes that if political actors and institutions place less emphasis on the search for absolute truths and on fundamental conflicts, there is potential for dealing with new situations in a constructive manner.

PART II

Political Institutions, Innovation and Social Change

CHAPTER 4

The 'Centrality' of Political Institutions

Can contemporary political institutions and organisations respond effectively to challenges like the disquiet about the environment? Can they defuse the conflict between environment and development, and then implement ideas like sustainable development? This chapter and the following one focus on concepts developed by social and political theorists which have guided discussions about the limits and likelihood of political action in general. This chapter will begin by giving further consideration to the notion of institutions. I will also concentrate on how social and political theorists frame their analyses of institutions and organisations. Do they, for instance, assign to political institutions and organisations a 'central' status in the social system? The final part of this chapter will centre on the relevance of traditional concepts for analysing institutions, and on the tendency of social and political theorists to formulate problems in dichotomous terms. Chapter 5 will then consider the problems of communication between political institutions and other social systems, and explore the possibilities for overcoming these difficulties.

Defining Institutions

There has been a renaissance in the study of institutions influenced by writers like March and Olsen (1984; 1989) and by many others (Evans et al. 1985; Brennan and Buchanan 1985; Hall 1986; Shepsle 1989; North 1990; Ostrom 1990). This literature views institutions as structures, comprising rules and standardised procedures, for shaping both individual and collective behaviour. This includes political behaviour and other forms of social behaviour and communication between individuals. The focus is not simply on the legislature, the legal system, the state and formal organisations – although all of these can be described as institutions. Rather, it is on the rules and organisational forms associated with these structures that organise political life and 'transcend individuals and buffer or transform social forces': 'When individuals enter an institution, they try to discover, and are taught the rules. When they encounter a new situation, they try to associate it with a situation for which rules already exist' (March and Olsen 1989: 160). This study adopts a similar approach, particularly the distinction made by North (1990) between political institutions and organisations (see chapter 1).

The 'new institutionalism' draws attention to the 'autonomous role for political institutions', and to bureaucracies, legislatures and courts as 'collections of standard operating procedures that define and defend interests' and are 'political actors in their own right' (March and Olsen 1984: 738). Although sociologists make other distinctions between types of institution, like the 'new institutionalists' they have drawn attention to rules, social practices and the continuous repetition of certain patterns of behaviour as some of the distinguishing features of institutions (see Abercrombie et al. 1988: 124). In some respects, there is nothing new about all this. The *Oxford Dictionary* defines an institution as 'an established law, custom or practice', or 'the action or act of instituting something'. The novelty of recent debates simply lies in the emphasis on the influence of institutions.

For the purposes of this book, the focus on institutions is directed towards how they organise political life and make things happen. Although I will continue to differentiate between political institutions and political organisations, I also want to draw attention to the interplay between institutions and organisations. In the following account, Putnam merges the concepts of institution and of organisation to make the following point about their purpose:

> Institutions are devices for achieving *purposes*, not just for achieving *agreement*. We want government to *do* things, not just *decide* things—to educate children, pay pensioners, stop crime, create jobs, hold down prices, encourage family values, and so on. We do not agree on which of these things is most urgent, nor how they should be accomplished, nor even whether they are all worthwhile. All but the anarchists among us, however, agree that at least some of the time on at least some issues, *action* is required of government institutions. This fact must inform the way we think about institutional success or failure (Putnam 1993: 8–9).

There is one important qualification: institutions also contribute to decisions not being taken and to preventing things from happening (Schattschneider 1960; Bachrach and Baratz 1963; Lindblom 1977; see also Luhmann 1990a: 44).

Whether it is framed in a positive or a negative way, the fundamental argument is the same: *social forces are shaped and ordered by institutions* (March and Olsen 1989).[12] By 'social forces' we mean public opinion, social movements and individuals, in so far as they act outside the constraints imposed by membership of or adherence to established political institutions and channels for the intermediation of interests (namely, political organisations). This also leads us to explore the contraposition to the one presented by March and Olsen, namely, how far *social forces reshape and influence the rules and procedures of institutions*. This may come about through the activities of social movements and other challenges to established institutions (see chapter 6). The argument that social forces shape institutions is recognised by some institutionalists. An empirical study of civic traditions in modern Italy finds that institutional structures and socio-cultural practices are 'mutually reinforcing' (Putnam 1993: 180). Drawing on Plato's *Republic*, Almond and Verba's *Civic Culture* and de Tocqueville's *Democracy in America*, Putnam concludes that '*social context and history profoundly condition the effectiveness of institutions*' (1993: 182).

The Centrality of Institutions

This chapter explores two approaches that, for different reasons, assign to political institutions a central role in bringing about social change. The first approach is closely tied to the new institutionalism and concentrates on the influence of political institutions on social change, as in the study by Putnam (1993) of civic traditions in Italy. His account is useful because it emphasises the significance of patterns of rules and practices in political institutions, and then attempts to link this to a detailed empirical study of political life over several centuries. The second account, by Jänicke (1990), also argues for the centrality of political institutions but concludes that the state has failed to implement policies for the benefit of most people. Jänicke does not draw the same distinction as writers like North (1990) between political institutions and political organisations. Like most writers, he conflates institutions (as defined by North) with organisations. Jänicke tends towards a more traditional (neo-Marxist) view of the state as a structure that imposes itself on other structures. The value of the accounts by Putman and by Jänicke is that they highlight arguments about the centrality of political institutions and political organisations, and they attempt to relate theories either of new institutionalism or of state failure to empirical studies.[13]

For writers like Putnam, tradition can be a good thing. Institutional history can provide a solid foundation for adaptation to new challenges and for shaping social change. Political scientists have adapted the term 'path dependence' from economic historians, and argued that 'where you get to depends on where you're coming from, and some destinations you simply cannot get to from here' (Putnam 1993: 179; see also North 1990). In other words, institutions are shaped by history:

> Whatever other factors may affect their form, institutions have inertia and 'robustness'. They therefore embody historical trajectories and turning points. History matters because it is 'path dependent': Whatever comes first (even if it was in some sense 'accidental') conditions what comes later. Individuals may 'choose' their institutions, but they do not choose them under circumstances of their own making, and their choices in turn influence the rules within which their successors choose (Putnam 1993: 8).

Putnam demonstrates how the performance of institutions is reinforced by history, and how 'social capital' (in other words, the trust, the norms and the social networks that have accrued) is 'self-reinforcing' and 'cumulative'. This corresponds to the claims by Luhmann about the 'reproduction' of political systems (see below). Putnam refers to 'virtuous circles' that affect the introduction of new institutional arrangements at the regional level in Italy: 'Where the regional soil is fertile, the regions draw sustenance from regional traditions, but where the soil is poor, the new institutions are stunted.' The regional traditions are those of civic humanism, namely of 'republican virtues and practices' (Putnam 1993: 182). The focus by new institutionalists like Putnam is therefore not only on rules but also on customs.

There is at least one thing that the new institutionalists have in common with the 'old' structuralists: they both tend to privilege certain political organisations as the agents of social change. Similarly, in sociology, there has been an enduring search among Marxists and neo-Marxists for a central agency. Thus Touraine (1974), for a long time a leading writer on social movements, argued that social movements were the harbingers of a new class that would replace the working-class movement of the nineteenth century in shaping a 'post-industrial' society.

What if political institutions and organisations cannot always become *the* central agencies for social change? This issue is raised by poststructuralist and postmodernist writers and by systems theorists like Luhmann. Although he has little in common with the postmodernist writers, Luhmann shares their reservations about notions of social structures with a central, guiding principle (Neckel and Wolf 1994: 70). According to Luhmann (1990a), political theorists have struggled to visualise modern society as a system without a central agency. Drawing on the classics, they have attempted 'to conceive the state or politics as the guiding centre for everything that occurs in and with it' (1990a: 32). If, as Luhmann argues, this is not the case, we are faced with a difficulty. To focus on the responsiveness of political institutions and organisations may raise unrealistic expectations about their capacity to address problems.

By contrast to Luhmann, Jänicke (1990) assigns a significant role to political organisations. However, like Luhmann, but unlike the new institutionalists, he implies that in contemporary societies the state and politics play a limited role in determining policy outcomes.[14] Though he promotes the centrality of political organisations, Jänicke argues that they can become effective only if they adopt a 'radically reformist' approach (see below) rather than the prevailing one. The latter he characterises as 'impotent' because of 'the inability of elected politicians to take and implement decisions that run counter to the prevailing trend' (1990: ix). He maintains that the masterminds behind environmental and other policies are large-scale industrial and bureaucratic organisations.

That the bureaucracy undermines the influence of elected officials has been an enduring theme in political analysis ever since Weber. His account was reinforced by other studies of oligarchy, notably the theory by Michels on the 'iron law' of bureaucracy in the development of political parties (Michels 1962). The concept of bureaucratic control over the political process has been adapted to explain the development of increasingly 'complex' political structures. Though it is widely accepted that the role of government has expanded over the past few decades,[15] there is a paradox in that the expansion of government is accompanied by a decline in the influence of politics: 'the increased complexity of the public sector, and the transfer of many functions from direct ministerial supervision in departments of statutory authorities under less stringent scrutiny, may have reduced government influence in some policy areas' (Davis et al. 1993: 124).[16] Jänicke refers to the state as 'a colossus with feet of clay' and thereby joins the line of writers who are apprehensive about the legitimation crisis of the modern state (Habermas 1976), the crisis of democracy (Crozier et al. 1975), government overload (Rose 1980), and the fiscal crisis of the state (O'Connor 1973).

These writers describe similar problems, but suggest different solutions. For instance, we can distinguish between neo-liberal and social democratic or radical reformist approaches. Neo-liberals emphasise strong leadership and freedom for market forces from the restrictions imposed by the state. Jänicke, a radical reformist, favours decentralised control (through local government), consensus government, preventive policies, and government taxes, duties and scales of charges (rather than massive public expenditure). All these strategies, he argues, could and should be applied to deal with environmental problems.[17]

The 'impotence' of elected officials in implementing these strategies is apparently determined by several factors. The dynamism of capitalist industrialism creates problems and 'externalises' them, in other words, passes them on to the state. The state, in this case the government and the politicians, is obliged to address the repercussions of the industrial system, and takes on the increasing burdens of regulation, legitimation, provision of infrastructure, and nuisance abatement (namely, dealing with the side effects of industrial production on the social and physical environment) (Jänicke 1990: 8–9). The state has only limited involvement in the creation of some problems. Yet it has to address issues like the disarray associated with unemployment, the needs of a growing aged population, and the apprehension about environmental protection and the quality of life.

Although it may seek to address the dysfunctional effects of capitalism, the state cannot neglect the industrial system. It depends on the industrial system to promote economic growth and prosperity, which in turn ensures that the state can deal with the consequences of industrialisation. As I shall claim later, this can present opportunities for a constructive dialogue between different interests and between groups driven by different logics of action. However, at this instant, I want to articulate the more pessimistic perspective that the state faces numerous obstacles to the effective implementation of policies arising from the tension between competing goals and from a variety of other constraints.

One of the most frequently cited constraints on government and politicians is the power of the bureaucracy, notably its capacity to define problems and its subsequent influence on the strategies developed to solve problems (Jänicke 1990: 13). However, Jänicke does not mention that interest groups may also disrupt or set the agenda for government (see Brittan 1975; Olson 1983). Jänicke and writers adopting a liberal or social democratic approach would question many of the arguments about the dysfunctional impact of interest groups on policy-making (Crouch 1983; Marsh 1995). Both Jänicke and Marsh suggest that new issue movements, or at least those that champion 'new politics' issues like environmentalism, feminism and civil rights, enrich the policy-making process.

Any effort by government to implement radical reforms apparently has to contend with a formidable coalition between industry and the bureaucracy on certain matters. Jänicke refers to 'bureaucracy–industry complexes', in other words to coalitions between industry and bureaucracies dealing with military supplies, finance, environmental protection, roads, energy supplies and security services. Coherence is facilitated by the shared outlook and interests of industry and bureaucracies. According to Jänicke:

- Both types of organisation prefer to deal with symptoms rather than underlying causes.
- Both are characterised by strong central control and a division of labour.
- Their solutions to problems tend to be global and routine.
- They tend to intervene only when problems become 'visible, prolific and calculable'.

- They have similar economic interests, to the extent that the bureaucracies want a larger budget and industry a greater market.

Jänicke argues that these 'structural affinities' result in defining problems in particular ways. First, the emphasis on specialisation directs attention away from the variety and complexity of problems. In effect, it reduces the pool of people who develop a broad vision. Second, the focus on symptoms rather than causes means that problems are tackled after they have manifested themselves. Efforts to anticipate and prevent problems are weak. Third, the solutions tend to be expensive because they are large-scale and standardised rather than 'one-off' and 'non-routine' (Jänicke 1990: 38).

Besides the problems associated with the operation of large industrial and bureaucratic organisations and the 'impotence' of elected officials in dealing with these powerful structures, Jänicke tries to demonstrate that 'common interests' in peace and the quality of life (like environmental protection) are only weakly represented and organised (1990: 18). Drawing on Offe (1976), he distinguishes between the organisation of interests in the 'employment' and 'residual' sectors; between the sphere of 'production' and that of 'consumption'; between the powerful, centralised, specialised, highly professional groups that represent the interest in economic growth and the amateurs, who are weakly organised, poorly represented in parliament, and have small financial resources.

Although Jänicke acknowledges disputes between 'capital' and 'labour' in the employment sector, he wants to draw attention to the conflicts associated with the 'new politics', to the divisions between materialists and postmaterialists or green movements. He identifies three sources of 'countervailing power' to the dominance of industrial and bureaucratic interests, namely, the legal system, the media, and political opposition (from 'new politics' parties). Parliaments have become instruments of government. Politics has become 'subservient' to the industrial system (Jänicke 1990: 25). Politics serves as a 'scapegoat' for problems caused principally by industrialism.

Politicians apparently have considerably less power than the bureaucrats in managing the affairs of the state (see also Thompson 1990). Jänicke identifies six dimensions of unequal power in the state by comparing 'politics and politicians' to 'administrators' (see table 4.1). These factors have been recognised by other writers on public policy. Bureaucrats are said to enjoy the advantages of having time, history, official networks, professionalism and greater scope for dealing with complex issues in a discretionary manner (Davis et al. 1993: 123). Jänicke argues that administrators are 'under no constraint to prove their legitimacy, and do not have to fear for their jobs' (1990: 27). Most bureaucrats survive changes of government. Politicians, particularly ministers, are usually held accountable for the mistakes of public servants. In an attempt to illustrate the power of bureaucrats, Jänicke points out that between 1950 and the 1980s in West Germany the number of public service employees doubled while the number of parliamentary deputies remained almost constant.

These arguments and the sharp distinctions made in table 4.1 represent a partial account of power relationships and of how institutions operate in practice. There are numerous mechanisms to restrict the power and influence of bureaucrats. The

Table 4.1 Factors of unequal power in the state

Politics and politicians	Administration
Diffuse base (electors)	Specific base
Amateurism	Professionalism
Public action	Behind-the-scenes action
Need for legitimation	No need for legitimation
Short tenure	Usually a job for life
Small number of agents	Plethora of agents

Source: Jänicke 1990: 26, table 2.

ties between politicians and the bureaucracy and between industry and politics are not represented in his typology. It also tells us little about the context for the formulation and implementation of particular policies. These obviously need to be closely scrutinised, as do the rules and practices within institutions. There is also considerable scope, as I shall affirm later, for dialogue between groups and organisations with different interests and for innovation which is of mutual benefit.

In an empirical study of environmental policies, Jänicke and his collaborators (1989) discovered that advanced industrialised capitalist countries experienced both high levels of economic growth and a reduction in damage to the environment (as recorded by an index measuring use of cement, energy, crude steel and freight transport by road). By contrast, less advanced nations (Portugal, Greece and countries in Eastern Europe prior to the collapse of communism) experienced low growth rates and an increase in damage to the environment (as measured by this index). Even more significantly, Jänicke et al. acknowledge that a more consensual style of government (one that seeks to achieve consensus between different groups, including industry, environmentalists, labour organisations, the bureaucracy, and so on) is positively related to better environmental standards. In some respects, this confirms his argument about the centrality of politics. In others, it weakens the rigid categories and dichotomies that he used to differentiate between politics and industry. It also confirms the expectations articulated in chapter 1 about the likelihood and desirability of constructive dialogue.

Jänicke (1990) presents rigid dichotomies and categories in order to simplify and strengthen his argument for a less subservient role for politics. His restatement of traditional fears that the market undermines the state or that bureaucracy diminishes the influence of politics leaves him open to the criticisms of traditional structuralist accounts made by new institutionalists. Ostrom, for instance, criticises approaches that treat 'the government' as an 'omnicompetent entity' and as the only significant policy actor, and are based on idealised notions of markets and states which impose their solutions on others (Ostrom 1990: 216). Still, Jänicke makes a valuable contribution by drawing attention to forces other than 'the government' (like the new politics parties), to 'public discussion of the causes' of various problems, and to the neglect by the education system of 'social discoveries and institutional innovation – the field of quality' (1990: 37).

His focus on innovation suggests the possibility of challenging the traditional dichotomies. Similarly, the interest in 'quality' reflects the reconceptualisation of the quality of life which I referred to in chapter 1. Jänicke also links traditional Marxist preoccupations to the radical reformist agenda of the 'new politics'. This agenda raises some of the problems associated with state intervention without falling into the trap of abandoning the state, an approach advocated by some neo-liberals (see Jänicke 1990: x). To that extent, his agenda transcends some of the traditional dichotomies evoked by left- and right-wing approaches to politics.

In arguing for a stronger role for politics, for the 'power of politics' at all levels of society and for the decentralisation of power (1990: 131), Jänicke claims that his model is 'realist' rather than 'idealist'. The realist model apparently 'pays less attention to ideas than to interests, less to individual actors on the small stage than to the large agents or macroagents in society and their relative positions of strength' (1990: 139). Nevertheless, the dichotomy he evokes between realism and idealism is unduly restrictive. In actuality, some of his prescriptions reflect ideas and values and they appear to play an important role, a point he himself acknowledges (1990: 139–40).

Though he offers useful insights into the limitations of contemporary institutions and into possibilities for reform, Jänicke draws the same distinctions as many other writers between apparently irreconcilable goals (state/market, politics/administration, realism/idealism). These attempts to simplify political reality and to reduce complexity are scrutinised by Luhmann.

Outmoded Concepts and the Limits of Politics

Luhmann has been described as 'the hard-headed analyst of a complex world, putting uncertainties into circulation even where others cling doggedly to their ideals or become melancholy' (Neckel and Wolf 1994: 73). The following account of the work by Luhmann represents a paradox. It suggests that out of his pessimism we can still derive an optimistic account of the influence of politics. His ideas are interesting because they provide insights into the difficulties of implementing policies and a stimulus for thinking in a constructive way about environmental problems.

Even the harshest critics acknowledge that Luhmann's conceptual schemes, whatever their apparent defects, can be used 'to produce rich and robust substantive insights' (Turner 1986: 125). Lempert, who criticises Luhmann for the lack of specificity and incompleteness of his theories, recognises their 'substantial metaphorical value' (1988: 188). His concepts can be used to improve our awareness of social processes even if we abandon some of their jargon or 'functional trappings' (Turner 1986: 125). Similarly, in this book, I use some of the work by Luhmann as a heuristic device and not as a complete theory.

Rather than being principally concerned about the function of political institutions or organisations as central agencies for the whole of society, Luhmann (1990a) is intrigued by the political system's function as just another 'sub-system' of society, as posited by his theories on social systems. The notion of a social system is used to refer to the communication that takes place within different areas of society. Our interest is primarily in the communication that takes place within the political system (and between political and other systems). Whereas we have so far drawn the distinction between political institutions (the rules of the game) and political organisations (comprising actors who influence the rules of the game and are influenced by these rules), Luhmann draws a broader distinction, namely between a social system (arising from a certain unity based on communication) and its 'environment'. Luhmann's account involves a reformulation of Parsons' systems theory. He develops systems theory 'not as a theory of specific objects but rather as a theory that observes reality using a specific distinction, namely the system/environment distinction' (Luhmann in Sciulli 1994: 38). This represents a crucial conceptual distinction for Luhmann (1982). Its significance is summed up by Turner:

> all social systems exist in multidimensional environments, which pose potentially endless complexity with which a system must deal. To exist in a complex environment, therefore, a social system must develop mechanisms for reducing complexity. Such selection creates a boundary between a system and its environment, thereby allowing it to sustain patterns of interrelated actions (Turner 1986: 103).

Luhmann's theory of social systems posits the existence of multiple sub-systems (the political, educational, economic, scientific and other sub-systems) which operate through 'communication' rather than 'action'.

His notion of a social system has several implications. Some of these will be explained more fully in the following chapter on the circularity of political communication and dialogue. In this section the focus is on the relevance of Luhmann's ideas to our concept of the significance of politics and society.

First, one of Luhmann's principal aims is to draw us away from the rigid dichotomies and outmoded concepts of the past, notably the distinction between state and society (which has had a particularly strong influence on constitutional lawyers). Luhmann proposes the following alternative to this distinction: 'Society is the all-encompassing social system that orders all possible communications among human beings. The political system is one of its sub-systems alongside other sub-systems for religion, science, economy, education, family life, medical care etc.' (Luhmann 1990a: 30).

Second, the reformulation of the distinction between state and society by Luhmann reflects the unease felt by many social scientists in using the term *society*. For instance, many sociologists are dissatisfied with the 'common-sense' usage of society, which refers to the boundaries of nation-states.[18] They have therefore moved away from the notion of society in so far as it implies a unitary concept linked to a particular territory or an attempt to divide 'society' into different parts or levels (Mann 1986).[19] Similarly, Luhmann places little value on distinguishing between societies purely on the basis of territory.[20] Instead, the notion of independent entities within an 'all-encompassing social system' lies at the core of his conceptualisation of society. As noted above, the political sub-system is simply another entity alongside the educational, economic, scientific and other sub-systems.[21] (The implications of this argument and the question of the autonomy of sub-systems from one another are explored in the following chapter.)

Third, for Luhmann society is made up not simply of human beings but of the communication between them. Communication between human beings is what makes society a reality. Furthermore, each sub-system (for instance, the political system) produces (through its actions) society from a specific point of view. However, this view is made up of two perspectives – one that is particular to the sub-system and the other which reflects environmental factors.[22] For instance, 'the economic and education systems belong to the environment of education and the economy' (Luhmann 1990a: 30).

Fourth, his 'systems' approach serves to highlight the challenges facing the political system and the possibilities for meeting them. Rather than prescribe the elevation of politics as a central force in society, Luhmann (1990a) attempts to understand the dilemmas confronting the political system. He has long identified the weakness of politics (Luhmann 1975). However, by contrast to Jänicke and other political scientists, he does not appear overly concerned about the subservient role of politics. For Luhmann, the government was there to protect and legitimate the bureaucracy so that the administration could 'concentrate on the actual task of running the country' (Jänicke 1990: 25).

Fifth, though not troubled by the subservient role of politics, Luhmann has misgivings about the theoretical justification for contemporary politics. He maintains that many of the theories that underpin contemporary politics are either obsolete or unduly restrictive, and that our institutions (and institutional practices) are, in many respects, a 'relic' of political theories. The formation of the modern state in Europe, he argues, 'was accompanied by a political theory that, in so far as it was visible, reflected its development, reacted to its problems and offered solutions of a legal and institutional kind' (Luhmann 1990a: 25). This political theory becomes part of the institutions: 'It descends, so to say, from the heights of pure theory into the murky atmosphere of reality and in this way is deflected, exploited, reified and thus becomes an aspect of whatever a new theory tries to discover. Our institutions are a relic of such processes and therefore need political reflection from time to time' (Luhmann 1990a: 25–6).

Sixth, among the ideas absorbed by the absolutist state were the notions of a constitution, the separation of powers, the democratic vote, and the term of office in parliament. In the nineteenth century the absolutist state responded to new problems by creating new institutions, notably the welfare state (Luhmann 1990a: 27). Although it responds to new challenges, the modern state is burdened by past practices and customs (tradition), some of which hinder it from confronting the problems arising from complex modern societies in an innovative manner. Theories absorbed by the state during the period of absolutism and into the modern era are apparently defective: 'As theories – not as legal forms and institutions! – they are historically surpassed' (Luhmann 1990a: 28).

Two aspects of this critique by Luhmann are pertinent to the focus in the book on tradition and innovation. The first is that, with the growing complexity of social systems, 'the past cannot serve as a guide to the present or future because there are too many potentially new contingencies and options' (Turner 1986: 116). The second is the preparedness by Luhmann to challenge and reassess old ideas as well as to develop new concepts. He does not deliver the standard Marxist critique of the state which focuses on the power of capitalists and the economy (rather than politics), and on the ownership of the means of production.[23] Instead, he not only questions the old nineteenth-century European assumption of a separation between state and society,[24] but goes on to suggest that the state is 'nothing' outside society. The implications of this challenge are far-reaching. The state, rather than assuming a central position in shaping society, is part of society. The notion that political institutions shape social forces therefore becomes less tenable. This has serious implications for any plans to tackle environmental protection simply by focusing on political action.

To sum up, the importance of Luhmann to this study is that he challenges preconceptions about politics being at the centre of the social system, that he represents a radical departure from the traditional worldview of political science or political sociology, and that he breaks the spell of many prejudgements about how to get things done effectively. Like Weber before him, Luhmann may appear to be a pessimist. Yet in challenging perceptions about politics as the centre of society, he may open for us new possibilitites for rendering politics more effective. For all these reasons, Luhmann's work can become a platform for innovative approaches. This is not to reject the value of the work by new institutionalists like Putnam or structuralists like Jänicke. Like Luhmann they are concerned about the limits and likelihood of effective action. Unlike Luhmann they pin their hopes on politics – in the case of Putnam on traditions and customs of civic virtue and political participation, and in the case of Jänicke on apparently radical reforms to organisational structures.

CHAPTER 5

The Circularity of Political Communication and Dialogue

The Responsiveness and Effectiveness of Institutions

After exploring further the implications of the investigation by Luhmann into social systems, this chapter discusses the central question of the obstacles to and possibilities for an effective response by political institutions and organisations to challenges like environmentalism. Although Luhmann, as indicated earlier, highlights some of the obstacles that prevent effective responses by government and politics, I will concentrate on the ways in which groups and organisations with divergent interests and driven by different logics (for instance, economic growth or environmentalism or political power) engage in some form of constructive dialogue or conversation or rational communication.

One could infer that the term 'rational communication' originated in the work of writers like Habermas because of the experience of Germany of the 'irrationality' of fascism. If that were the case, it could also be argued that the concept is of limited value, both as an ideal type and as a way of describing empirical instances outside particular social, historical and geographical settings. While these arguments appear plausible, the aim of this book is to demonstrate the usefulness of this concept, or at least of the concept of constructive dialogue (which represents an elaboration of the notion of rational communication), in a variety of social, historical and geographical settings.[25] This is not to suggest that the process of constructive dialogue will be smooth or easy.

One of the aims of this chapter is to continue to draw attention both to the impediments to and the possibilities for the successful implementation of policy. Although the focus will be largely on the work by Luhmann, the aim is to return to some of the underlying concerns of writers like North, Putnam and Jänicke about the possibilities for an effective politics. This will become apparent in the latter half of this chapter and in subsequent chapters, which provide detailed evidence of adaptation by political institutions and organisations to the challenges posed by environmentalists.

Luhmann's Systems Theory and the Problem of Communication

The focus by Luhmann on communication between sub-systems which realise action in society from a specific point of view is central to the concerns of this study. When new challenges emerge or when there are shifts in values, how do established political organisations react? How can empathetic understanding of divergent viewpoints or of divergent goals be achieved? What are the possibilities for adaptation, conciliation and compromise? How are apparently conflicting principles resolved in a pragmatic manner?

Luhmann believes that established political organisations find it hard to respond to new challenges, and that empathetic understanding between divergent viewpoints is extremely difficult to achieve. Besides discussing the problems of outmoded concepts and of political theories that have been overtaken by events, Luhmann, as I shall explain later, draws attention to the in-built limitations of political and other social systems. However, there are some gaps in his account that invite further comment. For instance, his account does not or cannot identify the mechanisms whereby systems respond to 'environmental factors' or how these factors bring about change in systems.[26] On the one hand, Luhmann suggests that sub-systems are sensitive to what goes on around them. On the other hand, he argues that this openness is severely restricted: in other words, sub-systems are open to what goes on in their environment only if they can translate it into their own language. There appears to be little scope for what goes on in the environment of a sub-system to bring about changes within the sub-system. Luhmann, in other words, is pessimistic about the likelihood of actors (operating within the framework of a sub-system as, say, politicians, lawyers, industrialists and so on) suspending their own view of reality in order to fully comprehend that of actors operating in the context of another sub-system. Later I shall argue that, to a degree, Luhmann ignores aspects of his own argument that political and other systems are sensitive to what occurs in their environment. He also overlooks the fora which, with varying degrees of success, sanction social actors from different sub-systems to sustain a dialogue.

On a more positive note, Luhmann draws attention to the key issue of action by human beings and its relationship to structural or systemic factors. Luhmann also conceptualises in novel ways the problems facing contemporary institutions. For instance, he develops the concepts of 'autopoiesis' and of 'self-referential systems'. Autopoietic systems are defined as 'systems that reproduce all the elementary components out of which they arise by means of a network of these elements themselves and in this way distinguish themselves from an environment – whether this takes the form of life, or consciousness or (in the case of social systems) communication' (Luhmann 1989: 143). Autopoiesis is 'the mode of reproduction of these systems'. Self-reference is used to describe 'every operation that refers to something beyond itself and this back to itself' (Luhmann 1989: 145).[27]

Even if we reject Luhmann's overall theory of functional evolution for its lack of specificity, his elaboration of the concept of autopoeisis draws our attention to a fundamental problem in all forms of communication between human beings, namely, to what degree we can view the world from the standpoint of another person. Again, it is worth emphasising that this focus on human beings is based on the notion of social actors operating within the framework of a sub-system (in other words, as politicians or lawyers or educators or the clergy, and so on) and that Luhmann is pessimistic about the possibilities for the empathetic understanding of a different point of view arising from another sub-system. How far can we suspend our own view of reality in order to fully comprehend that of another person?[28] The answer to this question is crucial to understanding the possibilities for implementing effective reforms, for instance in environmental policy.

As shown earlier, like poststructuralist and postmodernist writers, Luhmann takes distance from social theorists who conceive society in terms of 'central agencies' or an 'apex' or 'centre'. By focusing on processes of communication among human beings, he arrives at the 'radical' conclusion that: 'Modern society is a system without a spokesman and without internal representation' (Luhmann 1990a: 32). He adds:

> Time and again political theory – from Hegel through Treitschke to Leo Strauss and Hannah Arendt – has tried to counter this diagnosis and to conceive the state or politics as the guiding center for everthing that occurs in and with it. Typically – and characteristically! – this happens through recourse to the Greek, Platonic or Aristotelian, concept of politics. An outdated, long since superseded conceptual apparatus appears to gain new plausibility due to new kinds of demands. One of the basic questions concerning the theoretical and political orientation of the present is therefore whether one can tolerate the idea of a centerless society and see in this the conditions for an effective, democratic politics. Or whether, in view of the entire situation of the system of society, one believes one can or even has to attribute a central responsibility to politics that might possibly destroy its present boundaries and the laborious procedures of the democratic determination of opinions (Luhmann 1990a: 32–3).

Luhmann therefore addresses directly the question of whether or not political systems can cope with the demands being placed on them.

The capacity of the state to deal with environmental issues is linked, in a sense, to the development of the welfare state. The creation of the welfare state realised the principle of 'political inclusion'. The welfare state became responsible for a burgeoning number of problems (for everything from 'safer docking facilities for Sunday sailors' to 'hot-air hand dryers in public rest rooms') (Luhmann 1990a: 36). These developments place an enormous burden on the political system. It can no longer hope to represent the whole of society (Luhmann 1990a: 14). Since the eighteenth century, the old structures of authority, founded on a highly stratified system, have been replaced by a system based mainly on 'functional differentiation'. This creates a 'legitimation crisis' in the sense that every system is faced by 'the imperative to legitimate itself' (1990a: 19).[29] Politics, like all other systems, thereby becomes 'self-referential':

> Whatever can become politically relevant results from a connection with whatever already possesses political relevance. Whatever counts politically reproduces itself. And this occurs by encompassing and absorbing interests from the social environment of the political system. Politics conditions its own possibilities – and apparently becomes sensible thereby to what its environment offers or requires. It is not understood adequately as a closed or an open system. It is both at the same time.
>
> The difficulties that theory-formation and on-going scientific research encounter here are rooted in their object. We will subsume them under the concept of 'self-referential system.'

> A system is called self-referential that produces and reproduces the elements – in this case political decisions – out of which it is composed itself (Luhmann 1990a: 39–40).[30]

This has powerful ramifications for discussions about the capacity of the political system to manage demands for environmental protection, for economic development and for social justice.

It would be easy to dismiss the notion of self-referential systems as, in Luhmann's own words, 'logically circular and therefore empty' (1990a: 41). Still, this criticism overlooks several important applications of the notion of self-reference. First, as Teubner has proposed in his application of self-reference to the legal system, the notion of a system that is both 'open' and 'closed' enables us to transcend the limitations of theories which view (legal) change as 'either purely internal and independent or exclusively the result of external events': 'Legal and social changes are, for the neo-evolutionist, related yet distinct processes. Legal change reflects an internal dynamic, which, nevertheless, is affected by external stimuli and, in turn, influences the external environment' (Teubner 1983: 249).[31]

Second, Luhmann submits that criticisms about the circularity of his arguments overlook the origins and 'inevitability' of self-referential systems and the problems raised by these developments:

> Viewed sociologically, self-reference is a result of evolutionary system differentiation and political self-reference, a result of the social differentiation of specifically political systems. The development of self-referential modes of operation corresponds exactly to the requirements of this historical development. And it imposes them to the extent of its realization: self-reference makes possible system openness to changing themes with a relative constancy of the structures guiding the operations (party organization, ministerial organization, law etc.). And it makes possible the inclusion of the entire population within the scope of politics – regardless who determines what is a political theme. Therefore one has to begin from a practically inevitable development of structures that binds us to use social functions in this way (Luhmann 1990a: 41).

Openness to the environment is crucial to the survival of the political system. However, the 'real condition of operation' lies in self-reference, 'in the continual reference of politics to politics' (1990a: 42). For the modern state, the traditional bases – law and constitutional order – are no longer sufficient. Deficiencies in awareness by the political system of its environment cannot be adequately addressed by using the traditional legal and constitutional mechanisms. Again, Luhmann steers us away from reliance on tradition and, perhaps unintentionally, impels us to concentrate on innovation.

Political theorists attempt to grasp new situations by adopting traditional ways of conceptualising social systems and traditional forms of logic (notably the use of adversarial logic and of rigid dichotomies and categories). These efforts create several difficulties, some of which are identified by Luhmann in his analysis of self-referential systems. He shows that symbols like 'money', 'love', 'power' and 'truth' are organised into binary codes in order to achieve simplification in a complex environment (see my presentation of these symbols and codes in table 5.1). These symbols are used, respectively, in the systems of the economy, the family, politics and science.

Along with the advantage of simplification come many disadvantages. Binary coding, by definition, makes it hard to conceive of alternative ways of perceiving situations and processing information. I have already alluded in chapter 1 to some of the problems arising from the use of dichotomies in political debate, and to their impact on attempts to create more effective policies. Luhmann perceives this problem in all areas of communication. He notes that binary codes entail the use of the categories true/false in scientific discourse, and legal/illegal in the law. In politics, the most commonly utilised codes are government/opposition and progressive/conservative:

> A typical problem of self-referential systems (and, indeed, of those that are well-structured) lies in the tendency of self-reference to short-circuit, undercut. Political systems above all, with their formula of government/opposition, provide a good example of this. A lot of 'politics' is conducted within the scope of this difference. A mistake by the government is chalked up as a victory by the opposition and vice versa. An attack on the 'impotence' of the government proves the vitality of the opposition almost immediately. Short-circuiting, undercutting resides in the technique of representing itself in the critique of its counterpart (Luhmann 1990a: 43).

Binary codes do not allow any exploration of a wide spectrum of alternatives. They restrict our choices. Binary codes impose constraints on dealing with new situations, and on communication between existing sub-systems. Hence, the economy as a self-referential system may respond to concern about environmental protection only by 'translating' it into the language of 'payments and prices':

> These codes are totalizing in the sense that they exclude other possibilities of ordering information. A system can react to the environment only in terms of its code. For example, the binary code of the economy, payment/nonpayment, forces communications to be expressed in the language of prices and profits. This means that the economy can react to the environment, but as an autopoietically closed system it can do so only if it translates the language of nature into that of payments and prices. Whatever cannot be expressed in this language cannot be processed by the economy *qua* autonomous system (Fuchs 1990: 748).

The outcome of this 'structural blindness' of the economy to problems that cannot be translated into the language of payments and prices is illustrated by Luhmann: 'Even

Table 5.1 Symbols and binary codes used in different social systems

System	Symbol	Codes
Economy	Money	Profit and loss
Family	Love	Love and hate
Politics	Power	Government and opposition; progressive and conservative; democracy and dictatorship
Science	Truth	True and false
Law	Justice	Legal and illegal

if, for example, fossil fuels deplete rapidly it may "still not yet" be profitable to switch to other forms of energy' (Luhmann 1989: 57, cited by Fuchs 1990: 748). Under these conditions, how responsive can political institutions and organisations become to some of the challenges posed by environmentalism? Can they respond only according to their own self-referential logic, or are there ways in which they might be reshaped in order to meet the more fundamental demands of environmentalists? What fora exist to facilitate the translation of the different logics of the sub-systems?

Luhmann argues that political systems are a long way from resolving these problems under conditions of rapid social change: 'But the question is whether and to what extent politics can actually succeed in bringing its problems under control in a society where, as it is, things change very rapidly. The danger is that, using the option of this code, one can make decisions about one's options too quickly' (Luhmann 1990a: 44). Apart from making precipitate decisions, self-referential political systems also prevent change by not taking decisions: 'This means doing nothing as long as this does not put one in a position of "blame" ' (1990a: 44).[32]

This recalls our preoccupation with political effectiveness and whether or not we should expect the political system, as it is currently structured, to provide solutions. The use of binary codes by the political system apparently leads to political ineffectiveness and to a very limited form of political communication: 'Is it not the case that politics' own dynamics is guided too rigidly, too centrally by the code of government/opposition for it to provide enough possibilities for combining controversial societal themes like genetic engineering and financing the welfare state, or foreign relations, rearmament and currency policy and to put them to the vote?' (Luhmann 1990a: 239). Luhmann acknowledges that in books like *Ecological Communication* he finds himself holding more of a pessimistic than an optimistic view of modern society (though he adds that, in comparing modern society with any of its predecessors, 'there seem to be more reasons to be optimistic and to be pessimistic at the same time') (Luhmann in Sciulli 1994: 44). Luhmann's pessimism may, however, have led him to under-rate the possibilities for communication between the political and other sub-systems, a theme that is explored more fully in the following section and chapters.

The Problem of Coordination between Sub-systems

The dilemmas identified by Luhmann arise in all policy areas. They can be addressed only by breaking out of the self-referential mode of operation: 'All self-referential systems have to break up such internal circles – I'll do what you want if you do what I want' (Luhmann 1990a: 44). Luhmann suggests two techniques: a focus on the external environment ('externalisation') and a focus on history ('historisation'). However, he is principally interested in the external environment as a means of breaking up the 'circularity of political communication' (Luhmann 1990a: 45).

Despite his pessimism, Luhmann records that self-referential systems are subject to a variety of challenges, including 'public opinion' (see chapters 15 and 16). Public opinion may play a central role in 'transforming self-reference into communication'. It is principally through public opinion that the political system observes the external environment:

> Far more than other function systems, the political system depends on public opinion. For politics, public opinion is one of the most important sensors whose observation takes the place of direct observation of the environment. Topics of public opinion, reports and commentaries in the press and broadcasting possess an obvious relevance for politics which at the same time conceals with its obviousness what actually is the case. It simply has to appear in the papers (Luhmann 1990a: 215).

Public opinion is used as a mirror for the political system. However, in fulfilling this role, public opinion apparently reinforces the self-referential qualities of the political system:

> As a social system the political system, accordingly, uses public opinion to make itself capable of observing itself and developing corresponding expectational structures. Public opinion does not serve to produce external contacts. It serves the self-referential closure of the political system, the return of politics upon itself. But self-referential closure is brought about with the help of an institution that permits the system to distinguish self-reference and other-reference, i.e. politics and public opinion, in the performance of its own operations and with it to construct a picture of the boundaries of its own possibilities of action (Luhmann 1990a: 216–7).

Luhmann thereby returns to the central theme of the limits of politics in bringing about social change.[33] Again, this is in stark contrast to the new institutionalists like Putnam, March and Olsen, and to reformists like Jänicke who wish to restructure the connections between politics and the bureaucracy as well as those between the bureaucracy and industry.

From here on, rather than sanction the approach either of Luhmann or of the new institutionalists or radical reformists, I will question certain aspects of Luhmann's conclusions and show how the political system can both effect change and prevent or delay it. This is well illustrated by the efforts of social movements, interest groups and 'new politics' parties to bring about change in the area of environmental protection over the past thirty years, and by the endeavours to achieve dialogue between different sub-systems. It is possible for groups and organisations with divergent interests, with different logics (or symbolic codes) at their core and with different levels of power, to engage in dialogue or communication: for instance, for business groups to discuss issues with environmental groups or for lawyers to speak to educators. In other words, it is possible for them to communicate their concerns to each other, to influence each other, to set aside some of their prejudgements about one another, and to become aware of and act in response to a different point of view (see also the discussion below of the work by Miller (1994) on 'intersystemic discourse').

Luhmann himself offers solutions to the problems of communication, and mentions that systems theory can improve the instruments available to us for 'self-observation'. Teubner, for example, develops from Luhmann's work the concept of 'reflexive law' which 'will neither authoritatively determine the social functions of other subsystems nor regulate their input and output performances, but will foster mechanisms that systematically *further the development of reflexion structures within other social subsystems*' (Tuebner 1983: 275). Above all, the legal system could serve not so much to decide conflicts between competing policies but 'to guarantee coordination processes and to compel agreement' (Teubner 1983: 277). Teubner points out that the notion of self-referentiality 'does not mean that any contact between systems is excluded' (1986: 312). He suggests that it is possible to achieve a degree of mutual 'understanding' between sub-systems, despite the difficulties they face in acquiring social knowledge about each other (see also the discussion below on the possibilities for 'intersystemic discourse').

The concepts of dialogue and reflexivity can also be applied to environmental social movements (see Papadakis 1984; 1988). Luhmann himself suggests that society cannot do without the kind of 'self-observation' that arises from social movements. Some governments and established institutions have recognised that social movements may, through the process of observing society, make a valuable contribution to innovation and social change. This has led to a more flexible response by government to social movements and to recognition that they can contribute to addressing the problem of circularity of political communication. Social movements have evolved into green parties, have influenced the political agenda, and have contributed to the revitalisation of politics (Dalton and Kuechler 1990; Papadakis 1989).[34] Social movements may also be more effective innovators than established political institutions, and they have the potential to create new social arrangements (see chapter 6).

Luhmann only hints at the possibility of responsive and effective political institutions. As Miller (1994: 104) suggests, he has under-rated the potential of social communication for providing 'co-ordination of modern society's different function systems' (for instance, between the political sub-system and other sub-systems). Miller refers to this form of social communication as the possibility of 'intersystemic' discourse. If there were no communication at all, 'modern society would not merely be split up into different function systems, it would just fall apart reiterating the tragedy of the tower of Babel' (Miller 1994: 110). Luhmann does not explore the following possibilities: 'whether and to what extent an intersystemic discourse is empirically possible, how the logic of that discourse can be described and whether it makes sense to distinguish between forms of collective rationality and irrationality on the level of such an intersystemic discourse' (Miller 1994: 109).

Luhmann has dismissed attempts by green social movements to communicate with the rest of society about their concerns. Yet he 'could probably not deny that it [the communication of new social movements] did affect society and very much determined the increasing awareness of an ecological crisis at least in some countries' (Miller 1994: 110; see also chapter 16 in this book).

Luhmann's pessimism about the possibilities for coordination and meaningful discourse between function systems is open to several other challenges. Although different functional systems are self-referential, they also 'continuously try to make joint contributions to the solution of societal problems, for example, ecological problems – or at least, they are expected by the public to do so' (Miller 1994: 111). As Miller suggests, this leads to the institutionalisation of discourse between function systems, for instance, the 'concerted action' involving government, business and labour or the 'systems of negotiation for social policy'.

A parallel example in the area of environmental policy can be found in Australia, where the Labor government established numerous mechanisms for the institutionalisation of discourse. One approach by the Australian Labor Party (ALP), under

Senator Graham Richardson as minister for the environment, was to establish a dialogue with leading figures in the green movement (Bob Brown, the best-known green politician; Peter Garrett, a rock music star and president of the Australian Conservation Foundation (ACF); and Philip Toyne, the director of the ACF) and even to employ them as senior policy advisers (as happened with Simon Balderstone from the ACF) (see Kelly 1994: 527). Furthermore, the formation of the ecologically sustainable development (ESD) working groups represented one of the most comprehensive attempts to defuse conflicts between developers and environmentalists, and to integrate as many of the warring factions as possible into a process that was steered and monitored by government (Papadakis 1993). This concerted action encompassed government agencies at state and federal level, industry groups and environmental groups. For organisations like Greenpeace, involvement in this kind of corporatist process was unprecedented.

The final report by the ESD working groups contained around four hundred recommendations for new policies, many of which implied changes in individual behaviour and in business practices. On many of the issues there was consensus among the various groups. Some environmentalists, despite their resistance to market-based mechanisms for tackling environmental problems and their protests about certain aspects of the procedures used by the ESD groups, gained a better understanding of how a balance might be achieved between economic and environmental goals. The government had initiated a transformation of the institutional order. Whereas interest groups and social movements had emphasised the differences between their perspectives, the government persuaded them to identify the common ground, brought the two sides together, and gained greater control of the agenda by influencing arguments and by devising new institutional mechanisms. The impact of these changes was felt during the 1993 election campaign, when the focus by the ALP and by leading environmental groups was on both development and the environment (Papadakis 1994). These shifts in perspective could not have occurred 'if collective rationality had been completely disintegrated into the specific rationalities of the different function systems' (Miller 1994: 112). It could be argued that there is evidence to show that the different interest groups have, in the early 1990s 'reverted' to the rationalities of the different function systems and failed to engage in a fruitful dialogue. That does not, however, negate the evidence that it is *possible* for dialogue to emerge and that some policies have been put into place which reflect the success of this process.

Miller points out that individual social actors are capable of talking in the 'languages' of the different sub-systems, and explores the following possibilities:

> If industrial managers, politicians, lawyers, scientists, theologians and any other representatives of any other relevant function system of modern society talk to each other in order to find recommendations, programmes or even concrete solutions for dealing with ecological problems – a conversational round which, for example, is quite typical for the institution of 'enquête commissions' consulted by the German parliament – to what extent can they understand each other; and what do they have to accept collectively if they at least want to understand their differences; and if they understand their differences is there, in principle, any chance of finding collectively accepted answers to collectively disputed ecological questions? (Miller 1994: 115).

Luhmann rejects the possibility of 'substantial or teleological rationality' that could 'serve as a common denominator for an organizational co-ordination of different function systems' (Miller 1994: 115, referring to Luhmann 1989: 138). Miller argues that there are many examples of how to achieve, if not 'basic consent', at least 'co-ordinated dissent'. In other words, it is possible to achieve 'collective rationality', even if it is only 'formal and procedural'. The notion of coordinated dissent (and the 'logic of dissent' that underlies much of the process of functional differentiation of social systems) 'does not presuppose consent on all kinds of beliefs and semantic codes' or 'that anything that can be understood can also be accepted'. Rather, 'it only presupposes the collective acceptance of at least some common basic or elementary grounds (that constitute a joint universe of discourse, for example an empirical-theorectical or normative universe of discourse) because otherwise not even differences concerning particular beliefs or systems of beliefs could be mutually understood' (Miller 1994: 116).[35]

Luhmann, as Miller mentions, offers little or no empirical evidence to support his claims about the process of coordination between function systems. As I shall illustrate later, there are undoubtedly huge problems in coordination. There are also many possibilities for dialogue and coordination between function systems.

Support for this argument can be gleaned from various sources. At an ethical level, Bernstein (1983) has drawn on Arendt, Gadamer, Habermas and Rorty to explore the likelihood of dialogue in a community (see Handler 1988). Handler takes this preoccupation with dialogue further by focusing on the question of power, particularly between dependent people and the state. How can people or groups of people with different degrees of power and with different interests engage in a meaningful dialogue? As I suggested in chapter 1, underlying the concept of dialogue are the notions of trust and goodwill. Similarly, Putnam has drawn our attention to the importance of trust (as a component of social capital) in the performance of institutions. The concept of trust is also explored by Handler (1988). Drawing on empirical cases of informed consent in medical ethics, of special education and of community care for the frail, elderly poor, Handler shows the fragility of trust and its potential. Trust, and the dialogue that accompanies it, involves goodwill and friendly feelings, the willingness to listen, and discretion. It can alter power relationships. Handler notes that his examples of a 'dialogic community' represent 'tiny corners of the modern welfare state' (1988: 1091). He concludes that though the task of achieving greater dialogue is far from hopeless, it does depend on 'an extensive reconceptualization and re-structuring of the way we conduct our public business' (1988: 1113). A key element in this process is what Handler refers to as a 'supporting environment' for people undertaking such an exercise, since it is bound to conflict with many of 'our ideologies, traditions and practices'.

This brings us back to our central interests, namely the response by political institutions and established political organisations to new challenges and their effectiveness in implementing new policies. Putnam has posited a strong connection between effective democratic government and civic humanism or a strong civil society. His observations can be read as both encouraging and discouraging. He notes that 'most institutional history moves slowly' (Putnam 1993: 184). How effective can democratic institutions be, even when backed by a long history of civic humanism, in addressing the kinds of issues raised by environmentalism? If, as Putnam writes, history is very slow in 'erecting norms of reciprocity and networks of civic engagement', how can we address new challenges like environmental protection? Is Putnam presenting a barrier (additional to the ones suggested by Luhmann) to the successful implementation of new policies, particularly ones that go against the historic trend of decisions in favour of economic development at the expense of environmental protection?

Luhmann posits further hindrances. He argues that, in dealing with environmental problems, we should be more concerned with problems of 'social behaviour' than with issuing prescriptions about what we ought to do:

> Prescriptions of this sort are not hard to supply. All that is necessary is to consume fewer resources, burn off less waste gas in the air, produce fewer children. But whoever puts the problem in this way does not reckon with society, or else interprets society like an actor who needs instruction and exhortation (and this error is concealed by the fact that he or she does not speak of society but of persons) (1989: 133).

Luhmann has introduced another binary code: social behaviour versus behaviour influenced by prescriptions for individuals.

Despite the 'slow movement' of history, despite the character of social behaviour, and despite the significant problems in communication between function systems, there are still many possibilities both for coordination between sub-systems and for the influence of environmentalism on established institutions and of economics on environmental protection.

Political institutions and organisations can become more responsive to new challenges. There is no essential conflict between the slow movement of institutional history and environmentalism. The passage of time can play a vital role in consolidating the impact of new challenges. We can even adapt the findings by Putnam about a strong correspondence between effective government and civic humanism, and argue that as environmentalism becomes institutionalised (following any successes in challenging the established order) it can profit from the fact that most institutional history moves slowly. This is not to argue against innovation and design (see chapter 7).

Though Luhmann is correct to point out that prescriptions are often not enough, his argument can become a pretext for not doing anything, for not bothering to design solutions to pressing problems. Are there ways in which institutions can become more responsive to new challenges? How do we adapt, if we accept their validity, the claims by Putnam about a strong correspondence between effective government and civic humanism, in a context where society cannot adequately be construed in terms of the boundaries of a nation-state or territory? Are there mechanisms for political institutions to short-circuit the 'virtuous circles' of history and for addressing the social character of environmentalism? What are the possibilities for 'designing' solutions to improve the performance of established institutions? (See Israel 1987; Ostrom 1990.)

A focus on institutional design and on the need for political systems to break out of self-referential modes of operation suggests several options for innovation. The first is to explore more fully the mechanisms and possibilities for coordination and dialogue (as suggested by Miller, Bernstein and Handler). Second, we have perhaps relied too much on social movements to force the state into action. We may need to focus on how the state can introduce and facilitate innovations. There are enough examples of the possibilities for this (see both this and later chapters). Third, we can explore ways to generate ideas about tackling intractable problems or improving on current ways of doing things (see chapter 7). This may involve taking distance from traditional ways of conceptualising social systems and from traditional forms of logic (notably the use of adversarial logic and of rigid dichotomies and categories). Fourth, we can explore the significance of discoveries and conceptual innovations (like 'sustainable development', 'the limits to growth' and 'biodiversity') which have broken the virtuous circles of history (see chapter 7). Provided new concepts can be formulated and the opportunity arises, an issue that has smouldered in the background of political debate for long periods of time can rapidly become politically significant. Fifth, the previous point raises the issue of the context for change. An effective way of addressing conflicting demands on political institutions is to consider particular contexts and circumstances (rather than to focus on absolute truths and on fundamental conflicts between environment and development). This approach may help to achieve two things. It may direct expectations away from the state or politics as the guiding centre for everything that occurs in society. It may also create opportunities for the state to address the conflicts between the values we attach to the environment and to development.

CHAPTER 6

Disrupting the Circularity of Political Communication: The Role of Social Movements

Most institutional history moves slowly. One explanation for the slow movement of ideas, customs and practices is that political communication, like other forms of interaction, often operates in a circular or self-referential manner. This chapter, by focusing on social movements, explores how we can circumvent or break out of these circular patterns of communication, how institutions can become more responsive to new issues, ideas and challenges, and how social forces can reshape and influence the rules and procedures of institutions. Social movements can play a crucial role in challenging the slow movement of institutional history. There is general agreement among social theorists that the collective action by social movements 'involves a specific type of socially conflictual relationship' and that the types of social movement include the 'classical' workers' movement at the turn of the century, the student and civil rights movements in the 1960s and the 'new social movements' which, in the 1970s and 1980s, focused on or rediscovered questions of the environment, women's rights and peace (Renon 1994: 599). In the area of social movements the notion of the slow movement of institutional history is by definition subjected to a challenge: 'Most social theorists agree that this mode of collective action [social movements] involves a specific type of socially conflictual relationship' (Renon 1994: 599).

Sociology has spawned widely diverging views about the role of social movements. For a long time many sociologists felt that social movements did not exercise a positive influence on political debates. Traditional sociological approaches have tended to explain involvement in social movements in terms of irrationality and pathological behaviour by those who are alienated from society (Smelser 1962; Kornhauser 1959). By contrast, more recent approaches attribute to social movements a capacity to transform institutions (see Banks 1972; Touraine 1974; Habermas 1981a; 1981b). Social movements are also seen as protecting societies from the destruction of social life by 'economic rationalism' (Pusey 1991: 22).

Giddens has suggested that social movements are a major stimulus to the 'sociological imagination' and are, in some ways, more effective than established organisations. In comparing social movements to established organisations, he claims that they both gather knowledge about social life in a 'reflexive' manner. However, he sees the movements as more effective innovators, and therefore as having a greater potential to create new social arrangements and transform the established order (see also Touraine 1981; Habermas 1981a; 1981b):

> In organizations, information is systematically gathered, stored and drawn upon in the stabilizing of conditions of social reproduction. Social movements have more dynamism, and in some ways greater transformative potential, because they are specifically geared to the achievement of novel projects, and because they set themselves against the established order of things. If they are not always the harbingers of the future states of affairs they announce, they are inevitably disturbing elements in the present. Hence . . . they may identify previously undiagnosed characteristics of, and possibilities within a given institutional order (Giddens 1987: 48).

Other social and political theorists have credited social movements with the capacity to challenge and to bring about radical changes in institutional practices. Social movements are also regarded as useful for drawing attention to, if not necessarily solving, problems and crises. For Jänicke they contribute to the revitalisation of politics and to social discoveries and institutional innovations. Even Luhmann recognises their contribution.[36]

Social Movements and Reflexivity

Before exploring the role of social movements in the process of political communication, it is worth focusing on their origins. For Luhmann, the emergence of social movements hinges on the development of highly complex and differentiated social systems. With the rise of such systems it became apparent in the eighteenth century that all attempts at 'natural' representation (or 'a religious justification of representation') of the world were presumptuous: 'In the new order there are no natural primacies, no privileged positions within the whole system and therefore no position *in the* system which could establish the unity of *the* system in relation to the environment' (Luhmann 1989: 122). Still, according to Luhmann, society 'cannot do without self-observation', the kind of service provided (albeit inadequately) by social movements.

Like Luhmann, Banks (1972) has suggested that modern societies depend upon social innovation in order to survive.[37] For Banks, the emergence of social movements may include any of the following conditions:

- the rulers and the ruled are prepared to tolerate experimentation by some sections of society;
- governments foster innovative techniques; and
- governments are prepared to experiment in the manner suggested by those who challenge the established order.

Luhmann is less concerned about the particular vehicle for the self-observation or 'self-description' of society than that it should occur at all. If the sources and means of achieving innovation and self-description can be improved upon as we come better to understand creativity, two changes are likely to occur:

- Self-description and innovation can more easily arise from elements of the established order.
- Social movements, as they come to understand this process, may also provide an improved basis for self-description and innovation.[38]

Although the capacity for self-description, analysis and innovation may be vital to the established order in order to survive periods of rapid change, initially, established political institutions and organisations tend to ignore the provocations and challenges by social movements. In subsequent phases, if the movement has not receded as a political threat (especially at the ballot box), and if any attempt at suppressing it is unsuccessful, established organisations resort to cooption both of ideas and programmes and of leaders and followers. Recently, the trend has been to grant some social movements greater recognition.

Beyond Traditional Accounts of Social Movements

There has always been a tendency for social theorists and for political actors to posit fundamental conflicts between established institutional practices and the challenges or provocations by social movements. Social movements have themselves contributed to this perception by presenting established political organisations with 'fundamentalist' demands which could not be met without the dissolution or instant transformation of the political system. The 'fundamental' conflict pertains to everything from values and ideology (for instance, the apparent incompatibility of economic growth and environmental protection), to organisational structures (decentralised versus centralised; hierarchical versus participatory) (Papadakis 1988). This fundamentalism still pervades many debates over environmentalism (Papadakis 1993).

To a degree, these debates are connected to a long tradition of describing social movements as irrational and pathological responses to temporary problems faced by established political institutions and organisations. The literature on 'mass politics' (see Kornhauser 1959) evokes the dangers of allowing people to articulate protests outside the control of established institutions and organisations. There was an understandable fear that people who were alienated from social, cultural and political associations might be manipulated by demagogues, like the leaders of fascist or communist groups and movements in the 1930s.

However, this account also retarded our understanding of social movements. In the 1960s there were two influential responses to this approach and to its limitations.[39] The first (resource mobilisation theory) focused on the 'ordinariness' of social movements. The second (action or identity-oriented accounts) made strong claims for their 'novelty' and their transformative capacity. Although they offered many insights into the significance of social movements, these approaches paid little attention to how social movements may represent *both* innovation *and* continuity.

Writers who have emphasised the novelty of social movements have based their arguments on values and culture. Values and culture are said to shape interests and institutions and policy outcomes. By contrast, writers who focus on the ordinariness of social movements also stress organisation and the institutionalisation of social movements. Like instrumental 'rational' actors, they pursue their particular interests.

The arguments used to support these two accounts sometimes refer to different social movements operating in different contexts and sometimes to the same social movements.[40] The two accounts emphasise:

- how established institutions have embraced the ideas, the leaders and the followers of the social movements; and
- how the movements have engendered resistance and opposition and have been engaged in 'fundamentalist' disputes with the authorities.

While the resource mobilisation approach appears to neglect the importance of new ideas, of discontinuity and of design in bringing about social change, the fundamentalist approach often involves morally tendentious arguments and has difficulty in defining its opponent.[41]

The focus on the ordinariness or novelty of social movements has also diverted attention from an alternative account of social movements which may be far more relevant to understanding not only their character but their potential. The approach proposed here is based on the considerations that:

- institutions may thrive on the challenges presented by social movements;
- social movements rapidly display many of the characteristics of the established institutions and political organisations, especially with respect to complex organisational practices; and
- the institutionalisation of social movements need not conflict with its more fundamental goals to change values and perceptions as well as behaviour (Banks 1972: 37–8).

This approach is at odds with some of the more influential accounts of the relationship between established institutions and social movements. It also challenges the strategy of some social movements – namely, to confront established political organisations with their criticisms and then to hope for the best or to expect that the established political organisations will find solutions to the problems. It might even be argued that social movements, in so far as they fail to provide solutions to the problems they have identified, are failing to meet expectations; they are not making any positive contribution or being creative and innovative.

At the other end of the spectrum, there is the arrogance and complacency of political organisations. In dismissing some social movements, they have failed to recognise their significance in provoking new ideas and in prompting efforts to resolve issues. Social movements have often been used by established political organisations to justify prevalent institutional practices and values that support the status quo. Established political organisations have also engaged in adversarial politics rather than in dialogue. They have devoted attention to outmanoeuvring their opponents rather than to understanding their misgivings (see Papadakis 1984).

Evolution, Revolution and Design

The survival and effectiveness of political systems depends on qualities exhibited both by established political institutions and organisations and by social movements. It depends on evolution, and hence on 'some minimal government or order' (Crick

1993: 29); and on design, in other words on trying to find 'particular and workable solutions' to the 'perpetual and shifty problem of conciliation' of conflicting interests (Crick 1993: 22). Design involves inventing practical measures to deal with ever-changing circumstances.

The distinction between evolution and design is useful in framing the development of the environmental movement and the responses to it. Evolutionary change has been the favoured mode of operation in Western democratic politics. Not only is evolution far less destructive and disruptive than revolution, it corresponds closely to our traditional ways of thinking about problems.[42] In other words, evolution allows us to engage in critical assessment of ideas, to test their value over time. In the language of the 'old' politics, evolution is usually contrasted with revolution. In many ways the old politics is based on two fundamental premises – evolution (the preferred option), and revolution (the undesirable alternative). However, there is another contrast or alternative to evolution, namely design, or a deliberate attempt to shape the future which is not necessarily based on past practices. As De Bono points out, in this scenario evolution is still widely regarded as superior:

> Bad ideas will die. Good ideas will survive and become even better. We really like the method of evolution because it fits our traditional thinking habits. Change has its own energy and we can modify and control this by the use of our critical faculties because criticism is the basis of our thinking tradition. Evolution is also collective and seems democratic, whereas design always seems autocratic (De Bono 1991: 19).

Evolution is usually the preferred mode since it more easily fits a conception of change as orderly, ordained (as in a well-managed change for the better), and slow (involving a gradual adaptation to a changing environment). Historical events are often portrayed as part of an evolutionary process, even if they were haphazard and unconnected. It is easier for us to comprehend events as part of a continuum and a tradition.

Although the development of the environmental movement can partially be explained as an evolutionary process, we also need to devote attention to elements of design and innovation (chapter 7). The environmental movement has evolved over many years and therefore is not an entirely novel phenomenon. However, there is a danger in arguing that it (or any other social movement) merely reflects evolutionary processes, that the ideas it promoted, the actions it undertook and the policies it influenced were entirely understandable on the basis of 'path dependence' (see chapter 4). Evolutionary explanations of institutional behaviour are valuable in understanding even the behaviour of social movements. They can also divert us from the most interesting aspects of social processes, namely, the elements of accident, design and creativity. Focusing on these accidents and designs is, paradoxically, valuable precisely because of the impact they have on 'what comes later'.[43]

The path through history of the environmental movement can be explained by evolutionary models only in so far as one focuses on what comes after an important scientific breakthrough and a new way of conceptualising this discovery. The development of the environmental movement leads us to question evolutionary models of change, particularly when it challenges deeply held beliefs about the value of progress defined in terms of economic growth and material prosperity.

The impact of the environmental movement represents a puzzle when we frame change in terms of evolution or its traditional opponent, revolution. Evolutionary approaches are based on the assumption that the paths or trajectory of the past will, in a logical manner, determine the present. In order to explain the sudden rise of the environmental movement, we try hard to unearth a precedent. We then become wise after the event. The same applies to other phenomena that we could not anticipate, like the civil rights and student movements in the 1960s. To cope with these disjunctures, we employ the following mechanism:

> Every valuable creative idea must be logical in hindsight (otherwise we would never appreciate its value). So once the creative idea has come about we insist that it could indeed have come from step-wise logic. All valuable ideas that come about as a result of insight, chance or mistake must always be presented in the scientific literature as if they had come about by a process of careful step-wise logic, otherwise the paper would never be published (De Bono 1991: 217).[44]

On reading this passage, a colleague of mine observed: 'When I was a student my supervisor said to something to the effect that "Always give the impression that you are in control of the process – examiners like that!" '

The environmental movement represents a puzzle because it does not fit easily into either the evolutionary account of social change or the revolutionary one. Apart from a few fringe groups, the environmental movement has not sought to overthrow or destroy the state. Nor has it always complied with the evolutionary, reformist agenda of established parties. This attempt by the environmental movement to avoid some of the paths set by established reformers (who favour evolutionary change) and to desist from adopting traditional approaches (to revolutionary change) involves the abandonment of some of the more utopian goals of social movements. For instance, it questions whether we can create 'an undifferentiated community free of all power and all forms of inequality' (Cohen 1985). Rather, the new movements have drawn on several principles, including the struggle for individual autonomy, and some of the formal egalitarian and universalistic principles that characterise modern societies and parliamentary institutions (Cohen 1985).

Apart from its capacity for drawing on time-honoured principles, the impact of the environmental movement has been achieved not by embracing traditional evolutionary and revolutionary models for social action but by focusing on changing perceptions about what constitutes the quality and meaning of life. This occurred in several stages, during the 1960s, the 1970s and the 1980s. At different moments new concepts were created to articulate their concerns.

In the 1960s, for instance, the notion of a *Silent Spring* (Carson 1962) referred to the fact that, if we continued to treat our environment in a certain way, there would be dire consequences. Similarly, the notion of *The Limits to Growth* promoted by the Club of Rome in the 1970s contributed to a radical shift in perceptions of our way of life. In the 1980s and 1990s, concerns about social justice and economic development on a global scale, combined with growing anxiety about the depletion of the ozone layer and the emission of greenhouse gases, have led to intense efforts to define a new agenda based on the concept of sustainable development (World Commission on Environment and Development 1990). Many people are now conscious of the possibilities either for promoting development without harming the environment or for maintaining a balance between development and the environment (see chapter 16).

For those who are accustomed to an evolutionary model for explaining change, the survival of established organisations (political parties, interest groups and the agencies of government) is unsurprising. This is construed as another indication of the durability of norms and procedures for absorbing any challenges. Moreover, the durability of political institutions, the absence of any *coup d'état* executed by green revolutionaries, appears to verify the evolutionary model. For revolutionaries, there is of course only disappointment. Capitalism is thriving. The old parties are still in power. The environment remains under threat.

Adjacent to these two positions, however, we find that there has been, despite the appearance of normality, a fundamental shift in perceptions and behaviour both in business and industry and among the governors and the population at large. The shift has taken place in fits and starts. The environmental movement and its goals were written off on several occasions, only to return with a vengeance (framed by new concepts and ideas) to the political agenda. The underlying trend, however, with the benefit of hindsight, has been towards much greater acceptance of a fundamental shift in both values and policies.

Social movements present not only a challenge to evolutionary accounts of social change, they play a valuable role in disrupting the circularity of political communication. This can be ascribed to the following factors:

- political institutions, if they are to survive as a process of conciliation and as facilitators of political communication, need to demonstrate some flexibility by taking on board ideas and issues raised by social movements;
- social movements have frequently mobilised sufficient popular support effectively to compel established political organisations to heed public opinion;
- social movements have regularly attracted the support of, and even been led by, some elements within established political organisations; and
- the impetus to social movement activities has repeatedly come from conceptual advances based on discoveries by scientists, educators and other individuals.

We can identify elements of continuity and discontinuity in the development of the environmental movement. In dealing with new challenges to institutions, we can appreciate the importance of both. Without disruption, design and creativity, the circular character of political communication cannot be broken. Without institutional routines and procedures, we cannot ensure that new and desirable policies will be implemented systematically and successfully. Institutions often stand, ultimately, to benefit from innovations. Innovations can be effective only if they are supported by institutional structures. Established institutions can also ensure that new ideas, particularly if they appear to be far-fetched or impractical, are subjected to careful scrutiny. Political institutions can also be helpful as mechanisms for 'deliberate conciliation' between opposing viewpoints (Crick 1993: 19). This serves as a further reminder of the significance of political communication.

The following chapters will analyse the character of institutional changes that have accompanied the focus on environmental politics. The next chapter attends to arguments about evolution and design (or creativity) as outlined in the preceding pages.

CHAPTER 7

Design, Evolution and the Environmental Movement

There are some striking continuities in organised campaigns for environmental protection both within and among nations. It is easy to find historical precedents and cross-cultural similarities in the 'evolution' of environmentalism. It is therefore tempting to dismiss claims about the innovative character of environmentalism in our own time.

In the following sketch, which draws attention to elements of logical sequence and connectedness in environmental campaigns, my aim is less to prove the validity of evolutionary logic than to demonstrate:

- the value of institutions in perpetuating and reinforcing certain patterns of behaviour;
- how difficult it is for new issues to become conspicuous on the political agenda (especially if they challenge some of our cherished ways of conceptualising economic growth and material prosperity); *and*
- the need for design and creativity in conceptualising an issue which can then be placed on the agenda by sufficiently powerful political forces.

The last point can be linked to the earlier discussions about innovation and to the proposition about how, if new concepts can be formulated and the opportunity arises, an issue that has lain dormant for a long time can suddenly assume political significance.

For instance, as I shall illustrate in this chapter, the concern about the destruction of forests can be traced back to the turn of century. Yet, it is only from the late 1970s that the problem became politically important (see part III on how political organisations took up this problem; part IV on the articulation of this topic by the media; and part V, figure 17.1, third column).

Evolution and Innovation: Some Early Illustrations[45]

Ideas about environmental protection have been around for centuries. Political organisations have generally been slow in taking up these ideas. The settlement of this continent by Aboriginal people around 40 000 years ago reminds us of the enduring concern about the environment.[46] Though Aboriginals were harshly treated by the white colonisers of Australia, their way of life served as a reminder to the white settlers of the changing relationships between human beings and their natural surroundings. Some of the earliest white settlers were vaguely aware of differences between their own culture and that of the Aboriginals in relating to nature.

The awareness of different approaches to nature also manifested itself in the influence of the nineteenth-century romantic movement which had developed in Europe. Though Australians did not experience the reaction against 'rationality' and human reason on the same scale as the Europeans, a small number of the earliest white settlers regretted the influence of European civilisation and contrasted it with the serenity of the Australian landscape (Bride 1898: 239, cited in Heathcote, 1972: 88).

In the following sketch of the development of ideas about nature we find elements of evolution and innovation. With respect to the latter, it is worth emphasising the novel character of the romantic revolt in Europe against prevailing views about progress and the adoption of notions derived from Europe in representations of the Australian landscape. During the nineteenth century the romantic evocation of the bush became part of a culture shared by many settlers on the land, and by the turn of the century the bush had become a powerful symbol of nationalism shared by urban dwellers. A new idea, 'the bush', was promoted by artists and politicians who played a key role in shaping perceptions. Inadvertently, they also made it easier for environmental campaigns which began in the nineteenth century to gain momentum (see below).

In romanticising the landscape, the earliest white settlers tried to portray it as a European one. This is hardly surprising, given the origins of the romantic revolution. Led by Tom Roberts (who founded the Heidelberg school of painters in Melbourne), the next generation of artists and poets broke with the tradition of portraying the Australian landscape as a European one. Although artists like Roberts did bring some new European influences to bear on their work (notably the use of light and colour discovered by the Impressionists), their portrayal of the landscape and of the 'heroism' of the pioneering era helped both to promote Australian art and to change perceptions about the bush and about Australian nationalism.

Art and politics can be combined to promote a wide variety of ideologies. In certain contexts they have been used to advance communism or fascism. In Australia perceptions of the landscape were used to promote an egalitarian ideology, particularly in the cities. The emerging and powerful labour movement drew on traditional images of life in the bush, especially on ideas about mateship and rebellion. Writers and poets, through their creativity, were effective in making accessible to urban dwellers myths about life on the land (Heathcote 1972). The shift in perceptions about the bush contributed to the development of the environmental movement. The earliest organised groups concerned about environmental protection in Australia fastened on to the ideas about patriotism, equality and mateship. The Mountain Trails Club, formed in 1914, was regarded by its founder, Myles Dunphy, as a 'bush brotherhood'.

The Paradox of an Evolutionary Account

The sudden shifts by which environmental issues come to feature on the political agenda can be truly appreciated only if one takes into account the lengthy period of gestation of the environmental movement – at least as a politically powerful force.

The following antecedents to the environmental movement illustrate this paradox. In France, the Society for the Protection of Nature was formed in 1854. In Britain, the Commons, Open Spaces and Footpaths Preservation Society was founded in 1865; the East Riding Association for the Protection of British Birds in 1867; the Association for the Protection of British Birds in 1870; the National Trust in 1895; and the British Ecological Society in 1913. In the United States of America the American Ornithologists Union was established in 1883, and the Sierra Club in 1892. All these organisations influenced legislation for environmental protection, including the dedication of major national parks.

In Australia, organisations committed to environmental protection included the Royal Societies which were formed in Tasmania (1842), in Victoria (1859) and in other states in the late nineteenth century. Organisations like the Field Naturalists' Section of the Royal Society lobbied governments, attracted a small but influential group of supporters, and gathered information on conservation issues. Conservation groups campaigned successfully for the establishment of the first national park in South Australia and (from 1892 onwards) for the preservation of the Flinders Chase (which culminated in the Flora and Fauna Reserves Act, 1919) (Whitelock 1985: 125). Naturalists' organisations also campaigned successfully for the introduction of 'closed seasons' to protect wildlife in the nineteenth century, covering deer, antelopes and some bird species (Animal Protection Act, 1879), imported and song birds (Birds Protection Act, 1881) (effective for five years and subsequently for a closed season).[47] Other successes included the protection, in 1866, of the Jenolan Caves in the Blue Mountains and, from the 1860s onwards, the creation of reserves along the coast. The latter involved the reservation for public use of a strip of land 100 feet wide from the high-water mark (Heathcote 1972: 147). Campaigns to change perceptions about the environment can repeatedly be traced back to the nineteenth century. For instance, in Victoria, 176 000 acres were preserved as parkland largely through campaigns organised by conservation groups and by prominent scientists, politicians and bureaucrats (Powell 1976: 115). At the turn of the century foresters were criticised for obstructing the tide of progress (namely, land settlement). The foresters had campaigned for the protection of forests on the grounds of preserving timber for future generations. There is a parallel between their perceptions and the notion of sustainable development (World Commission on Environment and Development 1990).

Inevitability and Innovation

Most of these examples imply that governments may have responded to pressure for environmental protection. To a degree, these examples do undermine claims about self-referential political systems that are unable to engage in intersystemic discourse (see chapter 5). However, the issue raised by Luhmann about the effectiveness of the political systems and the questions that I have raised about the obstacles to and the possibilities for the implementation of policies will be considered more fully in subsequent chapters. In this section I want to retain the focus on the contrast between evolution (and the notion of inevitability) and innovation. Arguments about evolution lead to the following question: were the responses by governments (cited above) inevitable? When I was an undergraduate, one of the lecturers asked us to consider whether certain events (say, the failure of the Weimar Constitution, or the Cold War, or the construction of the Berlin Wall) were inevitable. For those who answered that these events were not inevitable, the collapse of communism in Eastern Europe in the late 1980s would perhaps have come as less of a surprise than to those who answered in the affirmative.

However much we try to focus on evolution, the historical record is full of surprises and of new ideas taken up by social movements that had not been anticipated by the previous generation. It is only in retrospect that the romantic movement and the discovery of the Australian bush by poets and artists appears to be logical. Who would have anticipated the long-term impact of the earliest environmental groups in Australia? The formation of the Wild Life Preservation Society of Australia in 1909, of the Mountain Trails Club in 1914 and of the National Parks and Primitive Areas Council in the 1930s challenged the predominant approach to land use which 'could see no cultural values in preserving naturalness and wildlife' (Strom 1979: 53). None of these organisations succeeded in changing perceptions on a massive scale, even though they articulated a clash in values that became more pointed after the Second World War (see the subsequent discussions on *Silent Spring* and on postmaterialism).

These early initiatives by activists like Dunphy were effective in promoting the creation of national parks and the preservation of wilderness. National campaigns often involve modifying ideas from other countries. Dunphy adapted from the USA the idea of large national parks. He praised the 'nationally-minded citizens' of that country who valued wildlife for more than their 'skins, meat or bloody "sport"' (Dunphy in Thompson 1986: 169). He described the parks in the USA as 'the greatest piece of work for purposes of recreation and general conservation ever accomplished', and then emulated these achievements. As a result of lobbying by the National Parks and Primitive Areas Council, between 1932 and 1962 Australian governments dedicated fourteen national parks and other schemes, and many others were approved in subsequent years.

None the less, it took several decades for governments to establish appropriate structures for managing national parks, and to incorporate these ideas into their party platforms and programmes. Dunphy, with his proposals for statutory intervention 'to guarantee perpetual boundaries for wilderness areas', appeared to be 'decades ahead of his time' (Thompson 1986: 198). Interestingly, it is only with the benefit of hindsight that we can 'substantiate' these claims.

Other innovations that were 'ahead of their time' include the view that the environment might become a resource for tourism. Dunphy anticipated a form of tourism which combined access to parks and wildlife by tourists and the preservation of these assets in perpetuity. He also developed the craft of bushwalking by using new methods and new equipment during his long treks through the forests.

Even though the development of environmentalism can be viewed from an evolutionary perspective, we face the paradox that this evolution was based on new discoveries, innovations and concepts, and that the 'path of evolution' was full of unexpected twists and turns. To sum up, few, if any, people anticipated that the following discoveries and breakthroughs would form the basis for environmental movements after the Second World War:

- the 'discovery' of differences between the lifestyles of European settlers and the indigenous population;
- the translation of this discovery through the language of romanticism;
- the creation of myths about the Australian bush by poets and artists, and the connection between these ideas and the ideas of nationalism, egalitarianism and patriotism;
- the novel practice of organised lobbying by associations of preservationists and conservationists;
- the adaptation of a model for the preservation of wilderness and national parks from the USA;
- innovations in ideas about tourism and environmental protection;
- the development of the craft of bushwalking;
- the early challenges to colonialist views of wildlife and of land use; and
- the rediscovery of the notion of preservation for future generations.

Most of these ideas did not feature at all in the agendas and policy speeches of major parties and leading politicians until the 1960s (see chapters 8 to 12). Moreover, support for environmental groups was not widespread.[48]

Following the Great Depression and the Second World War, there seemed little prospect of challenging predominant views about the connection between the quality of life and the achievement of economic growth and economic development. However, at an international level there were some notable initiatives, including the formation of the International Union for the Protection of Nature in 1948, the meeting of the United Nations Scientific Conference on the Conservation and Utilisation of Resources (UNSCCUR) in 1949 and the foundation of the World Wildlife Fund in 1960 (see McCormick 1989).

Again, each of these initiatives represented important breakthroughs and discoveries:

- the broad-ranging agenda of the UNSCCUR, which considered the availability of resources to meet growing demands;
- the success of the UNSCCUR in placing conservation on the agenda of intergovernmental business;
- the anticipation by the International Union for the Protection of Nature of the effects of toxic chemicals; and
- the idea of fund-raising in order to preserve wildlife promoted by Julian Huxley and taken up by the World Wildlife Fund (see McCormick 1989).

My understanding of these events leads to a focus on two developments. The first is the element of continuity in environmentalism, particularly in the demonstrated capacity of political institutions and organisations to take up new ideas, to reinforce patterns of behaviour, and to shape new social forces.[49] The second, which is easily overlooked when we have amassed evidence about continuities, is that innovations tend to occur in a random manner, and that institutions are often slow to respond to the fundamental challenges arising from these innovations and discoveries. These issues will be explored further by identifying scientific discoveries and conceptual advances which helped to promote environmentalism.

Scientific Discoveries, Conceptual Change and the Role of Elites and Experts

It takes more than a scientific discovery to bring about a shift in perceptions about environmental protection and to create mass political support for it. Few, if any, of the initiatives described so far were associated with mass movements for environmental protection. Some initiatives were poorly organised and enjoyed very limited funding. It was only in the late 1950s and early 1960s that a broader movement began to emerge which also rediscovered and posed fundamental questions about the relationship of human beings to their environment.

One of the most valuable breakthroughs was the articulation of the discovery that the quality of human life could seriously be threatened by economic growth and economic development. The publication of *Silent Spring* by Rachel Carson provides a striking illustration of how such a discovery can be effectively disseminated. This book is widely regarded as the source of inspiration for environmental movements in the latter half of the twentieth century. Although *Silent Spring* was a landmark scientific study, its impact is not solely attributable to its scientific character. Carson, who had worked for the USA government as a marine biologist, was disturbed by the effect of chemical pesticides and insecticides, notably DDT, on wildlife and their habitat, and the consequent dangers to human life. In sharing her findings with others, she did more than present scientific evidence. *Silent Spring* challenged the entire approach of the chemical and other industries, their 'arrogance' in assuming that 'nature exists for the convenience of man', and their failure to appreciate that 'The history of life on earth has been a history of interaction between living things and their surroundings' (Carson 1962).

The book stirred up the chemical industry, which spent hundreds of thousands of dollars in trying to discredit it. Publicity surrounding the book also led to the establishment of a special panel of the Science Advisory Committee by President Kennedy, which supported the arguments presented by Carson. The book served for many as a manifesto for questioning the prevailing approaches to progress and the quality of life. Hard-cover sales alone amounted to 500 000, and in 1963 it was published in fifteen countries.

Given that much of the scientific evidence about insecticides and pesticides was already available, why did this book make such an impact? There had already been warnings about the dangers of DDT to the environment, and in 1945 popular magazines like *Harper's*, the *Atlantic Monthly* and the *New Yorker* had featured articles on this topic (McCormick 1989). A crucial difference between prior accounts and *Silent Spring* lay in the ability of Carson to link scientific discoveries to fundamental questions about how people related to the environment. Although the timing of the work may also have been a crucial factor – in other words, there was a more receptive audience in 1962 than in 1945 – other works had appeared around the same time, without the same impact (see McCormick 1989).

Before considering the political context which may have influenced the reception of *Silent Spring* and the role of new social movements in challenging and shaping government policy, it is worth exploring the role of 'elites' in articulating new concerns. The term *elites* can be used to refer to leading scientists and educators, as well as to journalists, public servants and politicians. It can also be used to refer to 'expert opinion' or 'expert communities' (see Zaller 1992: 319–28). The founding members of conservation and environmental groups were often from established elites who understood the importance of a radical shift in attitudes, values and perceptions about the environment (see below).

The role of elites and of prominent, nonconformist 'outsiders' (see Noelle-Neumann 1984) is important not only during phases of mass support for social movements but also prior to their emergence. There is frequently a long gap between a scientific discovery or conceptual breakthrough and the emergence of a powerful social movement. During this phase elites can play a crucial role in maintaining and promoting interest in a new issue.

Many of the discoveries and conceptual advances referred to so far have been made by experts or promoted by expert opinion and expert communities. This often lends their claims credibility (see chapters 13 to 16). The importance of expert communities in maintaining interest in an issue after a breakthrough has been achieved was demonstrated in the 1960s by the support given by the scientific community to the International Biological Programme. The formation in 1964 of the International Biological Programme comprising biologists from several countries represented a response to the threats posed to the environment. The programme was innovative not only in providing documentary evidence of threats to the environment, but also in stimulating collaboration between researchers in different nations. The forty volumes of findings by the programme contributed to a climate of opinion in favour of environmental protection and, indirectly, to the first major international conference on the human environment, organised by the UN in Stockholm in 1972 (see McCormick 1989: 61).

All the major social movements of the 1960s were supported at crucial stages of their development by elites and expert communities. Some movements grew out of formal organisations which had been created by prominent members of the establishment. In Australia, for example, the initiative for the formation of the ACF in 1965 came from well-known members of the political establishment as well as from prominent scientists (Warhurst 1994a: 76). Its founding members included the Duke of Edinburgh and the Chief Justice of the High Court, Sir Garfield Barwick. The ACF was the first truly national organisation of its kind. It even received a small grant from the federal government. Barwick, who later became its president, sought actively to promote changes in perceptions and in the organisation of environmentalists as a lobby group.

Although the ACF was not a militant organisation, prominent members influenced perceptions about economic growth and development. Interestingly, Barwick was closely affiliated to the political party that had presided over the postwar economic development of Australia. Drawing on notions similar to the term 'sustainable development', Barwick argued that conservation was a *prerequisite* for sustained productivity and a 'paramount partner' of economic growth and development (Barwick 1974).

He questioned the one-sided preoccupation with economic growth for its own sake, and promoted a change in values. He also emphasised involvement by citizens, the community and industry in tackling environmental problems.

Support among elites and expert communities has been an important ingredient in the development of other social movements. In the USA elites and expert communities provided openings for various civil rights movements and contributed to decisive shifts in the direction of public opinion. The following examples by Zaller (1992) show how long it can take to get from 'scientific discoveries' to the articulation of these discoveries to political action and, finally, to changing public opinion.

The first example is from the development of the civil rights movement which tried to address the issue of racism in the USA. Racist attitudes at the beginning of the twentieth century were supported not only by most people but by the majority of the political elite. In 1930, however, the Supreme Court rejected a presidential nominee to the Supreme Court mainly because he had made a racist speech ten years earlier. The source of this shift, according to Myrdal (1944), lies in studies conducted by expert communities in the 1920s which challenged the prevailing scientific theories of race and the focus on biological explanations of human behaviour. These significant shifts in the direction of scientific research and of political elite attitudes towards race did not lead to an immediate change in either mass attitudes or behaviour. However, despite constant setbacks in race relations, over the past four decades there has been a decisive change in policies and in attitudes (Zaller 1992: 11).

The second illustration is from the movement for the rights of homosexuals. Groups campaigning for homosexual rights emerged in the nineteenth century. However, they had no influence on public attitudes until the latter part of this century. The first changes in attitudes occurred only in the 1940s and 1950s among a small minority of scientists. It took several more decades for the broader scientific community of experts (for instance, the American Psychiatric Association in the 1970s) to follow suit, and even longer for a broad shift in mass opinion (Zaller 1992: 321–5).

The previous chapters, which focus on political institutions and their self-referential character and on the role of social movements in challenging the political agenda, explain to some extent why it takes so long for some new ideas and issues (either through design or through accident) to assume a significant position on the political agenda. The following section considers specific examples of the crucial role played by environmental social movements in this process.

Social Movements and Innovation: Seizing Opportunities

The hostile response by industrial and other interests to new discoveries and to ways of conceptualising these discoveries, and the reluctance by governments to deal promptly and effectively with new issues, contributed to the emergence of new conservation and environmental groups. Later, the same groups would play a decisive role in influencing government policy and in the formation of new political parties.

Until the 1960s, concern about the environment was articulated by a small minority of scientists, administrators, politicians and activists. The re-emergence of social movements after the Second World War contributed to an increase in citizen involvement in political issues. The leaders of some of these movements perceived, in the 1960s and 1970s, a chance for using the environment as an issue for their broad campaign to reform established institutions. They seized a unique opportunity to embrace the cause of environmental protection, and they used it to attack complacency and corruption in political organisations and to establish an agenda for a 'new politics'. There has long been a strong emphasis on moral protest within these movements (Pakulski 1991). The origins of mass environmental social movements include student revolts and protests against the Vietnam War in the 1960s, civil rights movements, the women's movement, and the peace movement (dating back to the campaigns against nuclear weapons in the 1950s) (see Papadakis 1993).[50]

The terms *new politics* and *new social movements* did not arise simultaneously. New social movement was first used to describe protest groups that arose in the 1970s in Western Europe, especially the environmental and peace movements in countries like West Germany (Brand 1982; Brand et al. 1986). By contrast, new politics was used in the early 1960s to characterise the misgivings about patronage, corrupt practices and the lack of responsiveness by established political organisations to new issues and concerns (Burkhart and Kendrick 1971). The new politics apparently involved placing new issues on the political agenda, adopting a different political style, and restructuring governments along more realistic and relevant lines. The new political activists saw themselves as less concerned (than politicians in established parties) about power than about the public good.

It is easy to be swept away by claims about novelty: some of the fundamental issues addressed by a new politics are as old as the practice (and the study) of politics, and contemporary approaches to solving problems have often been foreshadowed in the past. However, this level of abstraction overlooks the need for innovation and design at particular moments in time.

Three significant areas of innovation by social movements are: their challenge to prevailing ideologies by creating new ones; their willingness to experiment with organisational structures; and their suggestions for dealing with social issues.

One of the conceptual advances and innovations which contributed to the rise of the environmental movement in the 1960s was that it turned the analysis of pollution and environmental damage into a dialogue about the concepts of life and death. *Silent Spring* is the best example of how environmentalists were able to combine an informative account of damage to the environment with an emotional and imaginative depiction of a new struggle for survival. The metaphor of life and death was extended by political activists in the 1960s to incorporate political life in general: the reformers distinguished themselves from 'corrupt and decaying' political regimes. This metaphor appeared entirely appropriate, given the long trail of environmental disasters—DDT, oil spills in the ocean, the extinction or threat of extinction of numerous species (peregrine falcons, whales, seals and many others), nuclear catastrophes (Chernobyl), the destruction of the ozone layer, the increase in carbon dioxide emissions.[51]

The dominant political parties initially found it difficult to change course, even though there was mounting evidence of changes in perceptions about the dangers to the environment. The preoccupation by the dominant parties with economic growth after the Second World War provided reformist movements with a unique opportunity to lead campaigns for environmental protection. Although the major parties have tried to respond to concern about the environment (see chapters 8 to 12), they have had to grapple with countervailing forces, notably the enduring preoccupation with economic security among interest groups and the majority of the electorate. Their failure to take adequate measures to prevent environmental degradation has therefore meant that alternative, green political parties continue to have a strong appeal (Richardson and Rootes 1995). A solid core of the electorate is continuing to vote for green parties, and a much larger group anticipates that environmental issues will one day need to be addressed much more urgently (ANOP 1991; 1993).

Another breakthrough by the environmentalist movement was to promote postmaterialist values. Although the notion of postmaterialist values is not an entirely novel phenomenon – it arises implicitly in Aristotle's *Politics* – the rise in these values from the 1960s onwards reflected a profound challenge to ideologies associated with the great transformation of the nineteenth century, including the industrial revolution.

The rise in postmaterialism is associated with environmentalism both in European countries and in Australia and North America (Inglehart 1990; Bean and Papadakis 1994). Despite significant differences in the contexts which gave rise to environmental social movements and in the responses by different political regimes to these challenges (see Kitschelt 1986), there are some striking similarities. In all cases, the conflicts between new social movements and established institutions and political organisations derived partly from differing perceptions of the character of economic growth. For instance, some groups in the Federal Republic of Germany sanctioned economic growth through the exploitation of nuclear power. Their faith in the 'ideology of growth' and in the central importance of continued material prosperity were questioned by the protestors. The apparent differences in the issues adopted by protestors in countries like Germany and Australia (nuclear energy in the former and rainforests in the latter) may serve to disguise a common preoccupation: they all questioned the values associated with a society that was, in their opinion, addicted to production and consumption. The protests for the preservation of wilderness areas in Australia were therefore driven by similar values to the protests against nuclear power in Germany.

The force of the shift in values is reflected in the creation of new political parties (Curtice 1989; Müller-Rommel 1989) and in speculation about new bases for conflict in Western democracies and a shift or realignment of voters (Dalton, Flanagan and Beck 1984; Dalton and Kuechler 1990; Inglehart 1990).

In Australia, as in many other countries, the initial reception to these protests by established political parties, business groups and labour unions was less than friendly. This comes as no surprise if we consider how organisations establish procedures to deal with challenges in a routine manner, and if we observe that the protestors were questioning the political and economic power, the ideology and the electoral bases of these associations.

In creating their own political organisations, many of the protestors used the skills they had acquired as members of the major political parties. In the Federal Republic of Germany the diffuse protest against nuclear power projects developed first into a challenge to the political system founded after the Second World War, and later into an attempt to acquire power through the established system in order to change it from within. In Australia, though it took much longer for the protest movement to move from the margins of established political organisations to their centre, the protestors did eventually exercise significant influence on policies.

It is valuable to document the diversity of environmental movements and their impact on different party systems. Yet the influence of environmentalism has been strong in many different types of political regime. The Green Party in Germany was regarded by most people as the most successful in the world during the 1980s. Still, its influence on policy, on values and on public opinion was not necessarily greater than in other countries with weak green parties. Although environmentalism has manifested itself in the activities of social movements and political parties, it does not necessarily imply a particular organisational structure (for instance, a green political party or a social movement opposed to nuclear power). Rather, environmentalism represents changes in political and social processes, values and attitudes, and the influence of ideas about the environment on political regimes.

We cannot ascertain the influence of environmentalism simply by examining electoral data. For instance, the setbacks experienced by the Green Party in the 1990 federal election in Germany were not attributable to a fundamental decline in interest in environmental protection. Apart from the concerns arising from the politics and economics of German reunification, a key determinant of the poor performance by the Green Party was the ability of established parties to adapt to and coopt the green agenda (see Papadakis 1989). Moreover, support for environmentalism is fairly robust, even during periods of economic recession (Papadakis 1994).

The influence of environmentalists can be estimated in several ways. Votes for a Green Party are one indicator. Another is to examine the policies of the major parties. Environmentalism has influenced policy even in countries where green parties have fared badly in elections. In Australia, where a Green Party was not even formed at the national level until 1992, environmentalism has been appropriated by other minor parties. Parties like the Australian Democrats have become strong proponents of environmentalism (see chapter 11). Likewise, as in many other countries, the dominant parties and other organisations have responded to environmentalism by adopting many of its demands.

History, Innovation and Opportunism

The success of green social movements in articulating postmaterialist values and in influencing policy reminds us of the paradox of evolution and innovation. Important factors are conceptual advances and innovation, and the capacity of social movements to seize new opportunities. So too is history. The success of social movements has set historical precedents. New patterns of continuity were established by the breakthroughs of the past. Because of the opportunism of the environmental movement in the 1960s and 1970s in seizing the initiative on issues like nuclear power, several generations came to identify strongly with oppositional movements and parties on environmental policy. Surveys show that when people are asked whom they trust most to solve environmental problems, scientists and technologists as well as environmental groups are rated far ahead of political parties and various levels of government (Papadakis 1993: 185) (see chapter 16).[52] Trust in environmental groups is partly based on public perceptions of their willingness and ability to take action.

The following account demonstrates the importance of opportunism and innovation for the development of the environmental movement. Of all the campaigns that mobilised support for environmental protection, protests against the development of nuclear power (either for military or civilian purposes) have provided some of the best opportunities for the development of new social movements. Disquiet about the dangers from nuclear fallout, following hundreds of tests of atomic weapons, originated in the 1940s. The tests were conducted by several major powers. The impact was felt by their own inhabitants and those of other nations. This environmental issue was truly global (McCormick 1989: 51). The proliferation and deployment of nuclear weapons and the testing of this technology provided opportunities for powerful peace movements in the 1950s and in the 1970s (see Parkin 1968; Papadakis 1984). Among the most innovative responses to the testing of nuclear weapons was the formation of Greenpeace in the early 1970s. Through the spectacular attempts of its members to interfere with the testing of weapons, Greenpeace attracted media attention; it was effective in delaying or preventing experiments, and also in generating mass support.[53]

The development of nuclear energy for civilian purposes provided further occasions for protestors to contest prevailing modes of political and social organisation. The emergence of green parties throughout Western Europe in the 1970s was based largely on the attempt to create a political organisation which reflected the widespread protests against the construction of nuclear power stations (see Papadakis 1984). Support for these social movements and political parties grew as people became aware of the history of nuclear accidents (like Windscale in the United Kingdom in 1957) and were informed about new ones (Three Mile Island in the USA in 1978). The disaster at Chernobyl in the Soviet Union in 1986 confirmed the vulnerability of all states (even those that did not have nuclear power stations) to the dangers of nuclear accidents.

Despite detailed knowledge about the effects of radiation and the risks involved in developing nuclear power stations, established political organisations, including governments, have been often slow to implement changes. Change has occasionally taken place when the dangers of nuclear energy have been highlighted by the media under pressure from powerful social movements.

Global Networks and Innovation

The nuclear issue is one of several that help to illustrate why the influence of environmentalism is both widespread and relatively autonomous of particular political settings, at least as far as Western democracies are concerned. There has also been a growing awareness of the global character of environmental problems.

Some people have observed that a small group of influential writers and thinkers (like Rachel Carson, Barry Commoner, Paul Ehrlich and E. F. Schumacher) have contributed to the transformation of public perceptions of environmentalism (see

Rubin 1994). The discussion of *Silent Spring* and the media focus on environmental disasters shows that it is not so much the scientific discovery itself that immediately attracts attention or leads to changes in policy, but the ability to develop it as a concept.[54]

This can be demonstrated by considering the concept of *The Limits to Growth* (Meadows et al. 1974). The thesis about *The Limits to Growth* represents another landmark in the the development of environmental politics and institutional change. The principal and dramatic conclusion of this study conducted by a team at the Massachusetts Institute of Technology (MIT) was that:

> If the present growth trends in world population, industrialization, pollution, food production, and resource depletion continue unchanged, the limits to growth on this planet will be reached sometime within the next one hundred years. The most probable result will be a rather sudden and uncontrollable decline in both population and industrial capacity. (Meadows et al. 1974: 23).

The study went on to argue that it would be possible 'to alter these growth trends and to establish a condition of ecological and economic stability that is sustainable far into the future'.

Apart from the controversial findings of the report, it is worth noting that the research had been initiated by a group of prominent scientists, economists, industrialists and government officials known as the Club of Rome. Although further studies pointed to the deficiencies of *The Limits to Growth* (Cole et al. 1973), the Club of Rome study made an immense contribution to awareness of environmental problems. Within five years of its publication, about 4 million copies of the book had been sold in thirty languages (McCormick 1989: 82).

The Limits to Growth was only one of several studies attributed to the 'doomsday brigade'. Others included *The Population Bomb* (Ehrlich 1968), with sales of 3 million copies in paperback by the mid-1970s (see McCormick 1989: 70); *The Closing Circle* (Commoner 1971); *Blueprint for Survival* (*The Ecologist* 1972); and *Small is Beautiful* (Schumacher 1973).

The success of these books lay not in the accuracy of their predictions – most were woefully off the mark – but in developing concepts that raised awareness about environmental issues. As in many of the cases mentioned above, neither the idea nor the methodology was entirely novel. The originality lay in the effective revival of old ideas: 'Like Smith, Malthus, Mill, Marx, and Keynes before them, the new prophets of doom touched off heated debate, so that their arguments became less important than the effects of the arguments' (McCormick 1989: 87).

It could be asserted that the alarmist approach by some writers retarded rather than advanced the cause of environmental protection. However, analysis of the membership of environmental groups and of the party platforms and policy speeches of the major parties suggests that the effect was not entirely negative (see chapters 8 to 16). The real difficulty in the approach adopted by some environmentalists lies in their all-too-hasty dismissal of established organisations. Some of the most valuable initiatives for change were to come out of these organisations.

Far from arguing that established associations are hopeless in bringing about effective change, this book suggests that these organisations, backed by the routine measures that are a characteristic of institutional structures, provide a foundation for implementing policies. While the evidence lends much support to the claims by the new institutionalists, two other issues remain pertinent. First, there are the abiding obstacles to dialogue between the political and other sub-systems as well as between the other sub-systems (like the economy and the environment). Second, established organisations do need to respond more flexibly to the challenges mentioned so far, including changes in values, scientific discoveries and conceptual advances in promoting these discoveries. To that extent, a focus on evolution, on social capital and on customs and traditions can take us only so far.

PART III

Political Organisations and Adaptation

CHAPTER 8

Inertia and Innovation

The tension between innovation and tradition, between new ideas and established institutional practices, pervades most areas of policy-making. The evolution of policies on the environment serves to demonstrate that, despite this tension, established organisations are capable of responding to discoveries about environmental problems and to new intellectual paradigms. The policies also demonstrate the capacity of political parties both to influence, and to be influenced by, public opinion (see chapters 9 to 16). The pace of responses by established political organisations has varied immensely. In some instances, there has been a huge effort by governments to shift public opinion in support of new, radical measures to tackle problems. In others, changes have been slow despite the obviousness of the problem.

For instance, as early as 1922 the International Council for Bird Preservation was worried about oil pollution of the oceans.[55] On the face of it, the British government responded quickly by enacting legislation against oil pollution in the same year. In the early 1950s an important discovery was made that oil being poured out of oil tankers into the ocean was the main cause of pollution at sea. At a meeting organised by the British government in 1954, thirty-two countries tried to promote an International Convention for the Prevention of Pollution of the Sea by Oil. After four years, the agreement had been ratified by only some of these countries. Its application was limited, and it faced further resistance from shipping interests, particularly in the USA. The problem of oil pollution became more acute in the 1960s. Some catastrophes received world-wide publicity (like the spillage of 117 000 tons of crude oil off the southwest coast of England from the tanker *Torrey Canyon* in 1967, and the blast from an oil platform off the coast of Santa Barbara, California, in 1969). However, the problem was even greater. It has been estimated that, in the late 1960s, there were on average 10 000 spillages of oil and other hazardous substances per annum in the navigable waters of the USA.

Despite efforts to regulate the industry, the disasters continue. On 24 March 1989 more than 10 million gallons of crude oil spilled into Prince William Sound, Alaska, from the *Exxon Valdez* oil tanker. The political response to this calamity appeared to be appropriate. The United States Congress obtained assurances from the oil companies that they would use only double-hulled ships in Prince William Sound.

However, this measure was never enforced by the government, since it was not prepared to challenge a powerful economic interest group. There is a history of similar behaviour by governments:

> Note the similarities between the *Valdez* oil spill and the circumstances surrounding the passage and implementation of the Oil Pollution Act of 1924. It is interesting that in both cases the federal effort grew out of public response to a perceived crisis (waste and pollution from oil and an earlier major ocean oil spill respectively) and resulted in congressional action with poor enforcement. Thus federal policy makers were able to satisfy their constituents without alienating an important and influential economic interest group (Smith 1992: 157).

It comes as no surprise to find that for over two decades scientists, environmentalists and local citizens had been warning of the dangers of an accident in Prince William Sound (Buchholz et al. 1992: 47–8).

The reluctance by governments to confront large corporations and the denial by established organisations of the existence of a problem are confirmed by the case of the chemical plant at Minamata, Japan, which released mercury into the ocean. Though severe neurological disorders and illnesses were detected among the local population as early as the mid-1950s, the company at first disavowed any connection. In the 1960s the company paid the victims some compensation, but rejected any connection between its practices and the health of the local population. It was only in 1973, following a protracted protest campaign and evidence of serious damage to the health of people living around another factory owned by the same company, that victims were paid more substantial compensation.

These illustrations demonstrate that, in the manner suggested by Jänicke and by Luhmann (chapter 4), established institutional practices and established organisations represent barriers to effective action in favour of environmental protection. Elsewhere, I focus on the ability of established organisations to respond rapidly and effectively. At this point I simply want to make the connection between the slowness of institutional responses and the problem of self-referentiality in organisations. Notwithstanding their successes in placing environmental issues on the political agenda, environmentalists are aware of the difficulty in changing institutional practices, and of the tension between these practices and new ideas. Nicholson comments on how institutions 'must from their nature be rooted in the past, and thus conflict with current thoughts and aspirations' (1987: 13).

The difficulty in changing institutional practices and in tackling self-referentiality in political and other systems can be illustrated by the response to *Silent Spring*. Although the book stirred some policy-makers, institutional inertia delayed appropriate action.

My own survey of a major weekly news magazine in Australia, *The Bulletin*, shows that the first serious report on the issue of insecticides and pesticides appeared only in 1969 (Hoad 1969). In this report, seven years after the publication of *Silent Spring*, Hoad anticipated 'one of the biggest storms of protest action' around the issue of poisoning by DDT. Besides noting the shifts in policy in the USA, the story reported on the use of DDT in Australia. It related that restrictions on the use of DDT in animal foodstuffs and for protecting cattle from insects were introduced in Australia as early as 1964. Yet, during the five-year period up to 1969, the amount of DDT being used had increased by a factor of four, to about two million pounds per annum.

Apart from confirming the inertia of institutions, the history of the use of DDT in Australia highlights the difficulties for communication between self-referential systems. In this case, knowledge about the damaging impact of DDT on the environment did not immediately lead to restrictions on its use. Rather, effective measures were introduced only when environmental concerns were translated into the language of economics. The USA Food and Drug Administration had decided to reduce the upper limit of DDT in meat from seven parts to one part per million. The Australian government acted only when it feared losing export opportunities for meat: 'The greater experience, greater knowledge, and greater concern of the U.S. in matters of pollution meant nothing to the Australian authorities, who were unwillingly forced to act on DDT through hard-headed economic consideration alone' (Hoad 1969: 27).

In 1971, the Liberal Party advocated for the first time in its platform the protection of 'the quality of our air, water and soil resources', in other words, measures for controlling pollution. The first mention of this issue in a policy speech was in 1972. Similarly, it was only in the 1970s that ALP party platforms alluded to some of these issues. The problem of DDT rated a mention in its 1971 platform. The same platform remarked on the problem of pollution from offshore drilling. The ALP platforms in 1973, 1975 and 1977 drew attention to the need to monitor 'toxic pollutants'. From 1979 onwards, the ALP sought to 'reverse the trend' in pollution.

These responses to environmental concerns show that political elites can become locked into certain ways of perceiving the world, and can then have difficulty in appreciating how concern about the environment and the quality of life might lead to changes in attitudes and behaviour. Changes in attitudes and behaviour can be imperceptible, especially if one is accustomed to focusing on continuities, on historical precedents and on the role of institutions in shaping social forces.

Environmentalists have themselves contributed to this problem. By making extravagant claims about the novelty of some of their actions, they have undermined their own credibility; they have also diverted attention from innovations (including scientific discoveries about the environment) and from conceptual advances in addressing environmental problems. Though often slow to take up the challenge, established organisations have none the less demonstrated that they are capable of adjusting to new circumstances. The question remains whether or not the process can be improved significantly, for instance, through changes in the political culture (from the principle of adversarialism to that of dialogue) and changes in political processes (the design of institutions that facilitate dialogue and make it possible to enact effective policies).

Inertia, Adaptation and Innovation

Chapters 9 to 12 examine the development of party platforms and policies and how they have addressed environmental concerns since the 1940s. In order to understand the patterns that arise from the analysis of these documents I will draw on the following concepts:

- the inertia of institutions;
- the adaptability of political parties;
- the relative autonomy of the political process; and
- the conflicting pressures on political parties.

All these concepts are closely linked to the discussion in parts I and II about political institutions, dialogue and self-referential political systems.

'The inertia of history' is often evoked to explain why the choices by governments are limited: 'Every government is constrained by its history, for the force of political inertia carries past actions forward, thus limiting present choices' (Rose 1989b: 15). Even governments that have a powerful mandate to carry out reforms are forced to moderate their plans because of inherited constraints (Rose 1989a; Hindess 1987). Putnam and North present similar arguments. It is tempting, when confronted by the evidence of inertia, to maintain that little has changed. In Australia, for example, there has been a vigorous debate over whether or not the ALP today represents the 'labour tradition' (see Maddox 1989; Johnson 1989; Kuhn 1989; Maddox and Battin 1991; Rawson 1991; Warhurst 1994b; and Beilharz 1994).

The predominant view is apparently that there has been no discontinuity, that 'today's Labor Party is recognisably the same party as a century ago' (Rawson 1991: 200, cited by Warhurst 1994b: 153). Yet, even writers who share this view have observed that Labor parliamentarians come from similar (middle-class) social backgrounds to other parliamentarians; that the modern ALP is under much greater pressure than in the past to involve parliamentarians in policy-making; that new values associated with opposition to racism, with support for environmental protection and with concern about equality for women have come to displace the old values that permeated the party (see Warhurst 1994b: 154–6).

Though the ALP retains its original name and some of its earlier goals, it has changed significantly over the past century, just as the electoral system under which it operates has been subject to many changes (many of them initiated by the ALP) (Papadakis and Bean 1995). Before turning to the issue of adaptation, however, I want to focus on the question of continuity (tradition) and change (innovation). As noted earlier, tradition involves a great deal of innovation. This applies as much to 'young' states as to old ones like England: 'Symbols of continuity often mask great changes in English life. Much of what we think of as typical of English tradition – the ceremony of the monarchy, the urbane detachment of a non-party civil service, and the global commitments of an empire – reflect nineteenth-century reforms or the conscious invention of tradition' (Rose 1989a: 16).[56]

The first impression we gain in examining patterns of policy development is one of continuity. With the benefit of hindsight, events appear to be logical (De Bono 1991). The occurrences in Eastern Europe in 1989, which took many experts on these countries by surprise, appear to be logical in hindsight. Political commentators, politicians and students of politics often overlook that all traditions follow from inventions, from discontinuities, from disruption to the pattern of evolutionary change. This is not to deny continuity and tradition. It is simply to stress that our analysis of history is often coloured by assumptions about logical continuity.

Turning to political parties in Australia, we find a strong element of continuity. By and large, we have the same parties that were formed around a hundred years ago. The share of the vote captured by these established parties has also been remarkably stable over this period, despite the formation of influential minor parties ever since the Second World War (Papadakis and Bean 1995). Consequently, it is easy to conclude that there has been little disruption to the pattern of evolutionary change. There have been no violent revolutions. Political regimes have not been overthrown by force. We have apparently experienced evolution. Yet much has changed, and each time this has happened we have quickly taken the shifts for granted. Take the case of the shift from the 'ideological' to the 'catch-all' political party. For many political sociologists, the classic work of Michels (1962) on political parties is one of the most perceptive approaches to understanding their rationale. Michels regarded parties as organisations for the attainment of power. In order to achieve this objective, they were prepared to modify their ideologies considerably. For writers like Kirchheimer (1956), this was part of a transformation of Western democratic party systems.

Today the apparent transition of these modern parties from 'ideological' to 'catch-all' parties (Kirchheimer 1956) is taken for granted: 'parties act as a link between citizens and their political leaders, providing a two-way flow of information. This link means that decision-makers remain aware [of] and more responsive to voter demands, while at the same time citizens are better informed about the reasons for elite decisions' (McAllister 1992: 109). This explanation is linked to the thesis of 'adaptability' (Mair 1983). Established parties survive by appropriating new issues: 'the history of single-issue parties demonstrates that if a grievance is raised and attracts significant electoral support, it will be readily absorbed into the platforms of one of the major parties' (McAllister 1992: 115). This, as I shall demonstrate, is a plausible scenario.

However, it is not an inevitable one. The thesis of adaptability is open to a number of modifications. If a party adapts to new circumstances, it does not necessarily remain the same party, in terms of either the values it espouses or the policies it implements or the membership it attracts. McAllister and Studlar (1995: 213), in examining the key role played by political elites in placing environmental issues on the political agenda, have acknowledged that by integrating 'new politics' issues into existing party divisions, 'they may also have added to the long-term instability of their party system'. The notion of adaptability can be further refined by drawing attention to the capacity of political parties to operate as part of a self-referential political system. Even writers who emphasise the adaptability of parties and their responsiveness to voters' preferences admit that parties exhibit some contrasting qualities, namely autonomy from 'society' and a tendency to want to set agendas rather than respond to the preferences of voters. Paradoxically, it is at this level (of non-responsiveness) that we might more plausibly talk about party traditions, continuity and, of course, inertia.

The concept of 'agenda-setting' by political parties corresponds to the notion that parties do not necessarily reflect the influence of social forces. Sartori (1973) describes this as the relative autonomy of politics. This notion has been challenged by sociology, by behavioural political science and by economics, all of which make strong claims for 'absorbing politics', for reducing politics to sociological or economic processes. In response, Sartori poses the following question: 'if we do not identify first the political structures – and particularly the party structuring – we are likely to miss this crucial question: *How is it that similar socioeconomic structures are not translated into similar party systems?*' (Sartori 1976: 180–1).

Political forces, he remarks, may exert some influence over the political environment. Using Marxist terminology, the (political) superstructure may shape the (socioeconomic) substructure:

> And from the vantage point of a science of politics – in its difference from a sociological explanation or reduction of politics – the question is precisely how the superstructure reacts upon the substructures. Cleavages are not 'givens' coming out of the blue sky: They may mold, and be reflected in, the polity; but they may equally be polity molded or polity restrained. The United States, with a strong potential of deflagration at the societal level as yet unreflected at the level of its political structures, is a good case in point (Sartori 1976: 291).

Political parties can therefore exercise control over the political environment by selecting issues for debate. This theme is taken up by many writers, for instance, with respect to electoral manifestos: 'at the heart of the notion of party control is the agenda-setting capacity of parties, as evidenced in their provision of election cues' (Mair 1983: 420, cited by McAllister 1992: 126).

This process involves parties 'constantly bringing issues before the public and seeking to benefit from doing so' (Rush 1992: 175). Following from this approach, the durability of political parties has also been explained in terms of 'the autonomy of the political' (Mair 1989, cited by McAllister 1992: 125). To a degree, this claim corresponds to the approaches covered earlier that focus on self-referential systems and on institutions and their enduring impact on social forces.

Just as adaptation is not inevitable, so politics is not necessarily autonomous; we can overcome the problems of communication posed by self-referential social systems, including politics. Most of the qualifications that I would attach to claims about the autonomy of the political have been outlined in earlier chapters (see also chapter 3, figure 3.1). They include both the role of expert communities and other elites in making scientific discoveries and in conceptual advances; and the role of social movements in appropriating these discoveries and advances and in mobilising popular support. In both instances, political parties are forced to respond to 'societal forces'. The third factor that contributes to breaking up the circularity of political systems is public opinion (Luhmann, 1990a).

Many writers argue that political parties exercise considerable control over the political environment in the manner suggested by political scientists like Sartori and Mair and by social theorists like Luhmann. The agenda-setting capacity of political parties can be demonstrated in many ways (see Zaller 1992). However, public opinion can have a significant impact on policy (Page and Shapiro 1983). There are situations in which opinion is framed by the agenda-setters, others in which opinion leads to changes in policy, and others still in which both opinion and policy are moving in a similar direction (Weissberg 1976).

In analysing opinion about environmental issues I will later make distinctions between 'top-of-the-head' responses to opinion polls and 'considered judgements' (see chapters 15 and 16). At this moment I want to distinguish between mass opinion (as measured by opinion polls) and the opinions of expert communities, elites and social movements. Some of the most dramatic changes in mass opinion began to occur only in the late 1980s. By contrast, shifts in opinion among expert communities, elites and social movements took place much earlier.

Later I shall analyse mass opinion and explain how it may or may not have been influenced by agenda-setting political parties. The following chapters examine the often belated recognition by major parties of discoveries and advances by expert communities, elites and social movements. The data are derived from the federal party platforms and policy speeches of the Liberal and National Parties and the ALP from the 1940s to the present, and of the Australian Democrats since their foundation in 1977. The rationale for this analysis is to consider the responsiveness of political organisations to environmental issues. As suggested above, political parties play two significant roles: they attempt to respond to new demands and to set political agendas in order to retain control over the political environment.

The value of analysing both party platforms and policy speeches is that they represent two distinct attempts either to set the political agenda or to respond to popular concerns. The platform, as some writers have argued, represents the 'fundamental philosophy' of a party, whereas the policy speech, presented by the party leader prior to an election, is a 'more direct, authoritative statement of party policy' (McAllister and Moore 1991: xi). McAllister and Moore argue for the superiority of the policy speech on the grounds that it is prepared for elections and is designed to compete with the policy agenda of the opposing parties. While recognising this, I am also interested in the broad philosophy of the party.

Each party attaches different value to its electoral platform and presents it in a distinctive manner. The ALP has been more consistent than other parties in producing its platform. Whereas the ALP reviews and changes its party platform at almost every biennial conference, the Liberal Party carries out less frequent revisions and the purpose of the platform is contested within the party (see Tiver 1978, referred to by McAllister and Moore 1991). McAllister and Moore regard as problematic the production of the party platform by the party organisation rather than by the leader. However, for the following assessment of the responsiveness of political institutions to environmental issues, both sets of documents, the platforms and the policy speeches, are useful. They provide a comprehensive picture over a lengthy period of the passage of environmental issues onto the political agenda. Though we have to be cautious in making comparisons between parties (especially when it comes to party platforms), the data are also useful for studying the pattern of change over time within a particular party.

The analysis in the following chapters focuses mainly on environmental policies. Each platform or policy speech contains a wealth of material on economic goals, and one could easily argue that these often contradict or undermine environmental ones. None the less, the advantage of examining trends over a lengthy time-span serves to demonstrate the articulation of the environment as an issue of national concern.

Readers who are not, at this stage, inclined to read in detail the analysis of party platforms and policy speeches may wish to go straight to chapter 12, which summarises some of the main findings, identifies when an issue first appeared on the agenda of a political party, and which of the established parties was the first to recognise its importance. The aim of the following chapters is also to draw attention to why we might, as discussed in the introductory chapters, be both pessimistic and optimistic about the possibilities for overcoming institutional inertia and for addressing new challenges.

CHAPTER 9

Missed Opportunities: The Liberal and National Parties

The Liberal Party

The Liberal Party of Australia was founded by R. G. Menzies in 1944 and formally launched in August 1945. The party initially represented a coalition of anti-labour parliamentary groups, including former members of the United Australia Party, which had suffered a catastrophic defeat in the 1943 election. One of the issues that united the new group was the opposition to socialism and to the ALP (see Jaensch 1992). The other key factor in the new union was the leadership by Menzies, who dominated both the parliamentary party and the extra-parliamentary organisation until his retirement in 1966.

The structure of the party had three distinct features. The first was the emphasis on federalism, which allowed each state division to enjoy substantial autonomy (for instance, with their own branches, constitutions, platforms, electoral committees and conventions). The second feature was the creation of a mass base and a large membership. In 1950 there were about 100 000 members in Victoria and New South Wales; in 1975 total membership reached a peak of 130 000, and it thereafter declined to 69 000 in 1990 (see Ward 1991; Marsh 1995). (The ALP experienced a similar, though even more rapid, decline in membership over this period.) The third defining feature was the division between the mass organisation and the parliamentary wing. This feature of the party has remained almost unchanged since 1945.

Unlike members of the ALP, liberal parliamentarians both at state and federal level are formally independent of the party organisation and are not required to adhere to party platforms created by federal or state councils. According to the 1974 platform of the party, members of parliament 'are responsible to their electors and should not be subject to direction by persons or organisations either inside or outside the Parliament'. Parliamentarians are supposed to be bound by their consciences. By contrast to the ALP, which enforces discipline over members with a pledge that binds them to decisions by Caucus, the Liberals have asserted the principle that delegates 'should not be pledged in any way which could conflict with the right of a member of Parliament to act independent of Caucus or party *control*' (Jaensch 1992: 264). A delegate who intends to cross the floor of parliament in order to vote on an issue of personal conscience is required to inform the parliamentary leader and colleagues (Valder 1983: 102). Another crucial difference between the Liberals and the ALP is that, although the party organisation draws up the platform, policies have, until recently, been the province of the parliamentary party (Valder 1983: 98–9).

One of the outstanding differences between the ALP and the Liberals has been the focus on leadership and, above all, on the electoral success of the leader. During the period when Menzies dominated the party, this did not pose any difficulty. However, since 1983 problems associated with personalities, organisational structure and ideology have been constant in Liberal politics. Among the organisational problems confronting the party is the relevance of the party platform. In 1946 the constitution provided for a Joint Standing Committee on Federal Policy, comprising six members of the parliamentary party and six non-parliamentary members chosen by the Federal Council. The committee was to 'consider all matters affecting the Federal Platform and to report thereon to the Federal Council and to advise the Parliamentary Party upon any matters affecting the implementation of the Platform' (Liberal Party Constitution 1949: 18). However, these mechanisms never functioned properly, even in the 1950s and early 1960s (Hancock 1995: 87).

Despite recent attempts to address this situation (for example, the 1994 Constitution stipulated that the federal parliamentary party should be 'bound to the Federal Platform, except in so far as the Federal Platform purports to determine Federal policy matters which are properly the province of the Federal Parliamentary Party as hereinafter provided'), the federal platform is not really binding on the federal parliamentary party. The platform has not been revised since 1982, although the federal secretariat has informed the author that a new platform is near completion. The prospects for resolving these issues are, at any rate, slight. The principle of the independence of parliamentarians from the party organisation remains entrenched.

The following issues are therefore relevant to any analysis of the attempts by the Liberal Party to adapt to environmentalism:

- the dominance of the party by a strong leader like Menzies at a time when there was an almost exclusive focus on economic development rather than environmental protection;
- the strong emphasis on federalism, which allows each state division to enjoy considerable autonomy and is reflected in the area of environmental policies;
- the difficulties experienced by the Liberal and National parties in adjusting from the almost exclusive focus on economic development in the 1950s and 1960s to the growing awareness of environmental issues since the 1970s;
- the difficulties experienced by the Liberals in accommodating the conflicting aspirations of their own supporters and those of supporters of the National Party on environmental issues;
- the difficulties experienced by the Liberal and National parties in adapting to aspirations of the social movements that began to emerge in the 1960s;
- the loss in support for the Liberals among those with tertiary education and in non-manual occupations in the 1970s and 1980s, in other words among groups

most likely to be concerned about environmental issues (see Papadakis 1993: 177, table 6.1);

- the decline in the mass base of the party; and
- the relevance of the party platform (because it is not really binding on the federal parliamentary party).

Notwithstanding this last observation, it is useful to examine how the mass organisation has, through the platform, responded to disquiet about environmental issues over a period of four decades.

The first federal platform of the Liberal Party was published in 1946. It remained substantially the same until 1971, and major changes were introduced in 1974. Despite the availability of scientific knowledge about the problems of pollution, it took several decades for the party to recognise this as a problem in its platform. From the 1940s through to the 1970s the focus was almost exclusively on development. There is therefore a strong likelihood that, because they were also the dominant party in government for a lengthy period, the Liberals would be less open to new normative influences arising from fears about destruction of the environment. In the 1940s the only references to the environment were to 'the preservation of existing forest lands and a planned development of afforestation generally'; and providing tax incentives to landholders to conserve and reticulate water, and to improve soil and conservation (1948: 6).

The 1948 platform focused on intensive land settlement, the 'full development' of mining and fishing industries, and the 'prosecution of an intensive search for oil'. It called for the 'maximum development, of Australia's natural resources' and of its 'power resources'. The platform also promoted 'the preservation of existing forest lands' and used the term 'conservation' (with reference to water and land) (table 9.1).

The 1971 platform represented a shift in policy and included:

> Recognition that improvement of the environment and enjoyment of life in the future will depend on the manner in which we use or misuse our physical environment. Appreciation of the need in the interest of future generations, to protect the quality of our air, water and soil resources and our unique flora and fauna. Encouraging methods of protecting and improving our environment from the threats inherent in all forms of pollution (1971: 12).

Environmental protection was also linked to 'the enjoyment of life' – for present and *future* generations. We have already noted that similar concerns had been expressed in the nineteenth century and during the first half of this century by conservationists. By contrast to the policy speech (see below), the 1974 platform persevered with the theme of environmental protection. The Liberals undertook to formulate policies 'to minimise and where possible eliminate air, water, soil, noise and visual pollution and the loss of natural resources' (1974: 54). They emphasised the importance of completing and publicising environmental impact studies prior to undertaking development by the Commonwealth. They referred to the conservation of energy and to the preservation of national parks, whales, flora and fauna. The 1982 platform drew attention to preserving Antarctica and to the conservation of marine resources. Since then the Liberals have not produced an electoral platform,

Table 9.1 Liberal Party Platforms, 1948–82

Issue	1948	1960	1971	1974	1982
Natural resources	d, d7	d, d7	d, d7	d	d
Water resources	d, d*	d, d*	d, d*	d, d*	
Land resources	d, e1	d, e1	d, e1	d, e1	
Atomic energy				d1	
Uranium				d1	
Other energy	d, d2	d2	d2	e1, e2, e3	e1, e3
Forests	d, e	d,e	d, e	e, e2	e, e2
Species diversity			e	e	e, e5
Waste management				e1	
Pollution			e	e	e
Whaling				e3	
Antarctica					e
Public education				e2	e2
Sustainable development					e2
Environment (general)			e	e, e9	e, e9, e10, e11, e12

For explanation of codes, see Appendix.
Source: Liberal Party Platforms.

thus reinforcing the impression that the notion of a national platform is highly contested within the party. At any rate the Liberals, as the title of this chapter suggests, did not follow up these initiatives.

By contrast to the platforms, the policy speeches provide more insights into the Liberals' view of environmental protection and development (table 9.2). Reflecting on the rapidity of economic development in Australia, Liberal prime minister Harold Holt noted that 'We have squeezed into seventeen years what some countries have taken 150 years to do; what some countries have never achieved' (Liberal Policy Speech 1966: 4). Analysis of policy speeches from the late 1940s to the early 1970s shows the emphasis on the expansion and development of natural resources. At the ideological level, the Liberals attacked socialism and communism as obstacles to economic development. The principal themes in policy speeches also included industrial relations, free enterprise and the development and expansion of national resources. In his 1958 policy speech, Menzies proclaimed: 'Our slogan is ''Australia Unlimited'', and we pronounce it with confidence. Progress has been almost incredible. Great discoveries have been made, and developments achieved' (1958: 4). He listed achievements in the discovery and development of uranium, bauxite, copper and other minerals, and promised government subsidies for oil exploration. He noted that 'we are entering upon a dramatic phase of development'. Table 9.2 shows that there was little concern about the consequences of development until the 1970s. Specific initiatives in the 1950s included proposals for establishing a Ministry of Development, support for the Snowy Mountains hydro-electric scheme, and the development of atomic energy and uranium mining for both civilian and defence purposes. Water and land were seen as precious resources for development both now and in the future.

It was only in 1966 that the term 'conservation' was used to articulate concerns about water resources, again in the context of development: 'One aspect of national development is vivid in our minds from the recent drought. This is the conservation of that precious commodity – water' (1966: 9). Today we would refer to this as sustainable development.

A preoccupation with the economic implications of environmental protection emerges in the 1969 policy speech: it foreshadows measures to protect the local fishing industry from Japanese fishing operations by claiming 'an exclusive 12 miles fishing zone for Australian fishermen' and enacting laws 'to give Australia control of the living marine resources of the Great Barrier Reef' (1969: 28). The Liberals were also firmly committed to developing nuclear power. In the 1969 policy speech John Gorton announced plans for the construction of an atomic plant at Jervis Bay to generate electricity, stating that the time had come for Australia 'to enter the atomic age'. Support for the development of nuclear power by governments in Western democracies soon gave rise to massive protest movements and to the formation of green parties in the 1970s. In Australia, where there were no nuclear power plants, the focus of mass opposition was on uranium mining.

In their 1970 policy speech for elections to the Senate, the Liberals made an effort to place the environment on the national political agenda. Gorton noted the 'mounting, and justified concern' at the risks of pollution. He saw pollution, not as an 'inevitable by-product of advanced technology and population increase', but as the 'failure to take fully into account the environmental consequences of our actions' (1970: 10). Given the dominance by the Liberals of government over a period of two decades, this represented an admission of error. Despite their enduring concern about the central role of the states in dealing with such issues, the Liberals now proposed the creation of a federal Office of the Environment under the control of the Prime Minister's Department to advise on how 'to prevent or reduce pollution arising out of the activities of any Commonwealth Department or Authority'. They also foreshadowed discussions with the states about the creation of a National Advisory Council 'to advise the Commonwealth, and the States, on action to be taken in areas where co-ordination can properly be achieved'.

The 1972 policy speech reaffirmed the commitments to protect the environment, to enlarge parklands, to purchase land for national parks and reserves, to conduct a biological survey of flora and fauna, and to require 'impact statements' for new development projects within the jurisdiction of the Commonwealth government. This appeared to signal the beginning of genuine competition between the major parties over the issue of environmental policy. Still, these efforts seemed to be transient and the Liberals appeared to block out the influence of the proponents of environmental protection. The logic of economic development combined with short-term electoral considerations appeared to prevail over any plans to tackle environmental issues.

In subsequent policy speeches, in 1974 and in 1975, the environment was dropped from the agenda; the focus was exclusively on development, on attracting foreign investment to assist in the exploitation and export of natural resources. Similar themes were articulated in the 1977 policy speech, though the environment was now restored to the political agenda. There were promises to initiate inquiries into uranium mining and the conservation of whales, to promote solar energy and fuel

Table 9.2 Liberal Party Policy Speeches, 1946–93

Issue	1946	1949	1951	1953	1954	1955	1958	1961	1963	1964	1966
Natural resources	d, d1, d2	d, d2	d	d	d, d3, d4	d	d, d5, d6	d, d7, d8	d, d7	d, d9	d, d7, d9
Water resources	d	d	d1		d, d1	d1	d, d1, d2	d1, d3	d3		d*
Land resources	d				d, d1	d2	d		d2		
Atomic energy					d1, d2	d1	d	d			
Uranium				d1	d1, d2	d1, d2	d1	d1	d3		
Other energy		d1, d2		d2	d1, d2		d1, d2		d2		
Forests											
Species diversity											
Waste management											
Pollution											
Whaling											
Antarctica											
Great Barrier Reef											
Franklin Dam											
Green groups											
Public education											
Sustainable development											
Environment (general)											

For explanation of codes, see Appendix.
Source: Liberal Party Policy Speeches. (In 1951, 1954, 1955 and 1961 the policy speeches were also made on behalf of the Country (later National) Party. The speeches delivered in 1953, 1964, 1967 and 1970 were for elections to the Senate.)

conservation, to declare the Alligator Rivers national park, and to fund conservation groups engaged in protecting species diversity.

In 1980 the Liberals announced initiatives in soil conservation, promoting renewable energy sources, nominating Kakadu national park and the Great Barrier Reef for the World Heritage List, protecting the Alligator Rivers region from the effects of uranium mining, and a National Conservation Strategy. A theme introduced in both the 1980 and 1983 policy speeches was the 'balance' between development and

1967	1969	1970	1972	1974	1975	1977	1980	1983	1984	1987	1990	1993
	d, d10, e	d, d4	d, d9	d, d11	d, d11	d, d11, d12, d13	d, d12	d	d	d, d7		d
	d*, d4		d		d	d5	d6	d6, d7				
	d	d2		d, d2	d	d2, d3	d2, e1	e2	e2	d	d4, e2, e3, e4, e5	
	d3							d4				
			d1			d1	d1, e1	d1, d4		d1*		d1
			d3	d2, d4		d1, d2, d3, d4, e1, e2, e3	d2, d4, d5, e1, e3, e4, e5, e6	d2, d4, d5, e1, e3, e5, e7, e8, e9				e1, e3
			e1, e2						e9		d1	d2
			e1			e2	e1	e1	e	e3	e4	
									e2			
		e1									e1	e2, e3
						e1		e2				
							d1	d1				
d1						e1, e2	e3, e4					
								e1				
						e1	e2	e2				
							e1					
							e1	e1*			e1	
		e, e1, e2	e, e13				e3, e4	e4, e5, e6	e4, e6, e14, e15, e16	e, e4	e, e4, e6, e7	e, e8

conservation and the 'interdependence' of these objectives. Among the new policies announced in 1983 were a National Soil Conservation Programme, a youth project in reafforestation, a National Tree Programme for 'Greening Australia' by 1988, a major national park in South-West Tasmania and a world-wide ban on commercial whaling. Although all these policies reflected the growing interest in environmental protection, the Liberals alienated environmentalists by focusing on the feasibility of a uranium enrichment industry and by their policy on the Franklin Dam. The Liberal government promised to offer the Tasmanian government $500 million towards the cost of building a power station using a source of energy other than the proposed

Franklin Dam. However, it left the final decision to the Tasmanian state government. This dispute contributed to the failure by the Liberals at the 1984 election.

Defeat at the 1984 election was followed by the loss of any impetus among the Liberals to place the environment on the agenda. Throughout the 1980s they squandered numerous opportunities to take the lead on new environmental issues. In his 1984 policy speech Andrew Peacock promoted exploration and development, and access to natural resources. The focus on development overshadowed the Liberals' commitment to a National Conservation Strategy, to maintaining species diversity, to World Heritage listing (subject to approval by the states), to creating a national environmental data bank, to the National Tree Programme, to controlling hazardous chemicals and waste, to establishing an Australian Environmental Corps (for unemployed people to volunteer their assistance in conservation projects), and to encourage school children to become involved in planting trees and shrubs.

The 1987 policy statement released by John Howard appeared to place minimal emphasis on environmental issues. There was even less effort to challenge the ALP's campaign to present itself as the natural ally of environmentalists. Much of the emphasis was on cooperation with the states and on allowing them to retain their responsibility for land-use decisions. One innovation with respect to development was to remove the veto by the ALP government on opening new uranium mines, in order to boost export earnings and employment opportunities. Still, the Liberals promised to retain their 'long held commitment to conservation of the natural environment and preservation and promotion of Australia's heritage', and to encourage the enactment of state legislation on controlling the trade in endangered species.

The 1990 federal election reflected significant shifts in opinion against a background of growing publicity for the concerns of scientists about the greenhouse effect and damage to the ozone layer. Environmental issues surged back onto the political agenda. The Liberals' policy statement was critical of the failure by the ALP government to defuse conflicts between environmentalists and developers. Like the ALP government, the Liberals emphasised the importance of achieving a balance between environmental protection and economic development. They promoted a National Conservation Strategy, a land-use inventory, the Landcare programme announced by the ALP government in 1989, and increases in funding for soil conservation. They also promised to tackle pollution of urban waterways and beaches, and to extend sewage treatment systems.

Like the ALP, the Liberals in 1993 paid less attention to environmental issues than they had in the 1990 election campaign. The political debate was dominated by economic issues, particularly the proposal by the Liberals to introduce a goods and services tax. Among the environmental issues articulated by the Liberals were the reduction in greenhouse gas emissions, identifying the sources of acid rain before it became a significant problem in this region, research into alternatives to the burning of fossil fuels, and savings in energy consumption. Proposals to extend projects for uranium mining, to reduce the fuel excise (which would lead to an increase in greenhouse gas emissions), to hand back to the Northern Territory government the management of the Uluru and Kakadu national parks, to develop mining at Coronation Hill, and to end quotas on woodchipping, were all regarded as serious threats by environmentalists. Other threats to the environment included proposals by both major parties to 'fast-track' development projects. The Liberals proposed a twelve-month limit on evaluations of the environmental impact of a project. None the less, the Liberals pointed to the apparent convergence between their stance on environmental issues and that of the ALP. They welcomed what they regarded as the new emphasis by the ALP on cooperation rather than confrontation between the Commonwealth and the states (for example, through the intergovernmental agreement on the environment signed in 1992).

For the first time in a decade, the Liberals perceived an opportunity for making up the ground they had lost to the ALP for support among environmentalists. They also saw a chance to overcome the institutional inertia that they had helped to create through their repeated electoral victories in the 1950s and 1960s, and through the symbiotic relationship that had evolved between those successes and the economic development of Australia.

National Party of Australia

The National Party originated in the wheat-growing regions of Victoria, New South Wales and Western Australia.[57] It presented its first federal platform in 1921. As in the Liberal Party, the organisational wing of the party has no power over the parliamentary party: 'The annual conference, for example, has no power over the parliamentarians; it merely decides the general guidelines of party policy. The Central Council has no power other than its approval must be sought before the parliamentary party joins the composite government. . . .the parliamentary party is, then, very much its own master' (Aitkin 1973: 420).

The federal conference of the National Party is much weaker than that of the ALP. For instance, the resolutions it passes are not binding: 'It can make recommendations to change Federal policy but these recommendations must then be approved by Federal Council for further consideration at a joint meeting of the Federal Council and the members of the Federal Parliamentary National Party' (Woodward 1985: 57). The 1988 constitution of the National Party acknowledges the possibility of differences in policy between the federal conference and the parliamentary party: 'If circumstances require the Federal Parliamentary National Party to act inconsistently with policy decisions made by Federal Conference or Federal Council, the Federal Leader shall advise the reasons for doing so to the Federal Management Committee.'

The key themes in the early platforms included the need for closer cooperation between state and federal governments, decentralisation and closer settlement. Another theme was the management of natural resources. It is hardly surprising that the National Party has always been concerned about such issues. Its constituents and supporters were more acutely aware than urban dwellers of the need for conservation. However, the Nationals did not explore the possibility of combining their preoccupation with preserving the land for the purposes of sustainable agriculture with a more visionary approach that included the preservation of nature for aesthetic, cultural and social purposes. The 1921 platform called for:

A comprehensive system of water conservation and power production to serve producing areas for intensive culture by irrigation and to assist in establishing industries. Scientific investigation, complete survey, and tabulation of the resources of the Commonwealth.

The 1927 platform focused on the development of mining and forestry. Under forestry, the party called for 'afforestation, conservation and research'. In 1933 this section was broadened to include the 'prevention of erosion'.

The 1949 platform promoted a water conservation policy that was 'to operate as a continuous programme until every stream which flows through areas of inadequate rainfall, and every stream which can be diverted into such areas, is brought so completely under control that no flood waters, which can profitably be used, are allowed to flow to waste' (1949: 3–4). Conservation was closely tied to development and the maximum exploitation of natural resources. The policy on forests emphasised 'cooperation with the States in research work into markets, tests, methods of production, and reservation of the most desirable areas for the conservation and reafforestation of indigenous timber' (1949: 2). The countryside was there for development. Calls

Table 9.3 National Party Platforms, 1921–91

Issue	1921	1927	1933	1943	1949	1953	1958	1966	1979	1984	1989	1991
Natural resources	d	d, d7	d, d7	d, d7	d, d7	d, d*	d, d*	d, d7, d9	d, d*, d9	d, d7, d9	d, d7	d, d9, d14, d15
Water resources	d, d*	d, d*	d, d*	d, d*	d, d*	d, d*	d, d*	d, d*, d1	d, d*	d, d*, d7	d*, d/e	d*, d8, d/e
Land resources			e1	e1	d, e1	d, d5	d, d5	e1	e1	d, e1	d, e1, e2, e3, e5	e1, e3, e5
Atomic energy							d	d, d1			d4	d4
Uranium									d	d1, d4	d1, d4	d1, d4
Other energy		d2	d1, d2	d1, d2	d, d1, d2, d6	d1, d6	d1, d6	d1, d2, d6	d6, e2	d4, d6, e2	d, d1, d2, d4, d6, e3	d2, d4, d6, e2, e3
Forests		d, d*	d, d*	d, d*	d, d*	d	d, e	d, e2	d, d*, d3, e2, e10	d, d*, e2	d, d*, d3, e	d, d*, d3, e
Species diversity						d	d	d, e	d/e6, e	d1, e	d, d1, d/e6	d, d1, d/e6, e
Waste management									e1	e1	e1, e2, e3	e1, e2, e3
Pollution										e	e, e2, e4, e5	e, e2, e4, e5
Antarctica											d	d
Great Barrier Reef									e5			
Public education									e2	e2	e2	e2
Sustainable development										e1, e2	e1	e1
Environment (general)								e17	e, e9, e17	e17, e18	e, e4, e17	

For explanation of codes, see Appendix.
Source: National Party Platforms.

for the decentralisation of industry and intensive land settlement reflected the aspiration to achieve greater prosperity for the rural population. In 1958 the party added to its support for coal, hydro-electric and other sources of energy production, the exploitation of nuclear power. Again, the focus was on the 'decentralised' development of this technology.

In 1966, for the first time, the party platform focused on 'Australian heritage', the conservation of 'Australian fauna and flora', and the creation of national parks. As noted earlier, campaigns with these objectives date back to the nineteenth century and gained official recognition only in the 1960s and 1970s. The 1979 platform gave more recognition than any previous National Party document to the environment and conservation. It called for the protection of Northern Australia, including Kakadu, the Kimberleys and the Cape York Peninsula. It also concentrated on recycling, research into solar energy, and protection of the Great Barrier Reef. It foreshadowed a code of practice for the humane treatment of animals.

By contrast to 1979, the 1984 platform was much more aggressive in promoting economic development, including the export of Australian minerals and energy reserves, protection of farmers and miners, and large projects for developing resources. Like their Liberal partners in opposition, the Nationals squandered opportunities to create a new vision for preservation of the landscape for aesthetic, social and cultural purposes. The ethos of economic development prevailed over other considerations. The 1984 platform stated that it should be 'a constant objective of government to remove barriers to, and restrictions on, economic growth' (1984: 11). These barriers included 'heavy taxation, excessive protection and unnecessary government regulation'. Still, the document also promoted the preservation of the Australian heritage and environment, the conservation of resources, the prevention of pollution, and the 'implementation of appropriate environmental standards and controls for major resource developments and major projects' (1984: 65).

By the end of the 1980s, the environment had become a key issue both for political parties and for many voters. The 1989 platform of the National Party articulated this shift by focusing for the first time on:

- a coastal management strategy;
- a national land use inventory;
- tax incentives for on-farm water and soil conservation programmes;
- advocacy of renewable energy sources;
- a ban on the use of chlorofluorocarbons (CFCs);
- a reduction in greenhouse emissions;
- protection of the ozone layer; and
- a Coordinating Committee on Climate Change.

Most of these issues remained in the 1991 platform, though some new clauses also reflected concerns about obstacles to development and advocated:

- the abolition of the Resource Assessment Commission;
- mining at Coronation Hill; and
- the abolition of Aboriginal veto rights over mineral exploration and development (whilst maintaining 'on-going consultation with traditional land owners').

Table 9.4 National Party Policy Speeches, 1946–93

Issue	1946	1949	1951	1954	1955	1958	1961	1963	1964	1966
Natural resources	d, d16	d	d	d, d3, d4	d	d, d5, d6	d, d7, d8	d, d17	d	d, d17
Water resources	d, d*	d, d*, d1	d1	d, d1	d1	d, d1, d2	d1, d3	d, d*		d, d*, d5
Land resources	d	e1		d, d1	d2	d		d		
Atomic energy				d1, d2	d1		d	d		
Uranium				d1, d2	d1, d2	d1	d1			
Other energy	d1	d2, d6		d1, d2		d1, d2		d2		
Forests	d	d								
Species diversity										
Waste management										
Pollution										
Antarctica										
Sustainable development										
Environment (general)										

For explanation of codes, see Appendix.
Source: National Party Policy Speeches. (In 1951, 1954, 1955 and 1961 the policy speeches were made by the Liberal Party on behalf of the Country (later National) Party. The speeches delivered in 1964 and 1967 were for elections to the Senate.)

The party platform provides us with a partial view into the willingness of the National Party to respond to environmental issues. The policy speeches, in other words the key statements made by party leaders in election campaigns, appear to reflect less enthusiasm by the leadership than by the federal conference for environmental protection. These differences may be partly due to the format of policy speeches, which tend to focus on a few key issues and ideological positions rather than on the details of policy. They also partly reflect enduring difficulties experienced by the Liberal and National parties in adapting to new normative influences associated with misgivings about the destruction of the environment and with aspirations for an improvement in the quality of life which extended well beyond traditional materialist values.

The 1946 and 1949 policy speeches promoted the concept of conservation for water resources (for the purpose of development). There was also a reference, in 1949, to soil conservation. (The policy speeches between 1951 and 1961 were joint policy speeches with the Liberals.) Throughout the 1960s the focus in policy speeches remained on development of all resources and of atomic energy and uranium mining. It was only in 1972 that the policy speech directly mentioned the environment and the problem of pollution.[58] For the first time the party acknowledged the shift in value priorities occurring in Australia and in other countries. Still, the primary focus was on the threats to material prosperity through over-exploitation of resources. The document also reflected arguments by the Club of Rome, with phrases like: 'putting

1967	1969	1972	1974	1975	1977	1980	1983	1984	1987	1990	1993
d	d9, d17	d, d*, d9	d, d17	d, d8, d9, d17	d		d, d7, d18	d	d	d, d*, d7	d, d7, d14
	d, d*	d	d	d, d*, d4	d, d*, d5	d, d*, d5	d, d*, d7	d, d*, d7	d, d*	d, d*	
		d		d, d*		e1, e2, e5	e1	e1	e1, e6	d, e2, e4, e5	
		d, d2									
		d1						d1	d1, d2, d4	d1, d4	d1, d2
		d2, d4		d3, e2, e3	d, d2, e1, e3				d2, d4		
				d, d3			e8		e9	d, d*	
									d/e6, e	d/e6	
									e2		
		e									
									d		
		e1								e1	d1, e3
		e									

too great a strain on the natural resilience of the environment', 'the danger of destroying the earth's capacity to sustain life at an adequate level', the need 'to work within natural laws, to avoid pushing the earth beyond its capacity', and the need to balance 'our desire for material goods and convenience with our responsibility to preserve the environment' (Country Party Policy Speech 1972: 6–7).

In parallel with the shift by the Liberals away from the normative influence of environmentalism, the 1974 policy speech represented a complete reversal. It concentrated on attacking the Whitlam government and did not acknowledge any of these environmental concerns. The 1975 speech was similar, though it did promote solar energy, other renewable energy sources and the establishment of a National Energy Council to assist in attaining these objectives. The 1977 policy speech added little on environmental protection, but the 1980 speech simply dropped these issues. The only novelty was the strong commitment (including tax concessions and specific funding arrangements) to soil conservation.

Although the 1979 platform had given greater recognition to the environment and conservation, this was reflected neither in the 1980 nor 1983 nor 1984 policy speeches. The 1983 policy speech added only a proposal to establish youth projects in conservation and afforestation. Despite the growing interest in environmental issues in the mid-1980s, the only notable addition in the 1987 policy speech was a reference to the control of hazardous chemicals and toxic waste. In 1990 Charles Blunt, the party leader, described the Landcare programme as 'not good enough' and promised to double the expenditure proposed by the ALP. Blunt also warned that he would not use the external affairs power of the Commonwealth to override state sovereignty over the issue of World Heritage listing, a statement that was apparently stronger than his Liberal coalition partner, Andrew Peacock, would have wished and one designed to anger environmentalists (see Warhurst 1990: 21). The 1993 policy speech focused on attaining a balance between environment and development. The party leader, Tim Fischer, proposed the creation of a new Department of Sustainable Development. Otherwise the Nationals again had little to say about environmental issues that were of concern to most people. This could only benefit parties like the ALP and the Democrats, and made it difficult for the Liberals to become more innovative in their approach.

The concepts outlined in earlier chapters, including the tension between innovation and tradition, the self-referential character of political systems, and institutional inertia, are all relevant to understanding the problems faced by the Liberal and National parties. In many respects these parties had suffered from the institutional inertia associated with their success in the 1950s and 1960s as the parties of government, particularly under the strong leadership of Menzies. The Liberal and National parties had played a key role in the institutionalisation of economic development. Their reluctance to take on environmental issues appeared to indicate how difficult it can be for a political organisation to take up new concepts. They seemed to be trapped by the rhetoric and reality of economic development. It also took them a long time to review the strong emphasis that they had always placed on federalism, and to consider the possibility of initiatives at the national level. Finally, the Liberal and National parties did not adequately address the issue of formulating policies that would appeal both to some of their traditional constituents (including sectors of the rural population as well as those with an interest in industrial development) and to those among the well-educated and professional groups that were becoming increasingly concerned about environmental protection.

The main hope for the Liberals and Nationals to gain more credibility on environmental issues has been through the growing emphasis on achieving a balance between conservation and development and on sustainable development, a factor which they welcomed in the 1993 federal election campaign and which provided them with a new opportunity to become much more credible as organisations that took environmental concerns seriously.

CHAPTER 10

Leading the Charge for the Green Vote: The Australian Labor Party

Background

Founded in 1891, the ALP is the oldest political party in Australia. As noted in chapter 8, there is disagreement over whether or not the ALP still represents a 'labour tradition'. Yet, tradition and innovation need not be treated as exclusive categories. A significant element of continuity in the ALP is the enduring influence of trade unions. The ALP was created as a political instrument for the trade union movement, and the ties remain close: 'The ALP was founded by trade unionists and it is still one of a small handful of true ''labour parties'' in retaining union affiliation and funding at the core of its organisation' (Jupp 1982: 103).

The 1994 platform retains the connection with the origins of the party by noting 'The recognition by the trade union movement of the necessity for a political voice to take forward the struggle of the working class against the excesses, injustices and inequalities of capitalism'. This does not settle arguments over continuity and change in the party. Democratic socialism, the term widely used to describe the ideology of the party, is interpreted in different ways by members and factions of the ALP.

The following issues are therefore pertinent to any analysis of the attempts by the ALP to adapt to environmentalism in recent times:

- the potential tension between the historic focus by the ALP on the needs of the working class and the attempt by the party to appeal to a broader cross-section of the population;
- the increase in support for the ALP among those with tertiary education and in non-manual occupations in the 1970s and 1980s (see Papadakis 1993: 177, table 6.1);
- the broader definition of quality of life adopted by the party, which has moved beyond a preoccupation with the economic welfare of a predominantly male and white working class to the social, economic and political concerns of Aboriginals, immigrants, single parents, homosexuals and women; and
- the influence on the ALP of social movements campaigning on issues like the

Vietnam War, peace and nuclear disarmament, and the prevention of the mining and export of uranium.

The most striking expression of the influence of new social movements was the sudden rise of the Nuclear Disarmament Party in 1984 (see Papadakis 1993: 180–3). The ALP adapted remarkably well to some of these pressures while retaining, at least in ideological terms, its commitment to the less privileged.

Similarly, the ALP managed to straddle the divide between accountability to the mass membership and executive power. The process of accountability has been described as follows: 'The Labor party, in theory, is committed to democracy, full participation and equality within its own organisation. Its organisational structure is an elaborate system of representation and responsibility, with every level of the party, in theory, accountable to a wider level below it, with final authority in the party conference, elected by the mass membership' (Jaensch 1983: 120). In practice, policy has been formulated in the first instance by a few interested members, then by informal committees. Since the mid-1960s the trend has been for policy to be formulated by committees appointed by the National Executive. Their proposals are circulated to all delegates and debated on the floor of the conference, sometimes vigorously, sometimes not at all. Since the late 1970s, national conferences have been 'stage managed' by powerful figures like the Party President, Party Secretary, federal and state ministers (including the prime minister and/or leader of the ALP) and shadow ministers, and faction leaders.

Labor parliamentarians must sign a 'pledge', committing them to the principles and platform of the ALP and obliging them to vote in parliament in accordance with decisions made by the majority of the Caucus. In reality, party discipline is not quite so tough:

> The national parliamentary Labor Party has considerable latitude to act independently of the party organization. It can largely determine which platform policies will be implemented and at what time, when in government. The prestige of the parliamentary leaders is usually, though not always, sufficient for them to have a decisive influence in the shaping of the party platform itself. Indeed, the Hawke government has shown how the party platform can be liberally interpreted in deciding government policy (Woodward 1990: 149).

These remarks suggest that the party platform does offer a useful guide to shifts in policy by the Labor Party, and that the actual implementation of policies may vary according to the circumstances as perceived by the party leaders.

As with other major parties, until the late 1960s there were only a few allusions in ALP party platforms to conserving water and land resources as well as forests. The 1953 platform tied the issue of conservation closely to development: 'The future of Australia depends in a great degree upon the intelligent use of land for primary production. The Labor Party believes in a public works program and agricultural policies designed to stabilise agriculture, conserve the soil and forests, provide irrigation and power, and to be the material basis of a prosperous rural community' (1953: 73).

Party Platforms

Though there was consensus among the major parties on the need for economic development, there was significant division over the development of nuclear weapons. In its 1963 platform the ALP opposed nuclear testing in the South Pacific and advocated a nuclear-free zone. It also opposed the foreign ownership and operation of military bases in Australia. The 1965 platform is significant to this study for several reasons. The theme of opposition to nuclear testing was again taken up vigorously, though the platform also promoted research into atomic energy for civilian purposes. Two innovations in 1965 were references to the problem of chemical pesticides and a new section on the use of natural resources:

> Australia's future, and the well-being of its people, depends on the scientific development of its natural resources. Development is not mere exploitation: it means wise use of natural resources. Non-renewable resources, such as minerals, should be used without waste, with research and planning for alternatives. Yields from renewable resources, such as soil, water, plants and animals, should be increased. Enough of both kinds of resources, and particularly of our natural landscapes, must be reserved for social, cultural, educational and scientific purposes' (1965: 13).

This focus on social, cultural and scientific values already placed the ALP ahead of the National and Liberal parties. In order to achieve these diverse objectives, the ALP undertook to:

- establish a division within the Department of National Development to carry out scientific assessments of natural resources;
- form a Natural Resources Council to assist in the formulation of policies;
- coordinate the activities of agencies involved in nature conservation and establish a nation-wide system of national parks and wildlife reserves;
- establish field study centres;
- carry out land research and regional surveys; and
- found a National Institute of Oceanography.

With respect to the chemical industry, the conference resolved to introduce controls on the use of insecticides, fungicides, weed-killers and fertilisers, and it called for a 'complete investigation into the chemical industry' to achieve minimum standards. There was no direct mention of DDT, but this platform appears to represent one of the earliest (indirect) references to the problem. Although the Liberal–National government was taking measures in response to these concerns, only the ALP Opposition was prepared to place this issue on its political agenda. Even prior to the advent of Gough Whitlam as leader, the 1965 platform represented some of the most significant statements by a major party for environmental protection. Notwithstanding the lasting attention by the ALP to economic issues, in the 1960s it began to emerge as the leader on environmental matters. This may partly derive from its opposition to the testing of nuclear weapons since the 1950s and from its proximity to protest movements against nuclear testing. Furthermore, as an opposition party, it could detach itself more easily from some of the institutional practices and inertia that the Liberal and National parties had created through their electoral

Table 10.1 Australian Labor Party Platforms, 1945–94

Issue	1945–51	1953	1955–57	1959–61	1963	1965	1967	1969	1971
Natural resources	d	d	d, d9	d, d7, d9	d, d7, d9, d17	d, d7, d9, d17	d, d7, d9, d17	d, d7, d9, d17	d, d7, d9, d17
Water resources	d, d*	d, d*	d, d*	d, d*	d, d*	d, d*, d/e1	d, d*, d/e1	d, d*, d5, d/e1	d, d*, d5, d/e1
Land resources	d, d5	d, d5,	d, e1	d, e1	d, e1	d	d, e1	d, e1	
Atomic energy					e1	d1, e1	d1, e1	d1, d2, d6	d1, d2, d6
Uranium									d1, d4
Other energy						d, e1, e3	e1, e3	d, d7, e1, e3	d, d2, d7, e1, e3
Forests	d*	d*	d*	d*		d, e16	d, e16	d, e16	
Species diversity	d	d	d	d	d	d	d	d, e, e1	e, e1
Waste management									
Sand mining									
Air pollution						e6	e6	e6	e, e16
Whaling									
Antarctica									
Great Barrier Reef								e1, e5	
Franklin Dam									
Green groups									
Public education									
Sustainable development									
Environment (general)						e	e	e, e17	e, e17

For explanation of codes, see Appendix.
Source: Labor Party Platforms.

1973	1975	1977	1979	1982	1984	1986	1988	1991	1994
d, d7, d9, d17	d, d7, d9, e	d, d7, d9, e2	d, d7, d9, e2	d, d7, d9, e2	d, d7, d9, e	d, d7, e	d, d7, e	d, d7, e	d, d7, e
d, d*, d/e1	d, d*, d/e1	d, d*, d/e1, d/e2	d, d*, d/e1, d/e2, e3	d, d*, d8, d/e1, d/e2, d/e3	d, d*, d8, d/e1, d/e2, d/e3, e9, e10, e11	d, d*, d8, e3, e6, e11, e12	d, d*, d8, e3, e6, e10, e11, e12	d, d*, d8, e3, e6, e10, e11, e12	d, d*, d9, e13
d, e1	d, e1	d, e1	d, e1	d, e1, e2	d, e1, e2	d, e1, e2	d, e1, e2	d, e1, e2, e4	d, e1, e2, e4
d1, d6	d1, d6, e5		e, e2	e, e2	e, e1, e2	e1, e2			
d1, d4	d1, d4	e2, e3, e4	e2, e3, e4	e2, e3, e4	d5, e5	d5, e5	d5, e5	d5, e5	d5, e5
d, d2, e1, e3	d, d2, e1, e3	d, d2, d7, e1, e3	d, d2, d4, d7, e1, e3	d, d1, d2, d4, e1, e3	d, d1, d2, d4, e1, e3	d, d1, d2, d4, e1, e3	d, d1, d2, d4, e1, e3	d, d1, d2, d4, e1, e3	d, d1, d2, d4, e1, e3
		d*, e/d1, e16, e25	d*, e/d1, e16, e25	d, d*, e/d1, e2, e14, e16, e20, e25, e26	d, d*, e/d1, e2, e14, e16, e20, e25, e27, e28, e29	d, d*, e/d1, e2, e6, e12, e14	d, d*, d6, e/d1, e2, e6, e12, e14, e16, e20, e25, e27, e28, e29	d, d*, d6, e/d1, e/d2, e2, e6, e12, e14, e16, e20, e25, e27, e28, e29, e30, e31	d, d*, d6, e/d1, e/d2, e2, e6, e12, e14, e16, e20, e25, e27, e28, e29, e30, e31, e32
e, e1	e, e1	e, e1	e, e1, e3, e5	d3, d/e6, e, e1, e3, e5	d/e, d/e6, e, e1, e4, e5, e21	d/e, d/e6, e, e1, e5, e21	d/e, d/e6, e, e1, e5, e21	d/e, d/e6, e, e1, e22, e23	d2, d3, d/e, d/e6, e, e1, e8, e22, e23
e1, e2	e1, e2	e1, e2	e1, e2	e1, e2, e15	e1, e2, e14, e15, e16	e1, e2, e15, e16, e17	e1, e2, e15, e16, e17	e1, e2, e15, e16, e17	e1, e2, e19, e20, e21
				e2	e2	e2	e1, e2	e1, e2	e1, e2
e, e16, e17	e, e16, e17	e, e16, e17	e, e16	e, e16	e, e16	e, e16	e, e5, e16	e, e2, e5, e16	e/d, e1, e5, e16, e20, e21, e22, e23, e24, e25, e26
		e2, e3, e6, e7	e2, e3, e7	e2, e3, e7	e2, e3, e7	e2, e3, e7	e2, e3, e7	e2, e3, e7	e2, e3, e7
				d, d1, e, e1	d, d1, e, e1	d, d1, e, e1	d, d1, e, e1	d, d1, e, e1, e5	d, d1, e, e1, e5
				e2					
				e1, e2	e1, e2	e1, e2	e1, e2	e1, e2	e1, e2
		e2	e2	e2	e2	e2	e2	e2	e2
e2	e2	e2	e2	e2	e2	e2	e2	e2	e2
e2	e2	e1, e2, e4	e/d, e1, e2, e4	e/d, e1, e2, e4	e/d, e1, e2, e4	e/d, e1, e2, e4	e/d, e1, e2, e4	e/d, e1, e2, e4, e5	e1, e2, e4, e5 e/d1, e/d2
e, e18, e20, e21	e, e15, e17, e18, e21, e22	e, e5, e13, e17, e18, e21 e22, e23	e, e3, e4, e17, e18, e20, e21, e23, e24	e, e5, e17, e18, e20, e21, e23, e24, e30	e, e4, e5, e16, e17, e18, e20, e21, e23, e24, e25, e26, e30	e, e4, e5, e13, e16, e17, e18, e20, e21, e23, e30	e, e4, e5, e15, e16, e17, e18, e20, e21, e23, e30	e, e4, e5, e13, e16, e17, e18, e20, e21, e23, e28, e30	e, e4, e5, e13, e16, e17, e18, e20, e21, e23, e28, e30, e31

victories and their almost exclusive focus on economic development rather than on environmental issues.

In 1967 the ALP undertook to form an expert working party on the problems of air and water pollution. In 1969 the ALP committed itself to the creation of a central organisation to control and coordinate the activities of nature conservation agencies; improved funding for research into the preservation of flora and fauna, and a system of National Parks and Wild Life Reserves, in cooperation with the states; and funding for the maintenance and care of all such parks and reserves (1969: 14–15). The platform also promoted the protection and preservation of the Great Barrier Reef; the suspension of the export of kangaroo meat for commercial purposes, pending further regulation and control mechanisms; and the 'civil' application of nuclear energy (including the construction of a nuclear power station).

The 1971 platform retained the emphasis on the development of natural resources, especially mineral resources, and the need to ensure Australian control of equity and policy. It focused on protecting the environment from pollution by fuel extraction and energy extraction. It promoted the establishment of a Conservation and Construction Commission, which would link conservation to development by acquiring pure water supplies, including treated and recycled waste water for agricultural, pastoral, industrial and urban development. Another objective was, in collaboration with the states, 'to achieve desalination of sea, surface and sub-surface water by solar and nuclear energy'. Besides maintaining its interest in nuclear power, Labor supported uranium mining and planned to develop a uranium enrichment industry. Still, it opposed the development, proliferation, possession and use of nuclear, chemical and bacteriological weapons.

Despite the relatively early response to concern about the use of pesticides in 1965, it was only in 1971, nearly a decade after the publication of *Silent Spring*, that the ALP (like the Liberals) referred explicitly to DDT and the desirability of 'broad long-term research into ways and means of controlling insect pests and plant diseases by means other than the use of DDT and other pesticides' (1971: 24). In a section on cities, the ALP suggested that the Commonwealth 'co-ordinate environmental preservation on a national basis'. The primary emphasis was on the provision of housing and urban infrastructure, reflecting the inclination by Whitlam to see environmental problems as an urban issue. Although economic development still remained the priority in the 1973 platform, for the first time there was a section dedicated specifically to 'the environment'. This spelt out general principles on environmental protection, including consideration of the human and natural environment as a 'key component' of all decisions which are made by government, and protection of natural resources (soil, air and water) in the interests of future generations (1973: 22–3).

The ALP advocated 'appropriate indices for measurement of general welfare in social, economic and environmental terms to be used in national planning' and 'environmental impact forecasting, analysis and accounting procedures for use in the normal machinery of Australian government decision-making for State, regional and local governments and the private sector' (1973: 22). The ALP appeared to demonstrate more vision than the other parties in calling for:

- cooperation with the UN, the Organisation for Economic Cooperation and

Development, the International Union for the Conservation of Nature and other international organisations in seeking 'comprehensive environmental protection';
- guidelines for industry in order to protect flora and fauna;
- education programmes to increase awareness of and concern for the environment;
- research programmes in the natural and social sciences and the humanities to address environmental problems; and
- controls on advertising products which represented 'a danger to human health' or made 'unreasonable use of scarce natural resources'.

The 1975 platform reiterated a commitment to including the value of environmental protection in the costs of production, distribution and exchange in order to discourage the use of materials and processes which damage the environment. It also promised that these costs would apply throughout Australia in order to prevent the development of 'pollution havens'. Though committed to the exploitation of mineral resources, the platform promoted a 'rigid anti-pollution code'. In renewing the commitment to the interests of future generations, the ALP undertook to develop 'national inventories of land, air and water resources' and, in cooperation with the states, to implement 'national approaches in the planning and management of these resources'.

The 1977 platform promised further changes. Preserving the environment was given, in theory at least, equal if not more weight than economic development. Included among the key policies and principles were:

- full consideration of the impact of economic development on the environment;
- regard for the needs of non-human species;
- cooperation with state governments over waste management and disposal;
- monitoring levels of pollution and creating 'ambient' air and water quality;
- preventing 'the development and use of environmentally damaging activities by an appropriate mix of both regulatory and pricing controls';
- implementation of policies on environmental protection prior to mining operations;
- environmental planning to monitor and restore land affected by mining;
- management of forest and water resources which recognised their multiple use character rather than the interests of one major use;
- opposition to the clearing of native forests for softwood plantations;
- support for an independent environment and conservation movement;
- conserving for future generations adequate samples of unique flora and fauna; and
- protecting marine animals by establishing a 200-mile offshore sanctuary for whales and porpoises.

The platform responded to several other concerns. To tackle the problem of harvesting rates for coastal fisheries, it proposed buying back fishing boats, joint management policies of fisheries (with the states), and the collection of data on the 'biology, population dynamics and ecology' of commercially important fish species, and on the economics of fishing operations. To address misgivings about uranium mining, the platform advocated a moratorium and the repudiation of any commitment of a non-Labor government to the mining, processing or export of uranium if it contradicted ALP policy. To respond to disquiet about the destruction of forests, the platform focused on their preservation, though it also stressed sustainable development which would provide 'a balance between economic, ecological and recreational considerations'.

The platform supported the following measures to tackle the depletion of non-renewable energy sources:

- education in 'energy awareness' in the public and private sectors;
- a program of energy conservation;
- a gradual shift to renewable energy sources;
- further exploration of fossil fuels;
- an investigation of present and future requirements for fossil fuel;
- regulation of marketing and export;
- investigations into gasification and liquefaction of coal; and
- labelling of consumer goods for energy efficiency (1977: 22–3).

The platform also suggested a National Fuel and Energy Commission, which would include representatives of the national and state governments and producers and consumers of energy. Its aims would be:

- to assist the government in developing a 'coordinated' fuel and energy policy;
- to prepare a blueprint for future energy needs and an inventory of energy resources, and to 'monitor exploration, development, price, marketing and use of energy hydrocarbons, fissionable materials and generative water';
- to coordinate, prioritise and fund research and development, including research relating to coal conversion and solar energy; and
- to stimulate oil exploration and production by providing guidelines for investment.

The 1979 platform maintained that the environment and development were compatible: 'Australia does not have to choose between environment and development. They are two sides of the same coin, one must be planned in the light of the other ... Labor's goals are for sustained environmentally sound humane development, planned within the constraints of and in harmony with the natural environment' (1979: 63). Full employment and environmental protection were also seen as 'compatible rather than conflicting goals'. The platform also reaffirmed most of the principles outlined in 1975 and 1977. Policies on land management were extended to cover desertification, the conservation of wetlands and forests, and the use of coastlines.

New proposals in 1979 included more effective legislation on the impact of development – the Environment Protection (Impact of Proposals) Act 1974–75 – an increase in financial and legal assistance to environmental centres and other voluntary environmental organisations, and more grants to the states for nature conservation and land use management. In promising to implement a national conservation strategy as part of the World Conservation Strategy, the ALP promised greater control over the trade in endangered and protected species. The platform also advanced an international ban on whaling, the conservation of all species, the prohibition of whaling in the economic zones surrounding Australia and Australian territories, and the prohibition of imports of whale products.

With respect to air pollution, the platform advocated uniform criteria for measuring pollutants and recording data for air quality standards in all major cities. In order to reduce pollution and to increase energy efficiency, it promoted innovation in the use of building materials and in the design of public transport as well as the creation of car-free zones.

Proposals on atomic energy included the repeal of the 1953 Atomic Energy Act and the enactment of legislation to create an independent regulatory authority responsible for environmental protection, health and safety. There was an emphasis on public debate prior to any official commitments to supply uranium to other countries. The platform reaffirmed the moratorium on mining, and opposed the establishment of nuclear power plants and all other stages of the nuclear fuel cycle.

Besides emphasising fuel conservation, research into alternative fuels and the need to identify 'institutional barriers' to the introduction of new energy technologies, the platform proposed an Australian Hydrocarbon Corporation to assist in developing oil and gas resources. The corporation would have strategic as well as commercial objectives and would perform the operations of an integrated oil company, including trading, refining and distribution (1979: 132). It would function independently or in joint venture with private companies. It would be funded by the Commonwealth and by loans and public borrowings. The platform also proposed legislation for regulating and exploiting all offshore resources within a 200-mile 'economic zone'.

The 1982 platform signalled further drastic changes. The minister for the environment would have the power to enact an Environmental Impact Study (EIS). The minister could initiate an EIS 'on any development project deemed of national importance'. The platform supported 'periodic public review of the scale, character and likely consequences of resource industries'. In order to encourage participation in environmental protection, the ALP would expand education programmes and increase financial and legal assistance to environment centres, other voluntary groups and trade unions engaged in environmental programmes and issues.

For the first time proposals were introduced on sand mining and on the protection of South-West Tasmania, Antarctica and the Great Barrier Reef. There was a new emphasis on water and soil conservation, on regulation of wastes, on energy conservation, and on research into alternative fuels. As in 1979, the ALP made the connection between full employment and environmental protection as compatible goals. It also linked environmental protection to 'democratic socialism': 'All Australians have a right to a healthy and diverse environment and accordingly environmental policies should reinforce Labor's economic social reforms and commitment to democratic socialism' (1982: 61). The platform called for 'periodic public review of the scale, character and likely consequences of resource industries'.

The platform reaffirmed opposition to uranium mining, and it promised to:

- phase out any involvement in the uranium industry;
- work towards international agreements on non-proliferation of nuclear materials;
- consider applications for uranium exports on a case-by-case basis;
- allow no new uranium mine developments; and
- prohibit the establishment of nuclear power plants and all other stages of the nuclear fuel cycle.

Influenced by growing public opposition to the destruction of forests, the ALP laid the foundations for policies that were to make it more attractive to many voters than the Liberal and National parties, at least on environmental issues. The platform stated that:

- an EIS would be required for any proposal to export woodchips;
- rainforests were a valuable and diminishing world and national resource;
- there were new employment opportunities in areas previously dependent on the exploitation of rainforests;
- an expansion of forests in national parks would protect all forest types;
- logging in rainforests should be phased out and they should be dedicated as national parks or nature reserves; and
- there should be a ban on 'mining or any other activity in National Parks which adversely affects the prime function of the park – nature conservation'.

In response to concern about energy resources, the platform included new proposals like: setting specific targets for reductions in energy consumption per unit of output in each sector; improving the average fuel economy of automobiles; the adoption by government agencies of energy performance standards for new buildings and appliances; financial incentives to homeowners and commercial and industrial enterprises to encourage investment in fuel conservation technologies; and ensuring that all government buildings attained high levels of energy efficiency.

In order to deal with problems of waste management, the platform proposed an Environmental Contaminants Authority. Cooperation with international agencies and other countries was extended, in 1982, to include the South Pacific Regional Environment Programme, the Association of South-East Asian Nations (ASEAN) Environment Programme and programmes to rehabilitate the environment of Vietnam and Kampuchea.

Over the Franklin Dam proposal, the ALP declared against the construction of a hydro-electric power scheme on the Gordon or Franklin Rivers, offered help to the Tasmanian government (to diversify the methods of electricity production), and undertook to assist in the expansion of the tourist industry in order to create employment. These policies were crucial in attracting green votes at the 1983 election. The ALP also promised to declare the Great Barrier Reef, as designated by the Great Barrier Reef Marine Park Act, as a marine park to the low-water mark and to extend the park north to the border with Papua New Guinea. Finally, with respect to the Antarctic, the ALP promised to oppose 'any development or exploitation of resources in the Antarctic Treaty Area which may cause damage to the marine or terrestrial environment'; to promote investigation of scientific, freshwater, meteorological and other resources in Antarctica; to provide financial support for new research projects (particularly in hydrology, glaciology and climatology); and to organise a scientific conference with all countries claiming rights or already having bases in order to coordinate and reassert Australia's leading role on the continent.

The 1984 platform included new clauses on forests, energy and uranium, waste management, species diversity, and water and soil conservation. Policy on water resources concentrated on protection of natural surface and ground water from contamination, the compilation of an inventory of wetlands, and monitoring of the impact of irrigation on ground water and surface water. The government would produce an annual State of the Environment Report as 'an objective annual monitoring of all key environmental indicators' (1984: 73). As in 1982 there was a proposal to work with the states and territories and the Commonwealth Scientific and Industrial Research Organisation (CSIRO) to carry out an Environmental Survey of Australia. The platform also aimed to provide grants to the states and territories for conservation and management of World Heritage Areas and of areas of national significance, and to complement the National Conservation Strategy by formulating 'other appropriate national strategies such as for energy and population' (1984: 74).

The ALP promised to introduce a national system of marine and estuarine reserves, to protect coastal regions and estuaries from contamination by land-based or derived effluents, and to institute water quality criteria for these coastal zones. Other proposals included the acquisition of critical areas of habitat for endangered species, reserving wilderness areas, and controlling feral animals (1984: 76). Furthermore, the government promised to 'discourage the siting of tourist developments inconsistent with conservation objectives in national parks and nature reserves and other areas of high conservation significance' (1984: 77). The platform suggested tax incentives for owners of a heritage area or item who undertook to preserve it in perpetuity.

As in 1982, though with some modifications, the ALP proposed an Environmental Contamination Authority to monitor the effects of environmental contaminants, set standards, coordinate and fund research, and record air and water quality. The organisation would manage a compulsory registration scheme for all chemicals used in Australia, develop national standards for labelling ingredients in commercial products, evaluate potential hazards of imported and domestically produced chemicals before their introduction, establish standard procedures for the transport and disposal of environmental contaminants, provide public information and advisory services to trade unions and community groups on environmental contamination in the workplace, and operate a national chemical waste furnace, capable of safe combustion of any environmental contaminant, including PCBs (1984: 79).

Under pressure from environmentalists within the ALP and from new political organisations like the Nuclear Disarmament Party, the ALP proposed new or revised policies on uranium mining:

- the export of uranium from the Nabarlek, Ranger and Roxby Downs mines under 'the most stringent nuclear non-proliferation conditions' to countries which observed the Non-proliferation Treaty and maintained strict safeguards;
- an end to the development of any mines, other than Nabarlek, Ranger and Roxby Downs;
- the prohibition of sales of uranium to France until it ceased testing nuclear weapons in the South Pacific region;
- a ban on the construction of nuclear power plants and all other stages of the nuclear fuel cycle;
- research into technology for the disposal of high-level nuclear wastes;
- no dumping of radioactive waste into the ocean;

- strengthening the International Atomic Energy Agency (IAEA) safeguards regime, including placement of an IAEA inspector on all sites covered by the IAEA; and
- the declaration of the South-West Pacific as a nuclear-free zone.

Again, and partly in response to pressure by environmentalists, the platform set new objectives on the development and protection of forests:

- to expand national parks to ensure protection of all forest types;
- to phase out of logging in rainforests;
- to dedicate rainforests as national parks or nature reserves;
- to conduct research into diseases like die-back that destroy native vegetation; and
- cooperation with international agencies in order to conserve tropical rainforests, particularly in the ASEAN and South Pacific regions.

The ALP also tried to modify the impact of development by seeking:

- to address the issue of employment in areas where the economy depends on exploiting rainforests by assisting states and territories in restructuring; and
- to issue licences for the export of forest products only if the forests were managed 'in such a manner which will ensure long term sustainable yield', if the project was based on forest types which were adequately conserved in national parks, and if the project was subject to environmental impact analysis and management.

The 1986 platform included a clause on integrating environmental objectives into overall economic strategies and industry development policies (1986: 109). Hence, policy proposals on water resources focused on:

- long-term consideration of both economic and environmental factors, with emphasis on research into the problem of salination;
- the efficient use of water resources through pricing policies, which would reflect 'the full cost of supplies and social equity'; and
- the adoption by landholders of water and land management practices which 'reduce the build-up and mitigate the effects of irrigation-induced and dryland salinity'.

Besides adopting the 'polluter pays' principle 'to ensure prices of products reflect the full social and environmental costs of their production', the 1986 platform promoted a national strategy to manage hazardous wastes, uniform national procedures to categorise hazardous waste, and monitoring of the generation, movement and disposal of such wastes.

Measures to address the 'urgent' need for the conservation, rehabilation and regeneration of wetlands included:

- the implementation of the Ramsar Convention on Wetlands (1974);
- the nomination of wetlands for registration on the List of Wetlands of International Importance;
- reservation of wetland ecosystems through incorporation in national parks and reserves;
- a national inventory of wetlands and waterfowl;
- advice and incentives to private landowners to conserve and manage wetlands; and

- the negotiation of further bilateral international treaties to conserve wetlands and waterfowl (1986: 113–14).

Once again reflecting the emphasis in the 1980s on protecting forests and wilderness, the ALP undertook:

- to support state and territory governments towards nomination of significant areas to the World Heritage List;
- the nomination of wet tropical rainforests as a World Heritage Area;
- to close and rehabilitate the track between Cape Tribulation and Bloomfield in the Greater Daintree Region;
- to reserve adequate rainforest communities in national parks and nature reserves;
- to promote research into the protection, conservation and utilisation of rainforest species in the South Pacific region; and
- to expedite the phasing out of logging in rainforests and their dedication as national parks and nature reserves by preparing studies of alternative employment opportunities and providing states with financial assistance to restructure regional economies.

The platform aimed to improve the ecological sustainability of silvicultural and harvesting methods; enhance employment opportunities and develop a plan for forest-related industries; to promote revegetation and reafforestation of marginal and degraded land in order to maintain the resource base of the timber industry; to provide funds for intensive plantations of softwood and native wood species; to expand national parks to ensure protection of all forest types; and to grant licences for the export of woodchips only if the project had been subject to environmental impact analysis, had provided net economic, social and environmental benefits, and excluded National Estate areas where logging or other forestry operations were inconsistent with the reasons for its listing. The platform also specified the need for regular public reviews of all projects, management of the forests on the basis of long-term sustainable yield, and a comprehensive survey by the Australian Heritage Commission of natural, archaeological and cultural values in all National Estate areas to which the project applies (1986: 114–15).

The principal aims with respect to nuclear power were to achieve acceptance of protocols to the South Pacific Nuclear Free Zone Treaty (1985) by nuclear weapons states; to promote the development of an Indian Ocean zone of peace; and to negotiate additional non-proliferation arrangements in the South and South-East Asian regions (1986: 226).

Two new issues in the 1988 platform were the ozone layer and the greenhouse effect. The ALP pledged action under the Vienna Convention for the Protection of the Ozone Layer 'to reduce the consumption of chlorofluorocarbons, halons and other chemicals which are causing depletion of the ozone layer', and to 'maintain research into the greenhouse effect, providing support and incentives for scientific collaboration and study into the effectiveness of alternative policies and adjustments' (1988: 86–7).

Proposals on forestry stressed the legitimacy of this form of primary production, the importance of forestry as a farm undertaking for the production of timber, and forestry development by private landholders as a 'viable alternative to other agricultural pursuits and as a major tool in addressing land degradation' (1988: 174).

The 1991 platform promoted an ecologically sustainable development strategy 'to ensure the integration of environmental and economic goals across all areas of decision-making' and 'the maintenance of ecological processes and genetic diversity in accordance with the principles of the National Conservation Strategy' (1991: 88). The ALP also aimed to 'develop a national strategy for the maintenance of biological diversity, to ensure the maintenance of genetic, species and ecosystem diversity', and to 'take a leading role in the development of an international convention for the maintenance of biological diversity' (1991: 87). Another innovation was the proposal to establish an Environmental Protection Agency.

The platform accepted that the 'impact of greenhouse gas emissions on global mean temperatures has been demonstrated beyond technical doubt, and the consequential long-term climate changes will be to the detriment of the global environment'. The ALP believed that these changes would require 'immediate and sustained action to minimise the potential regional and global effects and to adapt to unavoidable effects' (1991: 87). To tackle the greenhouse effect, the platform argued for a reduction in national carbon dioxide emissions by at least 20 per cent of 1988 levels by the year 2005, 'to the extent if necessary, of using international treaty obligations as a basis for requiring the compliance of States'.

The platform sought to address the problem of ozone depletion by:

- taking action under international forums to reduce consumption of CFCs, halons and other chemicals;
- continuing to implement and review the Ozone Protection Act and the Australia and New Zealand Environment Council Strategy for Ozone Protection; and
- supporting research into the effect of these measures and into the adoption of environmentally safe substitutes for ozone-depleting substances.

Policies on coastlines were amended in 1991 to focus on a 'comprehensive integrated system' of marine and estuarine protected areas in order to preserve their 'integrity and diversity'. The plan was to protect coastal regions from contamination by effluents, to introduce national water-quality standards, and to restore coastlines, even if this meant purchasing land 'into national ownership' (1991: 91).

To protect native forests, the platform promoted the completion of a National Forest Inventory and the National Wilderness Inventory and the creation of 'a reserve system which adequately represents all Australian native forest ecosystems' (1991: 91). With respect to rainforests, there was a proposal to restrict the import of tropical rainforest timbers 'other than those from sources where timber produce is ecologically sustainable and socially acceptable' (1991: 93). Production would be approved only if it did not threaten any species with extinction, did not 'degrade the ecological processes of forests', and was 'carried out with the consent and involvement of indigenous peoples' (1991: 93).

There was an emphasis on 'integrating' economic, ecological and recreational values in the use of forests by acquiring supplies of timber and pulpwood from both softwood and hardwood plantations, substituting softwood for hardwood timber in the building and construction industries, and creating employment, as well as being attentive to concerns about occupational health and safety. Another objective was for all state forestry agencies to operate 'on a fully commercial basis achieving a real rate of return to the State as owner of the public resource and allowing the profitable operation of competing private foresters' (1991: 188).

In 1991 the ALP suggested a ban on driftnet fishing and 'any other non-discriminatory methods of harvesting which have high impacts on marine biological systems', and the harvesting of species for commercial or recreational purposes 'at sustainable levels' (1991: 94). Finally, there was a slight modification to proposals for the Antarctic which involved working towards 'the concept of Antarctica as a World Park' and developing a treaty to protect Antarctica which would enhance its 'wilderness character' and prohibit forever all activities which could damage the environment.

The 1994 platform presented several innovations and placed greater emphasis than before on protecting and enhancing the environmental quality of urban areas in design, planning, construction and transport. There were new proposals on the ozone layer and greenhouse gas emissions and on Cape York Peninsula.

The ALP resolved to use the Endangered Species Act, the National Strategy for the Conservation of Australian Species and Ecological Communities Threatened With Extinction, and the Endangered Species Programme to increase the populations of endangered species and to protect their habitats. It also undertook to maintain genetic species and ecosystem diversity by 'fully' implementing the International Biodiversity Convention and the National Biodiversity Strategy. It also vouched that Australia would benefit 'from any international access to and use of its genetic resources'.

On the question of greenhouse gas emissions, the ALP committed itself to take 'a precautionary approach' and 'to minimise the potential national and regional impacts of Greenhouse-enhanced climate change' (1994: 115). The adoption of a 'precautionary approach' signifies an acceptance that some issues, though they may not represent a crisis that requires immediate attention, are important enough to warrant an instant response. In sum, this expresses a qualitative change in the approach by government to long-term problems along the lines suggested by Jänicke (1990) (see chapter 4 and also the discussion in chapter 17). The platform also indicated that the Department of the Environment would be responsible, in collaboration with the states and territories, for implementing a National Strategy for Ecologically Sustainable Development and for funding and coordinating research, development and demonstration projects related to the environment.

The department would also implement policies for biodiversity and 'provide national leadership on pollution issues including air and water quality, cleaner production and waste management and the development of appropriate management regimes for hazardous chemicals and waste', set 'national environmental standards', produce 'regular State of the Environment Reports' and develop 'resource accounting techniques and assessments for industries reliant on Australia's biological resources' (1994: 115–16). To improve the Environmental Survey of Australia, the ALP proposed the further development of the Environmental Resource Information Network, the Australian Biological Resources Study, and a new programme 'to document Australia's biological diversity by the year 2000' (1994: 116).

The Landcare programme had featured, in 1991, as part of a National Soil Conservation Programme. In 1994 the ALP pledged:

- to 'provide an integrated catchment approach to policy development and to all allocations of funds';
- to increase funding to community organisations;
- to enhance biodiversity through retaining native vegetation;
- to expand the National Corridors of Green programme to include major rivers in all states; and
- to ensure that any regeneration programmes re-establish species lost to an area (1994: 117).

As part of the continuing emphasis on international cooperation, the platform included proposals for participation in the Commission for Sustainable Development, contributions to the Global Environment Facility, and implementation of resolutions by the 1992 UN Conference on Environment and Development, including Agenda 21, the Convention on Biological Diversity, the Convention on Climate Change and the Statement of Forest Principles. The only new proposal on the Antarctic was to ensure that the Madrid Protocol and other treaties protected and enhanced the wilderness character of Antarctica.

With respect to coastal and marine protection, there were new clauses on completing regular State of the Marine Environment Reports to monitor the condition of Australian waters; the development and implementation of a national marine conservation strategy; the protection of coastal land areas as part of the National Reserve System; and public education programmes. Aquaculture was seen as offering 'a real opportunity to increase the value of Australia's fisheries products' (1994: 234).

The platform welcomed the moratorium by France on nuclear testing in the South Pacific. However, the ban on new contracts for the supply of uranium was maintained until the French became party to 'a comprehensive test ban treaty' (1994: 244).

New policy proposals on forests included the implementation of the conservation initiatives in the National Forest Policy Statement, the management of all forests in an ecologically sustainable manner by the year 2000, and the establishment of a comprehensive reserve system for all native forests by the year 2000.

The section on waste management was revised extensively in 1994. Under the title 'Cleaner Australia', the following issues were mentioned:

- the need to reverse wasteful industrial processes;
- the adoption of new techniques for waste management;
- the obligation by the Department of the Environment to work with the states and develop binding national environmental protection measures;
- the necessity for cleaner production processes;
- the reduction by 50 per cent of wastes to landfill by the year 2000 through recycling;
- the building of national facilities for the safe storage of hazardous wastes; and
- legislation for a national inventory of pollutants.

The platform suggested the need for innovative thinking on our treatment of water, the adoption of 'a total catchment management approach', and the recognition of water rights. With respect to air quality, it proposed a national programme for a reduction in vehicle emissions and a national strategy for lead abatement, especially in the light of revisions by the National Health and Medical Research Council of the minimum acceptable concentration of lead in blood from 25 to 10 micrograms per decilitre by 1998.

Reflecting the growing emphasis at the national and international level on strategies for sustainable development the ALP promised:

- to encourage local government to incorporate environmental concerns in local planning (and hence to build 'ecologically sustainable cities');
- to promote cooperation between government and industry, to reward companies that reduced their pollution and to penalise companies that did not; and
- to develop an environmental management industry 'to ensure that we build a capacity to address environmental problems now and in the future' and to promote the export of environment industry products (1994: 129–30).

To tackle depletion of the ozone layer, the platform advocated:

- phasing out, in accordance with the Montreal Protocol, the consumption of ozone-depleting substances;
- a regime for the management of hydrochlorofluorocarbons, methyl bromide and other ozone-depleting substances remaining after 1996 until their phase-out was complete;
- application and review of the Ozone Protection Act using other Commonwealth powers;
- innovation to find environmentally safe substitutes for ozone-depleting substances;
- the transfer of 'non-CFC' or ozone-benign technologies to developing countries through the Multilateral Fund of the Montreal Protocol; and
- bilateral programmes with countries in the region, creating opportunities for the export of technologies and expertise for ozone protection.

Besides wanting to ensure that Australia met its obligations under the Climate Change Convention, the platform upheld the need for:

- cooperation with the states and territories to implement the National Greenhouse Response Strategy, endorsed in December 1992;
- compliance by the states and territories with Australia's obligations under the Climate Change Convention;
- evaluation of development proposals in order to reduce greenhouse gas emissions; and
- promoting the national interest, including environmental, economic and foreign policy interests, in international flora on global climatic change (1994: 131–2).

Policy Speeches

Turning to ALP policy speeches which, as McAllister and Moore (1991) suggest, are much more geared than party platforms to electoral contests, table 10.2 shows that between 1946 and 1964, the era dominated by the Liberal Party under Menzies, environmental issues were not considered important enough to warrant any special mention. As with the Liberal Party, the ALP focused on economic development. The 1946 platform emphasised that the introduction of a resource rent tax on highly profitable resource-based projects would not deter investment in exploration and mining. In 1949 the ALP supported protection for and mining of uranium on the same basis as other metals. From 1955 the policy speeches usually referred to the development of Northern Australia. Like the other major parties, the ALP supported large-scale development projects without any mention of environmental safeguards. The only note of caution arose in a 1955 policy speech: though strongly in favour of the development of nuclear energy, H. V. Evatt mentioned the need to take care 'to prevent injury to this generation and future ones'. In 1958 he supported the suspension of nuclear testing as well as efforts by the UN to achieve agreements on disarmament. As noted earlier, this did at least indicate a greater proximity by the ALP than the Liberal and National parties to protest movements against nuclear testing.

In 1954 Evatt promised that Labor would discharge a 'sacred trust for the benefit of the children of today and tomorrow'. Part of his vision included the concept of conservation, which was tied closely to development: 'We believe in the great development programme, in the modernisation of transport and all its facilities, in the decentralisation of secondary industry, in the conservation of the soil and forests and in the provision of irrigation and power' (ALP Policy Speech 1954: 25). Notwithstanding these strong commitments to economic development and modernisation, the ALP was more attentive to environmental issues than the other major parties from the mid-1960s onwards. The 1966 policy speech by Arthur Calwell signalled the first significant statement in more than a decade on environmental issues. Calwell called for the acceptance of 'balanced development', of 'sound economic growth . . . based on the wise use of natural resources' and of 'a more responsible role' for the Commonwealth in a programme of reafforestation (1966: 11–12). The speech also set as objectives the 'establishment of National Parks and the protection of our distinctive flora and fauna'.

The 1969 speech by Whitlam included policy proposals to improve the quality of life in cities. It also advocated the suspension of all mining and drilling on the Great Barrier Reef. The 1970 speech alluded to the plight of cities 'choked with toxic gases' and to streams 'strangled' by sewage and industrial waste (1970: 7). The 1972 speech promised the creation and administration of several new national parks and wilderness areas. The 1974 speech represented an extension of the benchmarks established in 1972. There was also a statement on how the ALP had placed the environment on the political agenda:

> We are the first generation of Australians to become sharply aware of the conflicting demands between growth and preservation of the environment. Our government is the first Australian Government to attempt to develop sound environmental policies to reconcile these demands, to ensure that growth and development are not bought at the price of the destruction of the nation's natural and historical inheritance. We believe that the polluter must pay, not future generations of Australians (1974: 23–4).

The 1975 speech was dominated by the dismissal of Whitlam by the Governor-General. In his final policy speech in 1977, Whitlam focused mainly on the economy. The following environmental concerns also featured in the speech: the need to focus on fuel and energy conservation, opposition to uranium mining, and a ban on the slaughter of whales (especially by Japan and the USA). The 1980 policy speech by Bill Hayden focused even more on the economy and less on the environment. Very little effort was made to place the environment on the agenda.

This changed rapidly in the 1980s under the government led by Bob Hawke. A central theme of his 1983 speech was to achieve 'consensus' and to end 'the politics of confrontation' of the Fraser government. This concept was applied to environmental policy: 'It's not a matter of having to choose between environment and development. With sensible policies and a willingness to resolve problems through negotiations and consensus Australia can have both' (1983: 27).

The principal policy recommendations were:

- opposition to the construction of the proposed Gordon-below-Franklin Dam in Tasmania;
- preservation of Moreton Island through a ban on the export of mineral sand;
- declaration of the whole of the Great Barrier Reef area as a marine park;
- a campaign for reafforestation and regeneration; and
- an increase in funding for the National Soil Conservation Programme.

The 1984 speech focused on salinity control and water quality, the nomination of areas for World Heritage listing and national heritage (in connection with the 1988 Bicentenary of white settlement in Australia). The 1987 speech reaffirmed the commitment to environmental protection. Still, it noted the potential tension between environment and development (perhaps in an attempt to dampen the growing enthusiasm for restrictions on development): 'protecting the environment requires us to find a delicate balance with legitimate economic interests' (1987: 32). The speech emphasised that Australia relied considerably on the export of minerals and agricultural products. None the less, the ALP continued to promote environmental protection and placed the following issues on the agenda:

- saving the Daintree rainforest;
- proceeding with stage 3 of the Kakadu national park;
- nominating Uluru national park for World Heritage listing;
- completing zoning plans for the Great Barrier Reef Marine Park;
- introducing a programme to protect endangered species;
- developing a national forest strategy; and
- preventing sand mining on Fraser and Moreton Islands.

Reflecting flexibility and adaptability by the government (now that the environment was firmly established on the political agenda) the 1990 policy speech promoted:

- the protection of 'Australia's precious environment for all time';
- the prevention of mining by all nations in Antarctica;
- the end to driftnet fishing in the South Pacific;

Table 10.2 Australian Labor Party Policy Speeches, 1946–93

Issue	1946	1949	1951	1953	1954	1955	1958	1961	1963	1966	1967
Natural resources	d, d7	d, d7, d17	d	d	d	d, d9	d	d, d9, d17, d19	d, d9, d17, d19	d, d*, d7, d9, d17	d, d*, d7
Water resources		d, d1	d, d1		d	d				d, d*	d, d*
Land resources				d	d,e1	d	d	d	d	d, d6	
Atomic energy		d1			d	d	e1	e1	e1	d	
Uranium		d1			d1						
Other energy		d1, d6		d1, d6		d1, d2				d, d4, e1	
Forests					d*			d, d*, d4	d, d*	d, d*, d4, e2	
Species diversity										e	
Waste management											
Sand mining											
Pollution											
Whaling		e4									
Antarctia											
Great Barrier Reef											
Franklin Dam											
Public education											
Sustainable development											
Environment (general)											

For explanation of codes, see Appendix.
Source: Labor Party Policy Speeches. (The speeches delivered in 1954, 1967 and 1970 were for elections to the Senate.)

- strategies to tackle greenhouse and ozone problems; and
- public education on the environment.

Although, following a major economic recession, the ALP placed less emphasis on the environment in its 1993 election campaign, environmental protection remained on the agenda. The focus, however, appeared to shift towards an even greater emphasis on the compatibility between environment and development, reflecting recent initiatives like the creation of the ESD working groups.

The process of adaptation between the (politically) most influential environmental groups and conventional political parties was reflected in the 1993 election campaign, which showed that the concerns of environmentalists were accommodated by political elites and that there were still significant areas of conflict among these elites over the environment and development. Despite their efforts over a decade to attract

1969	1970	1972	1974	1975	1977	1980	1983	1984	1987	1990	1993
d, d2, d9		d, d2, d6, d8, d9	d, d7		d, d2, d7	d		d	d, d7		
d, d5		d, d*, d1	d, d*		d, d*		d, d*	d, d*		e1	d*, e2
		d, d*	d, d*			e2		d, d*, e1	d	e4	e1, e2, e4, e7
		e1						e1			
					e2						
			d, d2, d4		d, d4, e1, e2						e1, e2, e4
	d, d* e2	e2	e10, e11				d, d*	d, d*	d, d*, e/d, e10, e12, e13	e14	e, e14, e15, e16
			e3, e5					e7	e5		e5, e8
										e3	e1, e2, e3, e4
							e1, e2		e2	e2, e5	e2, e5
	e										e, e2, e3, e5
					e3						
e1		e2	e5			e2			e2	e2	e, e2
							e2				
										e2	
			e1				e1		e1, e4		e1, e5
e, e17, e19	e, e19	e, e17, e19	e, e13, e18	e, e17	e, e17			e, e16, e17	e, e4	e, e16	e, e16

the green vote, the ALP had not persuaded many environmentalists that they could effectively tackle some of the issues.

In the view of Philip Toyne of the ACF, the environment statement by the prime minister, released in December 1992, avoided the most contentious environmental problems. These included the establishment of firm targets for the reduction of greenhouse gases, the implementation of recommendations by the working groups on ESD (which had been sponsored by the federal government to conduct a major review of the environment and development), and the introduction of effective legislation to protect endangered species.[59]

The prime minister in his policy statement on the environment rebuffed this attack by arguing that the greens were not interested in 'brown' issues like salinity and soil degradation. These issues dominated his statement on the environment. Appended to the statement was a programme of measures (valued at $156 million over four years) for:

- cleaning up waterways like the Murray–Darling Basin;

- conservation reserves that would be representative of plants, animals and habitats;
- the development of alternative and renewable sources of energy;
- the creation of a National Environment Information Database;
- assistance to companies that would serve as models in the area of waste prevention;
- a halon gas storage and recycling facility; and
- the management of tourism in environmentally sensitive areas.

The ALP also reminded voters of its accomplishments over the previous decade, including the prohibition of the Franklin Dam in 1983, the creation of a huge World Heritage area in Tasmania, the tripling in size of the Kakadu national park and its inscription on the World Heritage List, and the protection of Uluru national park, the Queensland Wet Tropics, Fraser Island and Shark Bay. Other achievements included the extension of protective measures over the Great Barrier Reef Marine Park, and the refusal by the Australian government (along with the French government) to support mining and exploration in Antarctica.

Another feature of the campaign by the ALP was the rejection of any fundamental conflict between development and the environment, and of the need to choose between them. The ALP suggested that 'we can, and must have both'. Similarly, the statement on the environment by the prime minister concentrated on the economic value of environmental protection: 'the drive for environmentally friendly industries and the protection of our environment is part of the economic drive – part of the international competitive drive in which Australia is engaged' (speech by the prime minister, Paul Keating, Adelaide, 21 December 1992). Keating then praised the new cooperation between the Australian Council of Trade Unions and the ACF over a 'green jobs' strategy. He also stressed the economic costs of environmental damage, citing the example of the Murray–Darling river system.

All this shows the flexibility of the dominant parties, both in Australia and in other countries, and their willingness 'to steal' the green agenda. Above all, it reflects their ability to deal with ambiguities and uncertainties in trying to formulate policies. The ALP has not only 'translated' concerns about environmental protection into the language of economics (as suggested in the account by Luhmann of communication between economic systems and environmental concerns) but has also created the opportunities and the fora to promote a dialogue between the various sub-systems.

As regards a dialogue between political organisations, the most interesting response to the prime minister's statement came from the Liberal–National coalition which welcomed the proposed measures. The Liberals highlighted what they saw as a new emphasis by the ALP on cooperation rather than confrontation between the Commonwealth and the states (for instance, through the Intergovernmental Agreement on the Environment signed early in 1992). The Liberal spokesman on the environment, Jim Carlton, emphasised the 'convergence' in policies between the two parties. The Liberals were aware of the success of the ALP over the past decade in promoting itself as the more responsible of the major parties on environmental issues. They therefore snatched this chance to identify points in common with the ALP, and to try to reverse their previous failures to lead on environmental issues. For the ALP, being green has always been a struggle. Opinion polls conducted in

1994 and 1995 showed that as many, if not more, voters were inclined to regard the Liberal–National coalition as the most capable of handling the issue of the environment. For instance, a telephone survey by Newspoll in September 1995 (n = 1141) showed that 31 per cent of the sample felt that the Liberal–National coalition was best able to handle the issue of the environment, compared to 24 per cent for the ALP (*The Australian*, 20 September 1995: 6). Similar polls conducted in June 1994, September 1994 and June 1995 resulted in the following distributions for the Liberal–National coalition and the ALP respectively: 29 and 24 per cent; 34 and 21 per cent; and 28 and 28 per cent. This is not to say that the Liberals and Nationals will always succeed, in a national election campaign, in attracting the majority of green preferences.

Sustainable Development

Although environmental groups like the ACF were disappointed with the major parties for neglecting the environment during the 1993 federal election, they also emphasised the importance of development. In their own publicity campaign during the election, the ACF stated: 'Jobs and the environment. It doesn't have to be one or the other. Because the environment doesn't cost jobs, it creates them. With the right priorities, we can have jobs and a healthy environment.' The emphasis on development and the environment suggests a shift in perceptions by many environmentalists.

The ALP government had been engaged in a constructive dialogue with both farmers and environmentalists for several years, particularly in the development of a National Soil Conservation Strategy. Similarly, there had been efforts to promote a dialogue between trade union organisations and environmentalists, for instance, over the creation of 'green jobs'. Although there were significant differences in emphasis between the two sides, the 1993 election campaign demonstrated that the Australian Council of Trade Unions was concerned about the consequences of economic development.

The environment statement by the prime minister in December 1992 reflected the efforts by policy-makers to implement this idea. Though environmentalists were downcast about the omission of certain issues from the statement, they could hardly question the measures themselves. Besides the endorsement by trade union and farmer organisations, the statement won support among business and industrial groups for underlining the importance of the burgeoning environment protection industry, and of the market for treating and recycling waste, for reducing air pollution and for cleaning water.

The prime minister's statement on the environment was also welcomed by the Liberal and National parties. In their joint policy statement, issued in February 1993, they affirmed their commitment to 'A Better Environment – *and* Jobs' (emphasis in the original document). They advocated a new Department of Sustainable Development. The report by the UN World Commission on Environment and Development (1990) was cited in the policy statement by the Liberal and National parties to justify a focus on development and the environment. The two parties maintained that: 'There is no reason why we cannot have both high economic growth and a sustainable environment.' They also acknowledged the 'valuable work and recommendations' of the ESD groups established by the Hawke Labor government – though they proposed a new plan to coordinate activities in this sphere.

Analysis of policy platforms and of statements by prominent politicians and by social movement organisations reveals one of the most interesting features of the 1993 election campaign. It illustrates the consolidation and widespread acceptance of ideas about the complementarity of development and the environment. These ideas had been promoted by the ALP government (see Papadakis 1993). The outcome was an unprecedented level of collaboration between interest groups, each of which laid different emphasis on aspects of policies for development and the environment. Again, this serves to highlight the possibilities for overcoming some of the dichotomies that underpin different sub-systems and for achieving constructive dialogue between them. It points to the likelihood of overcoming institutional inertia, in this case, by weakening the exclusive focus on economic development that had, from the 1940s to the 1960s, been a feature of Australian politics.

CHAPTER 11

Fundamentally Green: The Australian Democrats

The Australian Democrats were founded in May 1977. The former Australia Party and the South Australian Liberal Movement played an important part in their formation. Their first leader, Don Chipp, had been a minister in the federal Liberal government. His leadership was crucial to the success of the new party: 'Chipp presented a quixotic figure and pledged, in characteristically earthy language, to "keep the bastards honest". Although . . . the policies of the Australian Democrats should not be discounted, the initial appeal of the party seemed to owe more to Chipp's ability to tap idealism and disenchantment than to rational commitment to Democrat policies' (Shamsullah 1990: 167).

The Australian Democrats are a national party with ancillary state divisions. The National Executive comprises the president, two deputy presidents, the leader and deputy leader of the party in the Senate, and two representatives from each division. All these officers are elected by a ballot of party members. In addition to the emphasis on participatory democracy, the Democrats insist on involvement by party members in deciding on policy guidelines.

Policy proposals, formulated by various committees, are published in the official journal. They become party policy only if supported by a majority of members: 'Policies shall be formulated with the maximum participation of members and shall finally be determined by the direct and equal say of the membership by a voluntary postal vote' (Australian Democrats National Constitution July 1978: 3; and July 1993: 5). Thus policy-making is a continuous process. Members of parliament are not necessarily bound to party policies. According to Section 11.3 of both the 1978 and 1993 national constitutions, an elected member of parliament must adhere to policies formulated by the party. However, they may vote according to their conscience or to what they perceive as their 'duty' to their electorate. In these circumstances, they must 'furnish a statement' to the divisional executive, explaining their stance.

Although parliamentarians are expected to implement party policies, rigid party discipline does not apply: 'You can keep them [other parties] honest by giving the Australian Democrats the balance of power in the Senate. . . . For us to have any impact at all we must be joined in any vote by at least 25 senators from other parties. Because we don't believe in strict party discipline, it doesn't even mean that all Democrat Senators will automatically vote as a bloc on all issues' (Don Chipp, Policy Speech 1980: 1–2). In general, Australian Democrat policies can be drafted into law only if their senators hold the balance of power and there is disagreement between the government and the opposition. The Democrats may also coalesce with other minority parties against the government.

Australian Democrat policies and ideology are within the welfare liberal tradition. The first policy objective in the national constitution states: 'to be beholden to no group or groups in the community but to serve the best interests of all Australians' and 'to seek improvement in the quality of human relationships in all aspects of society and the economy, through honesty, tolerance, compassion and a sense of mutual obligation' (Constitution 1978 [and 1993]: 1).

What makes the Democrats 'fundamentally green'? First, the Democrats have prominence for their environmental policies and their opposition to uranium mining and the nuclear industry. Second, concern for the environment is a fundamental objective: 'To accept the challenge of the predicament of mankind on the planet with its exponentially increasing population, disappearing finite resources and accelerating deterioration of the environment' and 'To seek the transition to a sustainable economy, in equilibrium with world resources and ecosystems, with a minimum of dislocation by planning the necessary changes in good time, and by increasing public awareness of the problem ahead' (Constitution 1978 [and 1993]: 1).

Third, in so far as the Democrats have a distinct social base, they are consistently supported by those with tertiary education, by younger rather than older age cohorts, and by women more than men (Bean and Papadakis 1995). This matches the social base that one associates with environmental movements. Fourth, the participatory approach by the Democrats to the formulation of policy is akin to the style espoused by environmental social movements. Fifth, supporters of environmental groups are more likely to vote for the Democrats than for any of the major parties (see Papadakis 1993: 200–1, table 6.3). Sixth, in recent elections, for instance in 1990, the environment has been the most important consideration for people who voted for the Democrats (see McAllister and Studlar 1995: 208). Finally, the commitment by the Democrats to environmental protection is also mirrored by their policies. This is not to argue that the Democrats have neglected other policy areas. Their strong performance in elections to the Senate and in negotiations with other parties in the Senate reflects their notable contribution to policy debates over many issues, including the economy and social justice.

The following analysis of their environmental policies covers the period 1977 to 1993. Table 11.1 has been divided into four cycles: 1977–80, 1981–87, 1988–90 and 1991–93. These periods tend to coincide with the acceptance of new environmental policies by the Democrats. They do not necessarily coincide with changes in leadership, although the first two cycles cover the 'Chipp years'. The Democrats were led by Senator Don Chipp between 1 July 1978 and 18 August 1986, Senator Janine Haines between 18 August 1986 and March 1990, Senator Janet Powell between 1 July 1990 and 19 August 1991, Senator John Coulter between 19 August and 1

October 1991(acting), and between 2 October 1991 and 29 April 1993, and since 29 April 1993 by Senator Cheryl Kernot.

The first column of table 11.1, which is based principally on the 1979 policy papers, shows that the Democrats were interested in the development of natural resources and in the exploration of oil and gas.[60] They were concerned about development which was in the 'national interest' and over which Australians had economic control. The Democrats were also attentive to the consequences of development. Exploration of mineral reserves would have to be based on 'minimization of pollution and preservation of wildlife' (1979: 20), and all proposals for new projects would be subject

Table 11.1 Australian Democrats Policies, 1977–93

Issue	1977–80 (1979)	1983–87 (1984)	1988–90 (1988)	1991–93 (1993)
Natural resources	d, d7, e	d, d7, e	d, d7, e	d, d7, e
Water resources	d*, e2, e3	d*, e2, e3	d*, d/e, d/e2, e2, e3, e4, e5, e6, e7, e8	d*, d/e, d/e2, e2, e3, e4, e5, e6, e7, e8
Land resources		d/e (1987), e1	d/e, d/e1, e8, e9, e10	d/e, d/e1, e8, e9, e10
Atomic energy	e2	e1, e2, e3, e4	e1, e2, e3, e4	e1, e2, e3, e4
Uranium	e3	e3	e3	e3
Other energy	d1, d2, d4, e1, e2, e3	d1, d2, d4, e1, e2, e3	d1, d2, d4, e1, e2, e3	d1, d2, d4, e1, e2, e3
Forests	d, d*, e, e2, e5, e7, e17, e18, e19	e, e2, e5, e6, e7, e12, e14, e17, e18, e20, e21, e22	d, d*,e/d1, e, e2, e5, e6, e7, e12, e14, e17, e18, e19, e23	d, d*,e/d1, e, e2, e5, e6, e7, e12, e14, e17, e18, e19, e20, e21, e22, e23, e24
Species diversity	e, e5, e9, e10	e, e5, e9, e10, e11, e12, e13	e, e5, e9, e10, e11, e12, e13	e, e5, e9, e10, e11; e14, e15, e16, e17, e18, e19, (1991); e20
Waste management	e1, e2, e5	e1, e2, e5	e1, e2, e3, e5; e6, e7, e8, e9, e10 (1989)	e1, e2, e3, e5, e11, e12; e6, e7, e8, e9, e10 (1989)
Sand mining	e1	e1	e1, e3	e1, e3
Pollution	e, e1, e7	e, e1, e7	e, e1, e7; e8, e9, e10, e11, e12, e13, e14, e15 (1989)	e, e1, e7, e8, e9, e10, e11, e12, e13, e14, e15
Whaling	e2	e2	e2	e2, e5
Antarctica	e	e; e3, e4 (1986)	e, e3, e4	e, e3, e4
Great Barrier Reef	e2 (1977); e5	e2, e5	e2, e5	e2, e5
Franklin Dam		e2 (1983)		
Green groups	e3	e3; e4 (1987)	e3, e4	e3, e4
Public education	e2	e2	e2	e2
Sustainable development		e6 (1987)	e1, e6	e1, e6
Environment (general)	e, e13, e18	e, e13, e16, e18	e, e3, e4, e8, e13, e16, e18	e, e3, e4, e8, e13, e16, e18

For explanation of codes, see Appendix.

Source: Australian Democrats Policy and Electoral Statements (as listed in the References). At the top of each column, the figure in brackets denotes the year in which these policies and statements were issued unless otherwise indicated in the table itself.

to environmental impact studies (1979: 22). Analysis of the platforms and policies of all parties supports the view that the Democrats tended to anticipate efforts by the major parties to articulate environmental issues (see table 12.1). Above all, even if the other parties had already attempted to place an issue on the agenda, pressure by the Democrats and by new social movements ensured that the momentum was maintained for action and for more detailed policies.

The Democrats offered more detailed policies on energy than the other parties during the 1970s. They recognised some of the short-term problems (like the dependence of Australia on imported oil), and argued for long-term policies like:

- the development of renewable sources of energy for a 'sustainable economy';
- a reduction in the annual growth rate of fossil energy demand to less than 2 per cent;
- a decrease in oil imports from 700 000 to 400 000 barrels a day;
- a decline in petrol consumption;
- insulation of 90 per cent of residences at latitudes higher than 35 degrees and 50 per cent at lower latitudes;
- conversion of 70 per cent of all commercial, residential and industrial consumption to coal either directly or indirectly by electricity, synthetic gas or cogeneration;
- utilisation of solar energy for 5 to 10 per cent of all domestic and industrial heat use;
- funding of research by the CSIRO, universities and other agencies into developing renewable energy sources;
- tax incentives for the use of solar heating equipment;
- the development of emission control methods;
- the encouragement of car pooling and of the use of public transport;
- the imposition of a national speed limit of 100 kilometres per hour;
- setting guidelines for energy conservation in buildings;
- tax incentives to encourage industry and commerce to use energy-saving equipment;
- investigating the possibilities of converting gas from the North-West Shelf to methanol;
- the rapid conversion to coal by prohibiting industry and utilities from burning natural gas or petroleum in new boilers;
- the establishment of a federal Bureau of Energy 'to advise and co-ordinate the various federal and state government bodies concerned with energy'; and
- higher taxes on the registration of vehicles.

The Democrats also emphasised recycling products and stringent supervision over the disposal of toxic wastes.

Like the Liberals in 1972, the Democrats advocated that industries pay for pollution that they create. However, the Democrats were much more likely than the established parties to suggest specific policies and to press for their implementation. For instance, they proposed that fellmongeries and other unavoidably noxious industries be placed downwind of residential areas, and the introduction of 'more stringent and better policed' laws against the accumulation of rubbish and all forms of pollution.

The Democrats adopted the stand of social movements on issues like uranium mining and nuclear energy. Should the authorities permit the export of uranium, the Democrats promised that the mines would be operated by government and that all the profits would be devoted to the development of alternative energy. The policy on uranium was articulated strongly in policy speeches for the 1977 and 1980 federal elections.

In order to address some of the problems arising from the separation of powers in Australia, the Democrats argued that states should 'not be permitted to undertake works which will damage the environment in other States' (1979: 23). In order to achieve the key objective of clean rivers, the Democrats argued for non-polluting methods for disposal of sewage, like methane generation and composting, and for removing the run-off from pesticides and fertilisers and factory wastes (1979: 21–2). Like other parties, the Democrats were concerned about the salination in the Murray and other irrigation areas. In 1979 the Democrats proposed the formation of a coast protection authority 'to co-ordinate studies, surveys and necessary works to see that no authority performs works which have detrimental effects either locally or on other parts of the coast' (1979: 23). They advocated protection of the sea and coastline, including measures to prevent ocean dumping, operational discharge of ships, and the discharge of pollutants into marine waters from the land (1979: 22).

The Democrats pledged to declare the Great Barrier Reef and adjacent waters a national park. They also promised to preserve other areas of outstanding national and world significance, like the South-West Tasmanian wilderness, Cape York and Lord Howe Island. On the preservation of forests and of wildlife, the following proposals by the Democrats helped to set the political agenda:

- the introduction of a Wilderness Preservation Act, a Wild and Scenic Rivers Act, an Endangered Species Act, and a Sites of Special Interest Act;
- legislation to give individuals and community groups legal standing to take court action to protect the environment;
- a ban on woodchipping licences except for sawmill waste;
- a review, and possibly the cancellation, of existing wood-chipping licences;
- a convention, organised by the Australian government, of Pacific Basin countries to discuss the rapid destruction of forests in the region by Japanese woodchip interests;
- tax incentives or grants to private landowners for retaining approved areas of natural forests and the removal of tax incentives for the clearing of woodlands and forests;
- surveys of breeding and feeding sites of sea mammals and sea birds prior to action to protect these species;
- a total ban on whaling; and
- the use of natural methods like afforestation of catchment areas and the restoration of eroded and wetland areas in constructing flood mitigation works in order to avoid the dangers to fish breeding and water bird habitats.

During the 1977 election the Democrats had advocated the establishment of a National Parks and Wildlife Service to preserve fauna, flora, historical and archaeological sites. They had also called for a moratorium on whaling and the suspension of whaling contracts pending a full-scale inquiry into whaling.

On the issue of animal rights, the Democrats were again ahead of the other parties: 'we should allow neither avidity for material gain nor "sporting" instinct to override our concern and compassion for the rights of animals' (1979: 27). They offered an investigation along the lines of the inquiry convened by Professor Brambell in the United Kingdom, before enacting legislation on intensive animal husbandry, animal experimentation, and methods of culling excess populations of wildlife.

The detailed policy proposals by the Democrats were directed at raising awareness of the environment. The Democrats were of course in a better position to make radical promises because they were most unlikely to form a government. By articulating concern about the environment, they stimulated policy changes by the major parties. The Democrats sought cooperation with environmental organisations if their objectives were 'worthwhile' and aimed to 'encourage and publicise individual participation in the preservation of the environment' (1979: 22)

The 1979 policy papers represent a benchmark for later proposals by the Democrats. The data in the second, third and fourth columns of table 11.1 should be seen as cumulative – in other words, I have included most of the proposals already mentioned in the 1979 document and then drawn attention to new policies. The remainder of this section will focus on the additions to the policies adopted mainly in 1979. Most of the new proposals noted under column two arise from two documents published in 1984, namely the election policy speech by Don Chipp and the official policy on uranium mining and the nuclear industry.

The 1984 policy statement on uranium mining and the nuclear industry underscored the firm stance by the Democrats on these issues; it included:

- the immediate closure of existing uranium mines;
- a ban on the development of new uranium mines;
- the repudiation of existing contracts;
- an end to the export of uranium from Australia;
- the offer of financial compensation to Aboriginal people where uranium mining on their land has been prohibited;
- the offer of compensation and alternative employment to workers in the uranium industry;
- a ban on nuclear power stations, uranium enrichment plants, and other elements of the uranium fuel cycle;
- the prohibition of the passage of uranium and of the passage, storage and disposal of nuclear waste in or over Australian territory and its territorial waters; and
- the closure of nuclear reactors at Lucas Heights.

The Democrats also challenged the 'foolish' policy of destroying rainforests in order to 'provide cheap woodchips to foreign industrialists' (1983: 7). The 1987 platform promised to protect rainforests from 'commercial vandalism', to extend World Heritage listings, and 'to enforce this protection against State governments where they disregard it' (1987: 4).

The Democrats appear to have concentrated on the formulation of environmental policies in two distinct phases, namely the early years 1977 to 1980, and around 1988.

The following account focuses almost exclusively on documents published in 1988. In a document on 'Sustainability – Conservation and Development' the Democrats evoked the principle of caring for future generations, and described conservation as a positive value 'embracing preservation, maintenance, sustainability, utilisation, restoration and enhancement of the natural environment'. They suggested that conservation and development required 'an attitude of stewardship, especially towards those resources that could be destroyed if only short-term human interests are pursued'. The focus by the Democrats (in this and other documents) on long-term interests implies an approach similar to the one advocated by Jänicke (1990) for dealing with important issues (see chapter 4 and also the discussion in chapter 17).

The Democrats also wanted to address both the underlying causes and the complexity of some problems. For instance, they felt that the objectives of the National Conservation Strategy proposed by the Commonwealth in 1983 could be achieved only by:

- the integration of conservation and development through better understanding, improved decision-making and the recognition that such an integration is basis to human survival.
- focusing upon causes as well as systems; . . .
- the accumulation of knowledge for future application.
- the education of the community about the interdependence of conservation and sustainable development (1988a).

In the short run, the Democrats insisted on the preservation of the following areas as 'international parks': Willandra Lakes, the Great Barrier Reef, the South-West Tasmanian Wilderness, Lord Howe Island, East Coast temperate and sub-tropical rainforest parks, Uluru national park, the wet tropics rainforests, and Shark Bay. They also supported the inclusion on the World Heritage List of: Cape York Peninsula, the Australian Alps, the Blue Mountains, the Nullarbor Plain, the Central Arid Regions, Norfolk Island, Macquarie Island, Heard and MacDonald Islands, Fraser Island, the Great Sandy Region, and the south-western jarrah forests and wildflower country (1988b: 1). They also argued that there should be no grazing, mining or forestry practices in any national park or reserve.

New policies on water resources comprised the issuing of licenses for coastal fisheries, the protection of mangroves, the introduction of the user-pays principle and greater coordination and regulation in the management of resources (1988c; 1988d; 1988e). The Democrats also published new policies on soil conservation which covered a reduction in tillage farming, the use of new grasses, tree farming for windbreaks, water retention and the build-up of soil elements and biological systems for soil fertility and friability (1988f).

As noted earlier, the issue of forests was adopted by the ALP in the 1980s. It thereby gained an edge on the Liberal and National parties. The Democrats maintained the pressure on the ALP by issuing the following guidelines on forest conservation and management:

- achieving sustainability of the forest and timber industries without subsidies;
- establishing plantations on reclaimed and agricultural land;

- purchasing land for the development of hardwood plantations through a Timber Industry Development Fund, financed by a levy on profits;
- the exclusion (over a twenty-year period) of harvesting in all native forests of environmental significance, and a ban on harvesting in all national park and World Heritage areas;
- phasing out harvesting in virgin native forests over a five-year period;
- an end to new woodchip licences, except for genuine sawmill waste and plantation thinnings;
- the construction of pulp mills subject to strict environmental guidelines on the discharge of toxic materials;
- the reduction of existing woodchip licences to sawmill waste, plantation thinnings and domestic manufacturing only;
- a hardwood reafforestation scheme on cleared land, and an end to funding for new pine plantations;
- the cessation to forest clearing of steep lands;
- a ban on rainforest timber imports from countries like Malaysia;
- an immediate halt to logging in rainforests;
- acquiring of privately owned rainforests for inclusion in state reserves;
- funding by the timber industry of research on forest management;
- support by the public purse for research on forest ecology;
- expanding forests and plantations in order for Australia to become self-sufficient in forest products; and
- adoption of the concept of urban forestry (1988g).

In 1990 the Democrats also called for a ban on new pulp mills using the Kraft chlorine process (1990: 6).

Other documents reveal more detailed and scrupulous policies than before on species diversity (1988h), animal protection, and genetic engineering (1991). In order to protect wildlife, the Democrats proposed:

- a ban on the killing of any indigenous species (amphibian, reptile, bird or mammal) for any purpose, including scientific research;
- a Royal Commission into the 'kangaroo industry' and into criminal activities associated with the traffic in wildlife;
- improved enforcement of laws on trafficking, and the imposition of harsher penalties;
- a halt to the export of all indigenous species;
- a cessation of the import of all furs, of products from alligators and crocodiles, of ivory and animal products used in alternative medicines, as well all of species listed in the appendices of the Convention on International Trade in Endangered Species of Wild Fauna and Flora;
- legislation to implement the World Conservation Strategy developed by the International Union for the Conservation of Nature, and the National Conservation Strategy; and
- funds for government and non-government organisations for research into habitat protection, wildlife corridors and migration routes (1988h).

The Democrats opposed genetic engineering, particularly 'the transfer of genetic material between species, or the patenting of any species of plant or animal' (1991:1). They did, however, support interim measures, including the 'mandatory notification, assessment and monitoring of all genetic proposals', disclosure of 'all known potential environmental, social, economic, ethical and animal welfare implications' of the technology by its proponents, and an end to government funding of genetic engineering (1991:1).

The Democrats also developed new policies on waste management and pollution:

- controls on pest control and crop-spraying machines;
- a ban on all organochlorine pesticides;
- the relocation of chemical industries to industrial areas;
- a ban on the use of CFCs in aerosols and plastic, and a cut in their production by 95 per cent over a ten-year period;
- an end to the burial or incineration at high temperatures of intractable wastes;
- an educational campaign for a reduction of litter and pollution;
- the development of methods of disposal and recycling of sewage;
- an end to the flow of industrial wastes into the sewage system;
- a ban on dumping sludge into the ocean;
- full secondary treatment for all offshore sewage discharge, with the long-term goal of prohibiting this practice;
- restrictions on the use of motor vehicles in major business districts;
- the cessation of backyard burning in urban areas;
- the creation of pollution control commissions to monitor industrial pollution;
- a ban on billboards;
- extension of tree planting programmes and of tree preservation orders; and
- the requirement that building codes provide for noise barriers, deflectors or acoustic insulation (1989).

Two other key issues featured in Democrat policy documents in the late 1980s. The first was for public education (like the establishment of 'study centres' controlled by environmental organisations and the introduction of environmental awareness programmes into primary and secondary schools) (1988i). The second was on Antarctica: its inclusion on the World Heritage List, a ban on exploration for minerals and hydrocarbons, the regulation of commercial harvesting of krill, fish and squid, an end to commercial sealing or whaling, the regulation of tourism, giving up all claims of Australian sovereignty, and the total protection and conservation of the region by the creation of an internationally administered area (1986).

Between 1991 and 1993 policies were developed on energy, the greenhouse effect, national parks, World Heritage, forests, animal protection and genetic engineering. Some of the most detailed suggestions were again on forests, and reflected an attempt to balance environmental protection with economic development. They included:

- a shortening of the time-span for abandoning harvesting in all native forests from twenty to ten years;
- the removal of tax disincentives to plantation development;
- exemption from sales tax for paper products made from non-wood fibres;

- preventing the emission of organochlorines from new pulp mills;
- an excise duty on paper products bleached with chlorine;
- recycling of 40 per cent of waste paper by the year 1995 and 60 per cent by the year 2000;
- the establishment of a Wood and Wood Products Research and Development Authority to conduct research on softwood and hardwood mixed-species plantations, on dieback in forests, and on agroforestry and non-wood fibres; and
- the establishment of an Australian Wood and Wood Products Development and Marketing Corporation 'to develop and improve wood-based and non-wood fibre-based products and processing technologies' and to 'investigate market opportunities and facilitate export enhancement and import replacement programs' (1993a).

Proposals to protect wildlife comprised amendments to the Wildlife Protection Act to prevent the export of live native freshwater fish, and measures to prevent the exploitation of coral, shells and other shoreline species (1993b). Suggestions to defend animals included:

- establishing a National Commission to investigate the abuse of animals and to monitor animal experimentation;
- tax incentives for the advertisement and sale of cruelty-free products;
- phasing out advertising of products tested on animals;
- the cessation of recreational hunting; and
- a ban on all but the most necessary forms of experimentation on animals (particularly vivisection) (1993c).

In 1993 the Democrats developed a new 'action plan' on energy and the greenhouse effect:

- the implementation of the Climate Change Convention and the encouragement of all nations to become signatories to it;
- a small fossil fuel levy (not a carbon tax) to raise $500 million for sustainable energy and $250 million for upgrading transport;
- incentives for more fuel-efficient vehicles and alternative forms of fuel;
- the establishment of a National Energy Planning Authority and a Bureau of Energy Economics 'to assist in planning and analysing a nationally regulated energy sector based on least cost planning principles'; and
- tax incentives to accelerate the upgrading of energy-inefficient industrial plant and to encourage the adoption of sustainable energy technologies (including tax deductions for businesses to convert their power systems to renewable energy, deductions for expenses incurred in retrofitting existing buildings, exemption from sales tax for energy-efficient or renewable technologies installed by landlords at a higher capital cost than inferior alternatives, the acceleration of depreciation at a rate of 4 per cent for new income-producing buildings where they were energy efficient, reinstatement of taxation rebates for domestic insulation, and exemption of wind-power generators and energy-efficient light globes from tax) (1993d:2).

In 1990 the Democrats achieved their best-ever results in a federal election (12.6 per cent of first-preference votes in the elections to the Senate). This reflects the importance of environmental issues on the national political agenda in 1990. Interestingly enough, when the environment emerged as a less important issue than before, during the 1993 election, the Democrats scored their worst-ever result (5.3 per cent of first-preference votes in the elections to the Senate). The long-term prospects for the environment to remain high on the political agenda appear to be strong (see Papadakis 1994; and chapter 16 in this book). The Democrats have also shown that, although they are in many respects 'fundamentally green', they are also capable of adapting to changing perceptions and of exploring the possibilities of sustainable development. Their detailed policy proposals have contributed to the efforts by all political parties to respond to the challenges posed by concern about the environment. Above all, they have led the way in focusing on problems that do not require immediate attention but are unlikely to be resolved without a fuller appreciation of their complexity and of the need for a precautionary approach.

CHAPTER 12

Overcoming Institutional Inertia

The previous chapters bore out the growing interest by political parties in environmental issues. The aim of this chapter is to concentrate on three issues: when an issue first appeared on the agenda of a political party; which of the established parties was first to recognise its importance; and how patterns of continuity and change in party policies and platforms over a period of five decades lead one to be both pessimistic and optimistic about the likelihood of overcoming institutional inertia and introducing effective reforms.

In trying to explain the efforts by established political organisations to change institutional practices, an important consideration is the emergence of new ideas and of new political actors willing to place these issues on the political agenda. In the context of the analysis in this part of the book, the most significant new political actors have been the Australian Democrats. However, when considering the contribution by the Democrats, it is worth remembering that they were formed only in 1977 and that they represent only a portion of the contribution by new social and political movements to securing environmental issues on the political agenda.

The Democrats provided a significant impetus for change. None the less, the major parties had all demonstrated, even prior to the emergence of the Democrats, that they were capable of responding to situations perceived as crises (like the concern by the National Party about soil conservation dating back to the 1920s, or the efforts by the ALP to respond to new ideas about the quality of life and limits to growth in the late 1960s and early 1970s). These responses to new challenges are captured in table 12.1, which summarises the patterns observed in the previous chapters and enables us to identify which party appeared to want to take the initiative on a particular issue. The codes used in table 12.1 are similar to those used in previous tables (see Appendix) with one important addition, namely a code to identify when either the Liberals, the Nationals, the ALP, or the Democrats first took up an issue.

Previous tables showed that any mention of 'national resources' tended to focus on development rather than environmental protection, particularly in the 1950s and 1960s. The Liberals were the first, in 1970, to refer explicitly to the concept of considering environmental factors in the exploration of mineral resources. The ALP did the same in 1975, and in 1977 went further by recommending the restoration of the environment in areas affected by mining.

On the issue of water resources, in 1965 both the ALP and the Liberals focused on a coastal management strategy. The National Party followed suit twenty-six years later, in 1991. The Democrats raised this issue in 1988. The ALP was also ahead of other parties when, in 1977, it advocated ecologically manageable harvesting rates for coastal fisheries – an issue touched on by the Democrats in 1988 but not the Liberal and National parties.

Both the ALP and the Democrats broached, in 1979, the topic of a coast protection strategy. Still, the Democrats were ahead of the ALP when, in the same year, they undertook to clean up major waterways, in other words, to introduce 'rigid and enforceable controls' on 'ocean dumping, operational discharge of ships and the discharge of pollutants into marine waters' (1979: 22). The ALP raised the issue of cleaning up waterways in 1994 for the first time. The Liberals referred to the issue of urban waterways in 1990, though the Nationals remained silent on this problem. In 1984 the ALP took the lead by calling for a national system of marine and estuarine reserves and, in 1986, by advocating the user-pays principle for people using water from or discharging into river systems, and the preservation of wetlands. The Democrats led the way, in 1988, on the non-chemical control of exotic aquatic weeds, an inventory of all Australian rivers, and the protection of mangroves. In 1991 the ALP called for a ban on driftnet fishing, and in 1994 for a national marine conservation strategy.

Turning to land resources, the topic of soil conservation was taken up by the Nationals (then Country Party) in the 1920s and 1930s, by the Liberals in the 1940s, and by the ALP in the 1950s. Both the ALP and the Nationals referred to the National Soil Conservation Programme in 1980, followed by the Liberals in 1983. The issue of tax allowances and credits was first raised by the Nationals in 1980 and by the Liberals in 1990. In 1987 and 1988 the Democrats directed attention to the concept of sustainable agriculture and to the notion of tree farming for windbreaks. The Democrats also led, in 1988, on legislation to prevent grazing and cropping in marginal land, desertification, and limiting mining and quarrying in coastal regions. In 1987 the Nationals called for assistance to farmers for conservation and in 1990 all the major parties drew attention to the Landcare programme. The ALP, in 1994, referred to its own initiative for planting 1 billion trees.

In the areas of atomic energy and nuclear power, the ALP and the Democrats were the only parties to oppose nuclear testing. The Democrats were the first, in 1977, to declare their opposition to the development of nuclear power, followed by the ALP in 1979. In 1984 the Democrats were the only party to call for a world-wide nuclear freeze and for the closure of the Lucas Heights nuclear reactor. The ALP has experienced serious divisions over uranium mining, though since 1977 it has declared its opposition to the mining and export of uranium. In 1984 it also opposed the dumping of nuclear waste in oceans. The Democrats have always opposed the mining and export of uranium. By contrast, the Liberals and Nationals have been in favour of exploiting uranium and only once, in 1984, did the Liberals sound a note of caution by calling for an inquiry on environmental protection with reference to the Ranger uranium mine.

Table 12.1 The adoption of environmental issues as policy by the Liberal and National Parties, the ALP and the Democrats, 1943–94

Issue	1943– 1949	1953– 1965	1966– 1970	1971	1972	1973	1974	1975	1977	1979
Natural resources			eL (1970)					eA	e2A	eD
Water resources		d/eLA (1965)							d/e2A	e3AD, e2D
Land resources	e1N,L	e1A (1953)								
Atomic energy		e1A (1958)							e2D	e2A
Uranium									e2AD, e3A, e4A	e3D
Other energy		e1A (1965), e3A (1965)					e1L, e2L, e3L	e2N, e3N	e1N, e2A	e1D, e2D, e3D
Forests	eL	eN (1958), e16A (1965)	e2NA (1966)		e1L, e2L		e10A, e11A		e3L, e/d1A, e25A	eD, e2D, e5D, e7D, e10N, e17D, e18D, e19D
Species diversity			eNA (1966) e1A (1969)	eL	e1L		e3A, e5A		e2L	d/e6N, eD, e5D, e9D, e10D
Waste management						e1A, e2A	e1L			e1DN, e2D, e5D
Sand mining										e1D
Pollution			e6A (1967), eLA (1970)		eN	e16A		e17A		eD, e1D, e7D
Whaling	e4A						e3L		e1L, e2A, e3A, e6A, e7A	e2D

1980	1982	1983	1984	1986	1987	1988	1989	1990	1991	1993	1994
	d/e3A		e9A, e10A, e11A	e6A, a12A		d/eD, d/e2D, e4D, e5D, e6D, e7D			d/eN, e1A	e8D	e2A, e13A
e2AN, e5N		e1D, e2L			d/eD, e6N	d/e1D, e8D, e9D, e10D	e3N	e3L, e4ALN, e5L			e7A
			e1D, e3D, e4D								
e1L			e5A								
e4L, e5L, e6L	e2A, e14A, e20A, e26A	e7L, e8LN, e9L	e6D, e12D, e14D, e27A, e28A, e29A		e/aA, e9N, e12A, e13A	e/d1D, e20D, e21D, e22D, e23D	eN		e/d2A, e30A, e31A	eA, e15A, e24D	e32A
e5L		e4A, e13D	e21A, e7A, e11D, e12D	e3L	e17D	e14D, e15D, e16D,	e4L	e18D, e22A	e8A, e23A	e19D, e20D	
	e15A		e2L, e14A, e16A		e2N, e17A		e3ND, e6D, e7D, e8D, e9D, e10D	e3A		e4A	e19A, e20A, e21A
	e2A	e1A				e3D					
						e5A	e8D, e9D, e10D, e11D, e12D, e13D, e14D, e15D	e1L	e2A	e2L, e3AL	e/dA, e20A, e21A, e22A, e23A, e24A, e25A, e26A, e27A
		e2L								e5D	

(*continued*)

Table 12.1 The adoption of environmental issues as policy by the Liberal and National Parties, the ALP and the Democrats, 1943–94 *continued*

Issue	1943–1949	1953–1965	1966–1970	1971	1972	1973	1974	1975	1977	1979
Antarctica										eD
Great Barrier Reef			e1A (1967); e5A (1967)		e2A				e1L, e2LD, e3L	e5ND
Franklin Dam										
Green groups									e1L, e2A	e3D
Public education						e2A	e2L			e2DN
Sustainable development					e1N	e2A	e1A		e4A	e/dA
Environment (general)		eA (1965)	e17N (1966); e17A, e19A (1969); e1L, e2L (1970)		eN, e13L	e18A, e20A, e21A	e13A	e15A, e22A	e5A, e23A	eD, e3A, e4A, e9N, e13D, e18D, e24A

For explanation of codes, see Appendix. The capital letters indicate whether an issue was first taken up by the Liberals (L), the Nationals (N), the ALP (A), or the Democrats (D).

As early as 1965, the ALP expressed concern about the need to conserve fuel and energy and to develop renewable energy resources. The Liberals followed suit a decade later, in 1974. Consensus on this topic as an issue of importance appears to have been reached in 1975 when the Nationals also took it up.

The Liberals and Nationals both called for the preservation of forests in the 1940s and 1950s. In 1966 both the ALP and the Nationals called for the enlargement and/or protection of national parks. However, the ALP took the lead by a wide margin when, in 1965, it called for a national system of parks and reserves. Other initiatives proposed by the ALP were, in 1974, the protection of Northern Australia and the National Parks and Wildlife Conservation Bill and, in 1977, a ban on the clearing of native forests for softwood plantations and the development of a self-sustaining forestry industry. Nevertheless, the advent of the Democrats led to novel proposals, including the creation of a major national park in South-West Tasmania, an end to the issuing of woodchip licences except for sawmill waste, the protection of forests in Pacific Basin countries, and tax incentives for landowners to retain forests. Although the Liberals and Nationals came up with some constructive proposals (in 1979, on protecting the Alligator Rivers region and nominating Kakadu national park for World Heritage listing and, in 1983, for a youth project in reafforestation), most of the new proposals in the 1980s and beyond were made by the ALP and by the Democrats (particularly on protecting rainforests both in Australia and in other countries). The ALP was especially successful in responding to some of the proposals

1980	1982	1983	1984	1986	1987	1988	1989	1990	1991	1993	1994
e1L	eAL, e1A							e2A, e3D, e4D	e5A		
e4L											
	e1A, e2A	e1L, e2D									
e2L						e4D					
e1L	e2L		e2N		e6D	e1D		e1L	e5A		e/d1A, e/d2A, e3N e31A
e3L, e4L	e9L, e10L, e11L, e12L, e30A	e5L, e6L	e14L, e15L, e16AD, e18N, e25A, e26A		e7L	e3D, e4D, e8D		e8L	e4N, e28N		

by environmental groups and the Democrats on the issue of protecting forests, as demonstrated by its successful appeals to environmentalists at the 1983, 1987 and 1990 federal elections.

Similarly, the Democrats and the ALP took the lead on the topic of preserving the diversity of species. Both the ALP and the Nationals referred, in 1966, to the need for protecting flora and fauna. The Liberals followed suit in 1971. In 1974 the ALP called for legislation to control the trade in endangered species, and in 1977 the Liberals advocated funding for conservation groups engaged in protecting the diversity of species. In 1979 the Democrats enlivened the agenda by calling for a survey and protection of sea mammals and birds, and by supporting the rights of animals. In 1984 they suggested the cessation of the export of live fauna and the import of seal products and, in 1988, called for the prohibition of the killing of indigenous species, for a Royal Commission into the kangaroo industry, a total ban on the export of indigenous species, and an end to the import of furs and ivory. In 1991 the Democrats declared their opposition to genetic engineering. They also called for a halt to the export of live native freshwater fish and for a National Commission on Animals. The principal suggestions by the ALP were for the protection of plant genetic resources (1984), the conservation of kangaroos (1986), a national strategy and an international convention for maintaining biological diversity (1991), and implementation of the Convention on Biodiversity signed at the Rio Summit in 1992.

The issue of waste management was first mentioned in the early 1970s. In 1973 the ALP wanted to promote recycling and the control of hazardous chemicals and wastes. The Liberals drew attention to recycling in 1974 and the Nationals in 1979. The Democrats advanced the agenda in 1979 by advocating 'non-polluting' methods of sewage disposal. Above all, in 1989, they concentrated on controls over crop spraying and pest control machines and over herbicides and pesticides, on the resiting of chemical industries, and on the cessation of burning or high-temperature incineration of intractable wastes. In 1982 the ALP had taken the lead on informing the public about contaminants and, in 1984, on developing a system for identifying dangerous chemicals. In 1994 the ALP referred to the Basel Convention on the movement of waste between countries (1983) and proposed a 50 per cent reduction of wastes to landfill, the creation of national facilities for the storage of hazardous waste, and a national inventory of pollutants.

Only the Democrats and the ALP addressed the issue of sand mining. The Democrats led in 1979 by advocating a ban on the export of mineral sands. The ALP, from 1982, wanted a ban on sand mining in specific locations, notably on Moreton Island and Fraser Island. In 1988 the Democrats went further by proposing a ban on sand mining in all national parks.

On the question of pollution, the ALP and the Democrats were again ahead of the others. In 1967 the ALP supported a working party on air and water pollution. In 1970 both the ALP and the Liberals made broad statements about the need to address the problem of pollution (followed by the Nationals in 1972). The ALP drew attention to the possibility of developing systems for monitoring air and water quality (1973) and of tackling noise abatement (1975). In 1979 the Democrats attached to the agenda the pollution of urban waterways and of beaches by sewage. They also drew attention to the problem of 'visual' pollution. A decade later the Democrats presented a wide range of proposals on motor vehicles, on the introduction of unleaded petrol, on backyard burning in urban areas, on studies of health problems of people living near industrial complexes, on the establishment of pollution control commissions, and on the retention of airport curfews. The major stimulus to ALP policies on pollution arose from concerns about the depletion of the ozone layer (1988) and the emission of greenhouse gases (1990). In 1994 the ALP suggested comprehensive strategies for dealing with these problems. The Liberals and Nationals remained fairly tame in their response to all the misgivings about pollution.

All the established parties, apart from the Nationals, advocated the protection of whales. The ALP had called for the formation of a Whaling Commission in the 1940s. In 1974 the Liberals advocated the conservation of whales and, in 1977, a public inquiry into whaling. The ALP proposed, in 1977, the establishment of a 200-mile offshore sanctuary for whales and a ban on the import of whale products. On the preservation of Antarctica, it was the Democrats who took the lead in 1979. The Liberals and the ALP followed suit in 1980 and 1982. Stronger commitments were made by the ALP, in 1990 and 1991, on the prevention of mining and on establishing Antarctica as a World Park. In 1990 the Democrats suggested that Antarctica be placed on the World Heritage List and that Australia should renounce all claims to sovereignty over that territory. Since their foundation the Democrats have also been concerned about the protection of the Great Barrier Reef. Of the major parties, the ALP was a decade ahead of the Liberals and Nationals in advocating protection of the Great Barrier Reef. The ALP was also more robust in opposing to the construction of the Franklin Dam than the other major parties.

All the major parties have been in favour of raising public awareness about the environment and conservation, and all but the National Party have advocated support for or cooperation with environmental groups. All the established parties have embraced the notion of sustainable development, though the ALP has mentioned this concept most frequently and coupled it to a variety of issues.

The ALP was the first party, in 1965, to make a general statement in favour of environmental protection. The Liberals followed suit five years later and the National Party in 1972. In 1966 the National Party referred to the importance of the national estate. In 1969 the ALP promoted the concept of the quality of life. In 1970 the Liberal Party undertook to establish a Commonwealth office of the environment under the Prime Minister's Department.

In 1972 the Liberals advocated the polluter-pays principle, followed by the ALP in 1974. The following were some of the novel proposals by the ALP in 1973 for action on the environment: an examination of the impact of development projects, cooperation with international agencies, and support for basic research. In 1975 the ALP promoted the policy of creating a national environmental data bank. In 1979 it supported the concepts of a World Conservation Strategy and of a National Conservation Strategy. The Liberals followed suit in 1980. In 1982 the Liberals announced several proposals for considering the environmental impact of development projects. They also called for the conservation of marine resources. In the same year the ALP undertook to develop an Environmental Survey of Australia. In 1984 the ALP promised to produce an annual State of the Environment Report.

To sum up, these chapters on the response by established political organisations to discoveries about and perceptions of environmental problems have served to draw attention to the tension between innovation and tradition, between new ideas and established institutional practices. They have also shown both the obstacles to, and possibilities for, shifting the agenda for policy-making. On many issues institutional inertia, like the established patterns of concern about economic development, has been a formidable barrier to change. This applies especially to the Liberal and National parties for whom, in the 1950s and 1960s, the logic of economic development combined with short-term electoral considerations appeared to prevail over any strategies to deal with environmental problems.

On the other hand, the analysis of data over a long period of time can be used to demonstrate that political organisations are capable of adapting to social forces and that they can also operate independently of social forces in order to reshape the political agenda. This chapter has drawn attention to the contributions of different parties to this process over time, and to the leading role played by the ALP and the Democrats in dealing with concern about the environment. The ALP, notwithstanding its strong attachment to materialism and economic growth, was less encumbered by the institutional inertia that affected the Liberal and National parties. It managed to maintain a close connection with social movements and opposition groups that emerged in the 1950s against the testing of nuclear weapons and in the 1970s against uranium mining and other forms of economic development.

Paradoxically, this chapter also reinforces the observations by writers like Putnam (1993) that tradition can be a good thing and that institutional history can supply a firm basis for adaptation to new challenges and for shaping social change. In other words, as I suggested in chapter 5, we can accommodate the proposition by Putnam about a strong connection between effective government and civic humanism. We can propose that, as environmentalism becomes institutionalised (as documented in these chapters on policy speeches and party platforms), and as it succeeds in challenging prevailing institutional practices, it can actually benefit from the slow movement of institutional history. For instance, the dominance by the ALP in government during most of the 1980s through to the middle of the 1990s, and the influence on the ALP of new social and political movements and parties, have in many respects secured a powerful niche for environmental protection. The environmental movement has, in effect, become part of some of the social networks and the norms that constitute contemporary institutional practices.

Like the following chapters, the preceding ones need to be placed in the context of the emergence of new ideas and of discoveries, and of shifting intellectual paradigms about the value of economic development and environmental protection. The process through which parties take up these ideas and discoveries has been discussed in chapter 9 and forms an integral part of the framework for analysis outlined in chapter 3. The manner in which political parties articulate and disseminate these ideas and discoveries has been covered, to a degree, in this part of the book, particularly in chapters 9 to 11. The following part, on the media, also serves the purpose of focusing on the dissemination of these ideas and discoveries. Political parties play a crucial role in providing the media with cues and frameworks for discussing new issues. These cues and frameworks are crucial for raising public awareness about new topics, though not necessarily for resolving conflicts over these issues. The media, as we shall see, receives cues from expert communities and social movements. It also contributes in a distinctive way to creating the agenda both for political debates and for attempts to change institutional practices.

PART IV

The Media, Agenda Setting and Public Opinion

CHAPTER 13

The Articulation of Environmental Issues by the Media

So far I have concentrated on the significance for environmental politics of institutional practices, social movements and organisations. We now turn to the role of the mass media. Over time the mass media have variously been regarded as a threat to democracy and as agenda-setters for public opinion and for policy-makers (Lippmann 1922; Bachrach and Baratz 1962; Iyengar 1991; Iyengar et al. 1982). Many studies have attempted to gauge the impact of the mass media on policy making and public opinion (Cook et al. 1983; Erbring et al. 1980; McCombs and Shaw 1972; Page et al. 1987). Much research has been undertaken on whether the media set the political agenda or reflect it (for an overview, see Rosengren 1981).

The media represent a powerful force and have been used to great effect by social movements in trying to reshape norms and social values, as in the campaign to prevent the construction of the Franklin Dam in Tasmania and in other campaigns (see Burgmann 1993; Papadakis 1993; Sylow 1994). However, more than any other organisations, the established political parties depend on the media for their survival and influence. In order to understand how the media may assist political organisations in changing institutional practices, the analysis of media coverage of environmental issues will be guided by the following specific objectives:

- to acquire an understanding of how scientific discoveries, conceptual advances and new intellectual frameworks are disseminated to the wider community;
- to identify the key sources of information used by the media in disseminating information and opinions about environmental issues;
- to estimate the direction in which media reports might be moving public opinion;
- to identify trends over time, both in the direction of media coverage and in the intensity of coverage; and
- to pinpoint the issues that are most frequently covered by media accounts.

The mass media play a crucial role in society to the extent that they present information in ways that influence public opinion. Shifts in opinion about policy tend to occur when five conditions are met, in other words when information is:

- actually received
- understood
- relevant to understanding policies
- discrepant with previous beliefs
- credible.[61]

The media play a vital part in ensuring that information is received: 'They shorten, sharpen and simplify stories, and present pictures with strong visual impact so that a reasonably alert grade-schooler can get the point' (Page et al. 1987: 24). The media frequently ensure that the first four conditions are met. The issue of credibility is more difficult to evaluate because of the wide variety of sources used by the media, including 'popular presidents and respected commentators' as well as 'discredited politicians and self-serving interest groups' (Page et al. 1987: 24).

Page et al. use their analysis of eighty pairs of policy questions in opinion surveys over fifteen years to conclude that the impact on public opinion of news from different sources varies significantly. The greatest impact derives from the news commentary itself,[62] expert opinion and popular presidents; the least impact is made by interest groups unless, like environmental groups, they are 'thought to be concerned with broadly defined public interests' (Page et al. 1987: 37).

The last point is specially relevant to this study. When it comes to environmental problems, people are much more likely to trust environmental groups and scientists and technologists than governments and political parties (Papadakis 1993: 195, table 6.2). They trust trade unions and industry least of all, no doubt because these interest groups are seen, at least as regards environmental protection, to have a narrow interest.

Although people express less trust in political parties than in environmental groups to solve environmental problems, political parties do play a crucial role in setting agendas (see chapter 8). The media are widely regarded as crucial in articulating this agenda and in influencing public opinion (see Cook et al. 1983; Erbring et al. 1980; Iyengar et al. 1982; MacKuen 1984). Apart from their influence on opinions about policies over the long term, the mass media also change attitudes for limited, though critical, periods – for instance, by creating bandwagon effects during elections (Noelle-Neumann 1984).

The media also influence public opinion by making events easily accessible and then placing them outside the social and political context in which they occur. There is concern that television, by focusing on specific episodes and individual actors, 'inhibits the attribution of political responsibility to societal factors and to the actions of politicians' (Iyengar 1991: 5). This may represent an unrealistic expectation that the media can provide an entirely 'objective' account of events.[63]

Analysis of Media Coverage

Shifts in attitudes are obviously determined by the ideas to which people are exposed. The framing of issues by the mass media plays an important part in ensuring that certain ideas are 'at the top of a person's head at a particular moment' (Zaller 1992: 266). Assuming that the media do have a powerful influence on public opinion, I will explore the following issues: the intensity and selectivity of media coverage of environmental issues; the sources of information for the media; and trends over time. Since there are vast individual differences in knowledge and in the manner in which new information is received, I will not affirm a precise connection between individual opinions and the dissemination of new information by the mass media. What I am presenting is, in effect, a content analysis.

The Intensity and Direction of Coverage

Measuring the intensity of mass media coverage, let alone measuring the impact of the whole of the mass media, presents several problems.[64] Like other writers, I will proceed on an *ad hoc* basis using 'story-counting techniques' (see Zaller 1992: 295). This procedure is appropriate since this chapter concentrates on the articulation of environmental issues by the media rather than a detailed and complex account of how these stories are actually read. The following data attempt to capture the intensity and the direction of coverage of environmental issues. The analysis makes no claims to show how all of the mass media, including television, frame and articulate concerns about the environment. Rather it focuses on one source, over a period of thirty-five years, to illustrate how the mass media may influence and reflect public opinion as well as the aspirations of political parties and social movements. The source used in this case study is the popular weekly magazine *The Bulletin*, which is more likely to be read by people with tertiary education and by those in high-status occupations. Members of these social groups are more likely than others to be sympathisers or active supporters of environmental groups (see Papadakis 1993: chapter 5). Though *The Bulletin* is not meant to represent all of the mass media, it provides a good indication of trends.

The Bulletin was first published in 1880 as a local Sydney newpaper. Since 1960, when it was bought by Australian Consolidated Press, it has been offered as a weekly magazine. In 1984 *The Bulletin* was amalgamated with *Newsweek. The Bulletin (with Newsweek)* is the leading Australian news magazine as regards the size of circulation and readership. In March 1981 the readership was estimated at 706 000. Since then, there has been a decline – to 507 000 in March 1991 and 450 000 in March 1994. The circulation in March 1994 was around 104 000. Readers of *The Bulletin* are more likely to be from higher than lower socio-economic groups and to have professional occupations (see table 13.1).

Table 13.2 shows that the intensity of coverage of environmental issues rose steadily from 1960 onwards. Whereas in the 1960s there were only two stories featuring environmental issues, the number had increased to 16 for the period 1970–74 and to 18 between 1975 and 1979. In the late 1980s (1985–89) the number of stories rose to 40 and in the early 1990s (1990–94) to 61. The intensity of coverage also increased steadily if we gauge this by the number of pages devoted to environmental issues.[65] More importantly, inasmuch as we can speculate about the impact of news coverage, we find that most of the stories (68 per cent) were 'pro-environmentalist', with the remainder mostly 'neutral' (28 per cent). In the 1970s, 23 out of 34 stories (68 per cent) were pro-environmentalist, the remainder being either neutral or pro-development. In the 1980s 57 per cent (37 out of 65) were pro-environmentalist – a figure

Table 13.1 *The Bulletin*: readership, April 1992 – March 1993 (per cent)

Classification	Reader	Total population
Sex		
Female	43	50
Male	58	50
Socio-economic categories		
A/B	47	20
C	24	20
D	13	20
E	10	20
F/G	5	20
Occupation[a]		
Professional/Manager	45	21
Clerk/White-collar	39	37
Skilled/Trade	9	20
Semiskilled/Unskilled	6	18

[a] These figures represent the number of readers in formal full-time paid employment.
Source: Australian Consolidated Press Research.

which rose to 78 per cent in the early 1990s.[66] Overall, the number of pro-development stories was very small.[67] We can shed further light on these trends by examining the means by which the media gather information, and also their sources.

Key Sources

If we were to take our bearings from the systems theoretical approach proposed by Luhmann (see chapters 4 and 5) we might regard the mass media as a sub-system with all the characteristics of self-referential organisational behaviours. Like any other sub-system, the mass media translate into their own short, sharp and simple language the concerns that arise in their environment and in other sub-systems.

In this section I want to focus on how the media acquire their information and on how other sub-systems, notably the political one, impinge on them. The mass media often draw on a wide variety of sources not only for information but also for interpretations of the news: 'Even when the journalist is in a position to observe an event directly, he remains reluctant to offer interpretations of his own, preferring instead to rely on his news sources. For the reporter, in short, most news is not what has happened, but what someone says has happened' (Sigal 1973: 69, cited by Zaller 1992: 315; see also Cohen 1963; Gans 1980; Halberstram 1979). So far, these accounts suggest a number of things. They focus on the importance of perceptions rather than simply of 'objective facts' (see chapter 17). Second, they appear to undermine claims about conspiracies by the media. Finally, and most significantly for the following analysis, they draw our attention to the possibility of a high level of pluralism in news sources.

Table 13.2 *The Bulletin*: number and direction of stories on environmental issues, 1965–94

Year	Number of stories	Number of pages	Number of photos	Direction of stories		
				Pro-environment	Neutral	Pro-development
1965	1	2.25	2	1		
1969	1	2.25	3	1		
1970	2	5.5	5	2		
1971	5	9.25	8	4	1	
1972	3	6.5	5	1	2	
1973	4	11.25	10	3	1	
1974	2	7	8		2	
1975	–	–	–			
1976	2	8	7		2	
1977	11	69.75	79	10		1
1978	3	17.5	20	1	2	
1979	2	8	6	2		
1980	1	0.5	1	1		
1981	3	7.5	6	2	1	
1982	5	23	26	3	2	
1983	7	15.5	11	3	4	
1984	9	26.25	20	3	5	1
1985	2	2.25	1	1	1	
1986	3	3	3	1	1	1
1987	10	18	14	3	7	
1988	7	18.5	22	6	1	
1989	18	44	34	14	3	1
1990	4	21	23	4		
1991	7	20.5	17	6		1
1992	6	9.5	13	3	1	2
1993	13	15.25	29	10	3	
1994	31	60	76	25	5	1
Total	162	432	449	110	44	8

Source: Analysis of *The Bulletin*.

Among the key sources for the media are the expert communities – those who provide intellectual frameworks for interpreting the news and those who make significant discoveries (see parts I and II). Political organisations represent another important source of information and interpretation (see part III). Some writers emphasise this source and feel that government not only informs, but also provides misleading information and withholds key evidence (see Cohen 1963; Sigal 1973; Bennett 1990). For these writers, the possibilities of censorship exercised by political institutions fuel speculations about conspiracies by the media. Like Zaller, I find that these approaches place too much emphasis on established organisations: 'Government officials may be the proximate source of much of the information that reaches the public, but they are not necessarily the creators of the information, nor can they always control how information is framed by the press or what the press is interested in, nor are they equally important in all types of information' (Zaller 1992: 329).

These comments on sources of information for the press can be corroborated by examining the articles in *The Bulletin.* As posited by numerous writers, government sources play a crucial part in providing information which is then utilised by the media (table 13.3). Still, it is notable that all government sources constituted less than half of the information directly attributed to specific informants by writers for *The Bulletin.* Sixty per cent of the information is attributed to non-government sources. The bulk of information from government sources is from the federal government and from government agencies dealing with environmental issues.

The two other principal sources of information are the universities and interest groups. There is a heavy reliance on green politicians and environmental groups (20 per cent of attributed sources) and on business groups (15 per cent). Overall, the comments and information attributed to interest and lobby groups (35 per cent) amount to nearly as much as that derived from government sources (40 per cent).

Arguments about the significance of expert communities are strongly backed by the data. Twenty-one per cent of the comments are derived from this source. Moreover, apart from environmental groups, expert communities are in this case more likely than other informants and commentators to support environmental protection (83 per cent). This may be an important factor in explaining how issues come to be framed over time, and in the emergence of environmental protection as an issue on the political agenda. Expert communities rate very high in terms of credibility and influence over public opinion.

Predictably, nearly all the comments attributed to environmentalists are pro-environment. Turning to business groups, although they are less likely than other groups to comment favourably on environmental protection, the figure of 41 per cent is still impressive for a sector that has traditionally been mainly preoccupied with development. As far as government sources are concerned, the majority (61 per cent) are pro-environment comments. Table 13.3 shows that pro-environment comments are more likely to be attributed to the federal government and its agencies than to state governments. For instance, 72 per cent (709 out of 983 lines of comments attributed to federal government sources) are pro-environment compared to 57 per cent (237 lines out of 419 lines) in the case of state governments. Most of the comments by federal governments were made during the period 1983–94, in other words, under an ALP regime. Regarding state governments, it is well known that they have been less willing than the federal government to embrace environmental protection. Consequently, over the past decade, environmental groups have set a higher priority on lobbying the federal government than on lobbying state governments (Papadakis 1993).

The data in these tables are not meant to suggest that, overall, the federal government is more likely to favour environmental protection than development, or that business groups are almost as much in favour of environmental protection as they are of development. The principal interest is in the sources used by the media, the direction of their comments, and the comparisons among different sources.

The data can be used to support the argument that the media rely on a wide range of sources. Quite apart from the sub-categories shown in table 13.3, a more detailed description of the data shows that the media can and do draw on the expertise of a large number of scientists, business groups, environmentalists, politicians, and bureaucrats in compiling stories about environmental protection. Moreover,

Table 13.3 *The Bulletin*: sources of information, 1960–94

Source	Pro-environment	Neutral	Pro-development	Total
		(number of lines)[a]		
Government				
Federal government	709	141	133	983
Federal opposition	9	62	8	79
Government advisor	37	5	3	45
Government agencies	772	224	227	1 223
State government	237	34	148	419
State opposition	–	10	–	10
Local government	15	107	50	172
Sub-total	1 779	595	569	2 943
Greens/Environmentalists				
Green politicians	258	7	–	265
Environmentalists	1 168	28	–	1 196
Sub-total	1 426	35	–	1 461
Business groups				
Business (general)	419	50	635	1 104
Logging	–	4	38	42
Mining	–	–	16	16
Sub-total	419	54	689	1 162
Universities	1 039	190	9	1 238
Independent sources	225	60	7	292
Sub-total	1 264	250	16	1 530
Local residents	70	58	114	242
Think tanks	10		4	14
Total	4 968	992	1 392	7 352
		(per cent)[b]		
Government	36 (61)	60 (20)	41 (19)	40 (100)
Greens/ Environmentalists	29 (98)	4 (2)	– (–)	20 (100)
Business groups	8 (36)	5 (5)	50 (59)	16 (100)
Universities/ Independent sources	25 (83)	25 (16)	1 (1)	21 (100)
Local residents	2 (29)	6 (24)	8 (47)	3 (100)
Total[c]	100	100	100	100

[a] This part of the table represents the number of lines in *The Bulletin* which are based on information directly attributed in the form of either quotations from, or references to, specific sources. All these quotations and references were coded to show their direction, in other words, whether they might be construed as pro-environment or neutral or pro-development.

[b] This part of the table summarises the data in the first part. The row percentages are in brackets.

[c] The actual total may amount to more than 100 per cent because the figures have been rounded off.

Source: see table 13.2.

although 'local residents' are poorly represented, their views are captured elsewhere, namely in reports about the climate of public opinion.

Key Issues

Apart from the diversity of sources, analysis of *The Bulletin* is useful in identifying the range of topics that are deemed newsworthy. The following account provides a basis for comparisons with topics featured in public opinion surveys and with electoral platforms. The topics covered by *The Bulletin* are described and analysed in table 13.4. The topics have been sorted into seven groups. More details are provided in the notes to table 13.4. Measured by the number of pages devoted to a topic, forests came first (115 pages), followed by green politics (83 pages) and pollution (66 pages). Regarding the total number of stories, green politics came first with 36 stories. Most of the stories on green politics were neither pro-development nor pro-environment. However, most stories on conservation, forests, sustainable development and pollution were pro-environment. Overall, 110 stories were pro-environment, 44 'neutral' and only 8 pro-development.

Table 13.5 directs attention to patterns of reporting on the various topics over time. This provides a useful basis for comparisons with agendas set by political parties and with patterns of public opinion (see chapters 9 to 12, 16 and 17). For instance, until 1977 there had been no reporting on forests. Apart from the exceptional series

Table 13.4 *The Bulletin*: coverage of key issues and directions, 1960–94

	Pages devoted to issue		Direction of stories (*n*)			Total stories	
Issue	%	(*n*)	Pro-environment	Neutral	Pro-development	%	(*n*)
Conservation[a]	13	56	22	5	–	17	27
Nuclear power[b] and uranium	13	55	6	7	2	9	15
Green politics[c]	19	83	13	20	3	22	36
Forests[d]	26	115	22	6	–	18	28
Sustainable development[e]	12	53	24	2	2	18	28
Pollution[f]	15	66	21	1	–	14	22
Mining[g]	2	10	2	3	1	3	6
Total	100	438	110	44	8	100	162

[a] Most stories related to conservation in general and to endangered species.

[b] Most stories were about uranium and radiation safety. Other topics included nuclear power and testing nuclear weapons.

[c] Most stories focused on green politics and on politicians' views on environmental issues. There were two stories on 'eco-guerillas' (namely, on people who engaged in acts of sabotage), two stories about debates between environmentalists and their opponents and one story each on women in environmental groups and on the 'backlash' against conservation.

[d] There was a major series of eight stories on national parks. Other stories focused on forests and woodchipping, the Franklin Dam proposal, rainforests, and pulp mills.

[e] Six stories were about waste disposal and three stories concerned recycling. Other topics included eco-tourism, green consumer products and the Rio Earth Summit in 1992.

[f] Several stories focused on ocean and air pollution. Three stories were about salinity in the Murray River. There were also two stories each on the Great Barrier Reef, Antarctica, and the greenhouse effect.

[g] The three stories were about sand mining and other mining projects. (Uranium mining has been included under 'Nuclear power and uranium'.)

Source: see table 13.2.

of stories in 1977, it was only between 1982 and 1987 that forests were consistently taken up as an issue in *The Bulletin*. There is a strong correspondence here with the preoccupations of social movements and political parties in the early 1980s. Again, reflecting issues addressed by social movements and political parties, we find a cluster of stories on uranium mining and nuclear power between 1976 and 1978. Pollution has been an important issue ever since the early 1970s. Interest in this issue appears to follow a pattern of different 'cycles of attention', from 1969 to 1973, from 1981 to 1984, and from 1988 to the present. In the last cycle the focus includes new issues like the greenhouse effect. Similarly, one can identify cycles of attention to other topics. Reporting on topics like sustainable development reflects both cycles of attention (1987–89 and 1991–94) and the widespread interest in this issue created by political and intellectual elites in recent years. To a degree, the data seem to support the theory by Downs (1972) about the 'issue-attention cycle', whereby interest in issues, including concern about the environment, moves through various stages, culminating in their displacement from the political agenda. In reality, the notion of an 'issue-attention cycle' offers only a partially satisfactory account of interest in

Table 13.5 *The Bulletin*: year by topic, 1965–94 (number of stories)

Year	Conservation	Nuclear power and uranium	Green politics	Forests	Sustainable development	Pollution	Mining
1965	1						
1969						1	
1970						2	
1971	3		1			1	
1972			3				
1973		1	2			1	
1974	1				1		
1975							
1976		2					
1977		2		9			
1978		3					
1979				1	1		
1980	1						
1981	1					2	
1982			2	1		2	
1983			3	4			
1984	1	2	2	3		1	
1985				2			
1986			1	1			1
1987	2		3	2	1		2
1988	5				1	1	
1989	1		7	1	5	4	
1990		1	2			1	
1991	1	1	2	1	1	1	
1992					5	1	
1993	3		4		4	2	
1994	7	3	4	3	9	2	3

Source: See table 13.2.

environmental issues, since, as I shall show in chapter 16, environmental issues have remained high on the political agenda over a long period of time.

Table 13.6 is interesting for a number of reasons. It shows that until 1984 most comments attributed to business groups were pro-development. However, since 1984 the balance has swung the other way. Business sources are more often used in order to support pro-environment positions than pro-development ones in stories on the environment. The pattern for *all* government sources remains fairly mixed though, as shown in table 13.3, *The Bulletin* has used federal government sources more often than not to provide pro-environment statements. Further analysis (not reported here in detail) also shows that federal ALP government sources have, over the past decade, been key sources of pro-environment views.

To summarise, this chapter has shown that the mass media have focused with increasing intensity on environmental issues, and that the reports have been inclined to favour the point of view of environmentalists. The sources used by the media have

Table 13.6 *The Bulletin*: year by source of information, 1966–94[a]

	Government			Business groups		
Year	Pro-environment	Neutral	Pro-development	Pro-environment	Neutral	Pro-development
1966						
1969			45	6		6
1970		8				
1971	5					
1972	3	2				
1973	116	19	13			10
1974	13		7	19		65
1975						
1976		5	11			
1977	5					28
1978	239	41	106			
1979	37	8	9		4	
1980						
1981	6	13	4	8		7
1982		9				17
1983			24	21		107
1984	64	49	37	83		38
1985	13					
1986						
1987	31	543	36	3		19
1988	72			48		3
1989	62	89	16	82		51
1990	23	167	177	15		
1991	133		9	30		
1992	40		12	94		86
1993	158	90	7	11		16
1994	183	120	74	49	24	217

[a] See note a to table 13.3.
Source: See table 13.2.

tended to be diverse and suggest a high level of pluralism (see also Sylow 1994). Expert communities have been a significant source in this respect. So far, the detailed analysis of news stories suggests a strong correspondence between the content of news stories in terms of the issues that are featured and the policy speeches and electoral platforms of established parties. There are several indications, however, that the media have been taking their cues from political organisations in placing issues on the agenda. Yet the presentation of issues suggests that the media impose their own logic on events and tend to simplify complex issues in order to articulate a particular point of view – in this case a pro-environment one. This theme, of how the mass media articulate certain points of view or stereotypes, is tackled in some detail in the following chapter, which analyses the content of news stories.

CHAPTER 14

Media Stereotypes and Adaptation

So far I have examined hypotheses about media coverage of environmental issues with a statistical analysis of stories in *The Bulletin*. The following account explores the detailed content of news stories. It demonstrates how the media affirm old stereotypes, create new ones, and can take on board new concepts. The focus will be on conservationists as a 'lunatic fringe', the encouragement of expressive protest, free enterprise and money-making, growth versus environment, a paradigm shift and sustainable development.

In the early 1970s the environment was barely on the political agenda. Notwithstanding efforts to establish institutional procedures for addressing this issue, there was some scepticism as to whether anything would actually be done. In 1973 *The Bulletin* reported on the ineffectiveness of the NSW Department of the Environment. It quoted a young graduate who had recently resigned from the department:

> Apathy, inertia, inefficiency, incompetence and inactivity were the order of any working day . . . The department, created 18 months ago because the Liberal Government became aware that the issue of the environment was an attractive political platform, is powerless . . . And, I was told, I was to be trained in the skilful art of conveying half-truths, telling convincing white and outright lies to the public concerning its activities; in acquiring the gentle art of placating individuals and conservation organisations with grievances and complaints . . . (14 April 1973: 21).

Although this and other reports represent a critical account of governments and their reluctance to place the environment on the political agenda, 'balance' was generally achieved by creating another kind of stereotype, namely, by portraying environmentalists as out of touch with reality.

Conservationists as a 'Lunatic Fringe'

Traditional accounts of social movements have tended to portray them as irrational and pathological reponses to established political institutions. These characterisations are reflected in some accounts in *The Bulletin*. They refer to the 'rabid fringe of the conservationists' who 'virtually demand that industrial progress be stopped'

(5 June 1971: 55), and to conservationism as 'almost like a religious revival movement', comprising 'bushwalkers, speleologists, limnologists, bird banders, "men of the trees," anti-chemical "organic farmers", fish clippers, blackbutt savers and sanctuary minders' (8 May 1971: 26). Interestingly, an article that begins as a cynical critique of the excesses of conservationists ends with the suggestion that there are some genuine issues to be addressed: 'In Burnie's Emu Bay Valley several hundred residents are battling with an acid plant which has polluted the area with acid fumes. Iron roofs are pitted and corroded, plants and bushes have died and leaves on trees have gone brown. At the Myall Lakes, land sales were being advertised late last month – the last undisturbed watercourses in the State' (8 May 1971: 27).

Still, the tendency by the media to simplify stories leads to portrayals of different types of environmentalists as extremists. For instance, in a conflict over the decision by the Queensland government to capture crocodiles over 1.2 metres long because of the apparent danger to humans, we are instructed that 'The greenies are an unlikely mixture of the ultra-committed conservationists to whom the destruction of a single shrub heralds a national botanical disaster and money-motivated tourist operators to whom fewer crocodiles means less business' (15 September 1987: 66). In this instance, 'balance' is achieved by focusing on the negative traits of all kinds of environmentalists. This kind of reporting conveys an adversarial style of politics.

Another line of argument, which is far less scurrilous than the previous one, is to show that the 'extreme tactics' of conservationists could undermine their own goals. The former federal minister for the environment, Barry Cohen, argued that environmentalists were misusing the World Heritage Properties Conservation Act (1983), and thereby debasing its value and allowing future conservative governments either to ignore or to repeal the Act (24 May 1988: 54).

Poor political judgement was only one of the criticisms directed at environmentalists. Another was to focus on their appearance:

> In this sublimely peaceful setting, a ragtag mob of protesters who look as if they have been plucked from an Afghan bazaar are shuffling and chanting, psyching themselves up for the benefit of the media.
>
> Ragged young women with children at their breasts and others snotty-nosed at their heels, men with ponytails and earrings, many of them barefoot in bandanas and braids . . . (6 June 1989: 50).

Interestingly, in the same story, the print media blame the television media for being more open to exploitation by environmentalists: 'In the battle for public hearts and minds and votes, the forestry commission has run a consistent, distant last, not least because the gullible electronic media, hamstrung by the need to condense their reports into bite-size grabs of no more than 90 seconds, find it infinitely easier to go with the emotional flow pumped out by the Greens' (6 June 1989: 51).

However, as shown by the statistical analysis, the print media have not only devoted increasing amounts of column space to environmental issues, but have also portrayed them in a favourable light and provided environmentalists with many opportunities for presenting their point of view, as in a report by an animal rights activist and environmentalist on the 'Grass-roots rebellion' (31 October 1989: 55–6). The media have therefore played a key part in undermining old stereotypes, in contributing to a notable shift in values, and in changing institutional practices.

The Encouragement of Expressive Protest and the Critique of Progress

Among the most significant shifts in values has been the growing criticism of certain models of progress and the support for environmental protection. *The Bulletin* played a serious part in this. At first criticism was directed not so much at Australia but at other countries, notably the USA: 'The mightiest industrial civilisation the world has ever known is paying a bitter price in despoliation of the land and its natural life – hardly a major river that is not lethally polluted with toxic wastes, vast areas where birds have virtually disappeared, poisoned by agricultural insecticides' (4 September 1965: 38). Later the criticism focused on Australian issues. An article on 'Losing the Conservation Battle' articulated fundamentalist opposition to progress. The destruction of the sandbar around the Myall Lakes evoked these responses:

> Progress, as an over-riding conception, *does* destroy. Bulldozers rumble about the mining complex eked out of the sandbar, processing machines emit a smell not unlike an old gas works, fine angophoras lie logged in a pile to the side. But right down in your guts the scene is offensive. Some of us want to fight all beach mining ('if this is what it is like, from Gosford to Cape York, then God help Australia's east coast') (3 July 1971: 31).

A picture of a mining operation has the following caption: 'The rape of areas that are unique and valuable, in the name of progress' (3 July 1971: 30). Believing that they best represented the public interest, environmentalists had put business on the defensive in the 1970s. Besides employing science to further their case, environmentalists used highly emotive language. Most of the media encouraged their expressive protest. A story with the title 'The Pack Rape of our Forests?' described woodchipping as 'having the most profound effect on the Australian environment since the vast clearances that accompanied the original white settlement of this continent' (9 January 1979: 34). The report traced the origins of the woodchipping industry to 'the exploitive outlook of our forebears'. In the 1960s *The Bulletin* had already begun to articulate a critical view of the white settlers:

> It is only today that we are beginning to wonder just how limitless the land really is; to speculate whether the clearing of millions of acres of trees might have begun the process of desiccating an already dry continent; to regret the total decimation of the great cedar forests of the east coast; to blame our forefathers for the fact that Sydneysiders will never have a foreshore drive around the Harbor; to shudder at the outlook which permitted nearly a million koalas to be shot and clubbed to death for their fur in a single 'open season' declared by the Queensland Government in 1927 (4 September 1965: 38).

In a report on the dangerous levels of salinity in the Murray River, the farming practices and cultural habits of the white settlers are condemned:

> So the white settlers pushed careless fingers into the delicate web of the ecology of a vast catchment, shattering the old symmetry. . . .
>
> The fate of the rich fish life of the Murray is a familiar story. The white settlers, obsessed

> with the Old World, brought in animals and plants to make their new home more familiar. In 1859 that monumental idiot Thomas Austin brought in wild rabbits. The same obsession with the Old World led to the introduction of trout to a freshwater system amply stocked with more than 200 native species, a number of them ideal for anglers (28 July 1981: 70).

In 1982 another story about the Murray River warns that South Australia could, because of the destruction of the Murray River by salinity, be wiped out, just as the ancient civilisation of Mesopotamia was 'wiped out by salting' (30 November 1982: 72). The cause of these problems is identified as 'European man'.

Several metaphors underlie these stories, including the contrast between the early white settlers and the enlightened citizens of modern Australia and, paradoxically, the preservation of a civilisation. In the following account, these metaphors are juxtaposed with symbols derived from the animal kingdom, from psychotherapy and from industrialised society. Log dump tractors are said to have 'steel jaws' for sorting logs into two piles. Forests are described as a 'green oxygen tent for urban man'. The destruction of forests is placed in a 'historical' context:

> What our forebears did has been described as the rape of the forests: this is mechanised pack rape, under the name of therapy. . . .
>
> Some of the giants going through the chipper (the largest in Australia) may have been standing when the Dutch and Portuguese first sailed up the west coast. . . .
>
> Woodchipping takes place in the seclusion of the forests, almost wholly on Crown land. And trees have no votes. . . .
>
> But if we as a community don't soon wake up to what's happening behind the eucalypt curtain, we may find that although the operation to renew the forest is successful, the patient will never recover (9 January 1979:39).

The following account is from a report on 'The Fight to Save The Barrier Reef':

> The desire to destroy another living creature, preferably bigger than yourself, seems to be part of many men.
>
> Until then, like most people, I thought of fish only as a tasty embellishment to french fries and salads, but seeing all those beautiful colored creatures quivering away their lives on the hot boat decks sickened me. Many I know to be gentle herbivores whose brilliant colors and passive ways were matched by their trusting manner towards humans. . . .
>
> But there is another plague nibbling away at the reefs: *Homo sapiens*, the two-legged wilderness raper. . . .
>
> Our Great Barrier Reef is one of the world's major natural wonders. Home to the richest varieties of marine animals on Earth, it has stood for centuries untouched by the rape of progress and the greed of man.
>
> But progress, the god of big business, has turned its destructive gaze upon this great reef (31 August 1982: 57, 58, 62).

Another report, 'With the Greenie Guerillas on the Franklin Front', cites the conservationist and entrepreneur Dick Smith: 'Why build a dam that will supply 180 megawatts for the next 10 or even 20 years and destroy a wilderness that has existed for 20 000 years?' (1 February 1983: 38). In a similar vein, a report by Professor John Mulvaney concludes that: 'It is ironic that one decade of "progress" may submerge this entire world of ancient plants and people. The resulting 200 megawatts of electricity probably constitutes a smaller economic benefit than the tourist potential' (1 February 1983: 42).

Some of these reports elicited a negative reaction, for instance, a report by Robert Raymond on the threat to forests (9 November 1982). Dr Frank Podger, Senior Research Scientist in the Division of Forest Research, CSIRO, felt that the attack on forest managers ignored all the evidence of legislative action: 'Unfortunately, Mr Raymond's article disappoints any expectation which readers might have had of an accurate and balanced summary. The article can be recommended only for what it has to tell us about Mr Raymond's strange sense of journalistic fair play' (4 January 1983: 25). J. J. Landsberg, chief of the CSIRO Division of Forest Research in Canberra, voiced the following concerns:

> The establishment of the State forest departments checked the destruction and they make the greatest contribution to the preservation of our forests. It is an incorrect generalisation to say that their primary concern is the management of the forests to maximise the yield of wood. The forest departments are concerned with forests as water-yielding areas, as recreational areas and for their aesthetic value, as eco-systems and as wood-producing areas. Wood production is not necessarily first on this list and, in any case, management for sustaining wood production does not (by definition) involve destruction of the forests' (4 January 1983: 25).

The principal focus in stories about the environment was on saving it from developers. In an interesting reversal of rhetoric, it is the sawmillers rather than the environmentalists who are said to be issuing 'doomsday warnings' (13 March 1984: 48). Above all, the agenda is clearly to engage in a battle to save the rainforests from development: 'Along the rainforest front, the struggle to hold the shrinking islands of green continues. Australia may yet stabilise its holdings of this prime reservoir of life and set an example to other countries' (13 March 1984: 51).

The metaphor of life and death, of survival and extinction, is neatly captured in a report entitled 'Rare Melbourne butterfly awaits death sentence'. The story was about a planned housing development in Melbourne that would destroy the sole remaining habitat of the nearly extinct *Paralucia pyrodiscus lucida*; it would cost $1 million to preserve the land to try to save the butterfly. The story suggested that 'an endangered Melbourne area butterfly species finds itself tangled in a life-threatening web of lean budgets, bad timing and political expediency' (19 May 1987: 46).

The passion in the environment debate persisted throughout the 1980s. In 1989 the focus was on the Wesley Vale pulp mill in Tasmania. Politicians were accused of 'ignoring lessons learnt from elsewhere', of using the Bass Strait 'as a toilet for much nastier stuff than floats up on Sydney's beaches', of giving in to powerful vested interests, of providing secret subsidies to bulk power users, of poisoning rivers and planning to pump toxic organochlorine wastes into the ocean (10 January 1989: 29).

Coastal development was perceived as a major threat to the nurseries for fish and crustaceans (namely the tidal wetlands, salt marshes, seagrass beds and mangrove areas). *The Bulletin* pleaded for 'a passionately caring look' at the marine environment and for reversing 'the greed, ignorance and stupidity' which were threatening both the coastline and living standards, and ultimately life itself (24 January 1989: 42).

Following these reports on Wesley Vale and on coastal development, the focus of concern was extended to the depletion of the land, in a report by Dr Chris Watson, a CSIRO soil scientist:

> We have a culture that does not know how to respect and look after its land, a culture whose living and population patterns are inimical to the sustainable production of food and fibre in the long term. If our civilisation is to persist, and not to fall into further disarray because of declining productivity, radical changes must be instituted to stabilise population levels, encourage decentralisation, foster self-reliance, increase recycling, and promote the stewardship of the land (7 February 1989: 91).

The momentum was maintained in subsequent stories on toxic wastes, recycling, sewage, on the destruction of the ozone layer and the greenhouse effect. The common theme to all these stories is the enduring legacy of our current practices:

> The Greeks and Romans left temples and aqueducts. The Egyptians of antiquity left the Pyramids and Sphinx. Our most enduring artefacts are lethal dumps of dioxin, polychlorinated biphenyls, organochlorines, hexachlorbenzene and radioactive wastes.
>
> When the ancient Sydney Harbor Bridge is only four pylons crumbling away and the tunnels of the Snowy Mountains Hydro-Electric Scheme have long cracked and ceased to be useful, the intractable wastes of the 20th century will be as threatening to life on earth as they are today. Our worst rubbish will long outlast anything else we did (14 March 1989: 53).

What is striking about all these stories is how forcefully they express the environmentalist point of view; this expression occurs in the columns of a mainstream, mass-circulation weekly magazine and not just in the publicity leaflets of environmental groups and political organisations.

Free Enterprise and Money-making

The critique of progress emerges in popular criticisms (articulated by *The Bulletin*) of free enterprise and money-making: 'The muck-and-money syndrome spawned by the founding fathers of the industrial age as they watched the smoke pour out and the profits roll in, persists' (26 April 1969: 25). Oil pollution becomes a symbol of greed and blind faith in progress. The *Torrey Canyon* oil tanker disaster is described as a 'nightmarish example of progress for its own sake', when the ruptured tanks 'began to vomit oil and great slicks spread over the sea in the direction of the Cornish holiday beaches' (Lord Ritchie-Calder, 17 January 1970: 30). In the same vein, the report argues that the destruction of the environment represents 'prosperity' at the expense of posterity.

In the 1970s Jack Mundey, a prominent trade unionist, led an unusual and successful social movement against development projects in Sydney. It was called the Green Bans movement because of the refusal by builders' unions to work on some development projects. Mundey articulated the critique of a form of progress that created employment but destroyed the Sydney skyline. The Green Bans movement was subjected to some scurrilous attacks: 'There is something highly comical in the spectacle of builders' labourers, whose ideas on industrial relations do not rise above strikes, violence, intimidation and the destruction of property, setting themselves up as arbiters of taste and protectors of our national heritage.' (12 May 1973: 38, citing an editorial from the *Sydney Morning Herald*). Still more column space was devoted to criticising developers and to characterising the campaigns by environmentalists as a war, as in the following account by Malcolm Turnbull of the destruction of forests by the woodchipping industy: 'The barren emptiness of a hillside, its timber felled for woodchips, must be one of the most desolate and depressing sights outside the napalm-ravaged fields of Vietnam. Woodchipping isn't a controversy, it's a war' (26 February 1977: 17). The report added that the woodchipping industry, confronted by 'fundamental opposition' from environmentalists, could focus only on 'jobs and money', and that 'even the most sympathetic politician' found 'the arguments of the environmentalists drowned out by the ring of the cash register' (26 February 1977: 19).

The coverage by the media of environmentalist protest actions and of the critique of free enterprise was noted by business groups. Hugh Morgan, executive director of the Western Mining Corporation, remarked that protesters were 'seeking to raise emotions', to create 'media pageants', and to destroy employment opportunities: 'The hard core have a hidden agenda that's not full of milk and kindness . . . what they're really doing is destroying job opportunities and Australia's growth pattern and exercising enormous political power' (6 September 1983: 21–3). The theme of growth and environment features not only in this report but in many other accounts.

Growth versus Environment

Binary codes are constantly used by the media to simplify and dramatise stories. Information from intellectuals, politicians, social movements and interest groups has been used by the media to evoke a sharp contrast between economic growth and environmental protection. Reports on the findings of organisations like the Club of Rome (15 July 1972: 35) and on electoral politics (28 October 1972: 19) lean heavily on the hypothesised conflict between economic growth and environmental protection.

The conflict between developers and environmentalists had become so acute by the 1990s that the government created new mechanisms for consultation like ESD working groups and the Resource Assessment Commission. A report on these initiatives appeared in *The Bulletin* (14 August 1990). A similar theme, namely the gulf between environmentalists and developers, is taken up a year later. Hugh Morgan presented his views on the extreme claims made by environmentalists, their support for social revolution and for negative growth. By contrast, Christine Milne, a green independent parliamentarian in Tasmania, focused on the finite character of the fossil fuels and the extent of environmental degradation: 'Governments must reassess the whole concept of economic growth and recognise that air, water, soil, minerals, forests and genetic diversity are not free goods. They must be built into the cost/benefit analysis of new developments and national accounting generally' (6 August 1991: 32). For Hugh Morgan, the environmentalist agenda was just as threatening:

> Managers and businessmen and women are not usually well trained in politics or theology. The challenge facing the business community from the environmentalist movement is as important a challenge as we have faced since World War II. If, in national terms, as well as in individual enterprise terms, we are going to have prosperity rather than impoverishment, the environmentalist agenda for secular economic decline has to be decisively rejected (6 August 1991: 30).

Morgan tried to determine 'what is right and what is wrong in this great debate'. *The Bulletin* introduced the story with the following sentence: 'Despite all the debate it has generated in recent years, the essential gap between the green movement and the growth movement seems as wide as ever.' Yet *The Bulletin* has also reported on attempts to overcome this divide in stories about sustainable development.

The next two sections therefore present contrasting accounts. The first focuses on *The Bulletin*'s articulation of the fundamentalist concerns of environmentalists. In certain respects, this reinforces the suggestion I have made that the media have posited a fundamental conflict between environment and development. In other respects, the focus by *The Bulletin* on new ways of looking at the environment (in other words, from the environmentalist point of view) represents the capacity of the mass media to articulate and contribute to challenges to institutional inertia. The second (and concluding) section focuses on the adaptability of the mass media, to the extent that they can undercut their own tendency to cast issues in adversarial terms. Here I am referring to the way in which sustainable development has been articulated as a significant issue on the political agenda.

A Paradigm Shift

Since the 1960s *The Bulletin* has reported on new ways of looking at the environment. In the following account it has tried to convey the discovery of a new paradigm and a new philosophy:

> For a world which has had to become accustomed to the extinction of 10 million Russian kulaks, or six million Jews, should the disappearance of the brush-tailed rat-kangaroo, the pit-footed bandicoot, or the numbat cause any real concern? . . .
>
> For the answer it is necessary to look beyond the horizon of the kangaroo-shooter, to the encompassing vision of one of man's newest but perhaps most significant philosophies—ecology (4 September 1965:39).

In 1977 Robert Raymond produced for *The Bulletin* eight lengthy stories about forty-five national parks in Australia. The description of national parks in these stories reflects an attempt to shape perceptions and to communicate a new attitude towards the environment. The introduction to the reports suggests that they represent, 'for the first time', 'an intensely practical consumer's guide' to 'some of the most splendid national parks in the world with magnificent and varied scenery and natural features'. The report points out that 'too many people still don't know how to get the best out of them' (30 July 1977: 37).

The first report describes the parks as 'Scattered jewels across the ring-barked, cleared, burned-off and over-grazed landscape that characterises so much of this continent . . . '. The parks, Raymond suggests: 'offer a resuscitative breath of fresh air, an opportunity for the renewal of our fundamental links with the natural world, the refreshment of the sense of wonder – re-creation in the true sense of the word' (30 July 1977: 37).

The report cites the American naturalist Wallace Stegner, who described 'wild country' as 'a means of reassuring ourselves of our sanity as creatures, a part of the geography of hope'. It also cites Judge Hedges who influenced the USA Congress to create the Yellowstone national park. Hedges talked about the park as a creation of God for all people, which needs 'to be kept sacred always' (30 July 1977: 38).

In another report, a forest in Tasmania is compared to the magic forests described in 'European fairytales' (6 August 1977: 56). Tasmania was soon to become the focal point of one of the most significant conflicts over environmental protection. The site of this conflict was the Gordon River, which is described as follows:

> At first the river winds between low banks, clothed in paperbarks and fringed with reeds. But with every turn the walls grow steeper, and the river narrower. The drenching annual rainfall has clothed the gorge sides in an unbroken wall of rich vegetation, a towering green tapestry that has flourished for tens of thousands of years. . . .
>
> The water itself is the colour of strong tea, an indication of its origins in the high peaty valleys of the south-west. In the shelter of the gorge the dark water sometimes lies like a mirror, without the trace of a ripple, and produces the dream-like reflection for which the Gordon River is famous (6 August 1977: 60–1).

In the report on South Australia, Robert Raymond describes the interaction between human beings and wildlife at Seal Bay, Kangaroo Island, in terms of 'trust' and 'of a new and better relationship between the original inhabitants and the newcomers which our national parks are helping to create' (20 August 1977: 63).

All the reports, like the following portraits of Ayers Rock and Mt Olga, present a distinctive perspective on nature, one that conveys a sense of wonder and mystery:

> Approached by the road from Ayers Rock, and seen at first across the sea of waving spinifex and low clumps of mulga, the Olgas resemble a batch of giant eggs, carelessly heaped together by some prehistoric monster. The height of the monoliths is deceptive, for there is nothing to provide a comparison . . .
>
> As you come closer, however, the ramparts loom higher and more precipitous. As the sunlight and shadows play across the huge domes it is not difficult to understand how the Pitjandjara people came to invest this place, like the Rock across the plain, with powerful spirits, and called it Katatjuta – "The many-headed one." . . .
>
> It is a place of overwhelming presence, and to wander through the breezy valleys and over the rocky slopes is an unforgettable experience. . . . This place leaves something in the mind – a sense of awe and mystery (3 September 1977: 42).

Each report includes detailed information about the facilities in the parks, the climate, and how to get there. The report on Western Australia explicitly proclaims the invitation to Australians to share in these delights with the title: 'Where the Tourist is Won by the Wild'. The Hamersley Range is enticingly described as an 'endless layer cake' and much else:

> As you come closer you see that the layers are strata of ancient rocks, cut and sculptured by hundreds of millions of years of erosion, a great barrier of ray ridges, gorges and sheer bluffs in all shades of red, brown, yellow and black. . . .
>
> Its rim and upper slopes are clothed with trees, including the darkly dramatic native pines. Far below a shimmering expanse of water gleams through the trees, fed by a series of tumbling cascades at one end of the gorge. . . .
>
> A track has been cut down into the gorge, along the rock wall under shady trees and past overhanging ferns, to the top of the falls. Here, in contrast to the bright, hot glare of the rocky plateau above, all is cool and green. Ferns and mosses cling to the rock walls, wet with spray from the cascades (10 September 1977: 55).

To reinforce his message, Raymond points out how different the Cape Range national park is from the urban settings where most Australians live. Readers are reminded that the parks 'act as a last refuge for some of the more vulnerable of our native animals' (10 September 1977: 57) and that previous generations had been careless with nature all along the eastern seaboard: 'Lamington is an outstanding example of the kind of luxuriant rainforest that once extended from Cape York well into New South Wales. Little of it remains. First it was ruthlessly stripped of its magnificent timber trees, especially the red cedar, and then cleared for farming and grazing' (17 September 1977: 46). This carelessness has turned some plants into 'priceless assets': 'The Bunya Mountains, which are a national park of intriguing character, contain a priceless asset – the last remaining major community of bunya pines, those towering giants of the rainforest that were once widespread in south-eastern Queensland' (17 September 1977: 47).

It is likely that these reports, comprising a total of sixty-three pages with colour illustrations in a major weekly magazine, contributed to shifting public perceptions about the value of preserving national parks in Australia. The change in viewpoints over the past decade is mirrored in a story on native animals which are unlikely to survive:

> Spare a thought for the numbat, the potoroo, the bilby and the bettong. If you don't, they might cease to be there to think about. The gradual disappearance of these rare marsupials seems to concern few Australians. Ecologists and conservationists are fighting a losing battle to avert the catastrophe that is destroying our native animals.
>
> Forget the Pleistocene age when climatic changes and other factors wiped out the dinosaurs, or the arrival of Aborigines about 40 000 years ago when numerous species of animal were eliminated. The changes wrought in two centuries of European settlement are unprecedented and a stark reminder of the ecological disaster facing our continent.
>
> Ecologists around Australia have unearthed startling evidence of a new wave of extinctions coming in the next three decades. Native populations of many species have reached bedrock, with 70 mammal, bird, reptile, frog and fish species likely to be lost within 30 years unless urgent action is taken. Australia has already lost 18 species of birds and mammals and 78 species of plants in the past 200 years.
>
> A severe drought could have tragic consequences for native fauna and flora, while the greenhouse effect is expected to have a substantial impact in the next few decades (25 October 1988: 48).

All these examples show that *The Bulletin*, a well-established mass-circulation magazine read mainly by professionals, managers and white-collar workers in the higher socio-economic brackets, articulated many of the concerns of fundamentalist environmentalists and made a significant contribution to challenging institutional practices. Although the articulation of fundamentalist positions sits easily with the tendency by the media to simplify issues and to adopt an adversarial style, this section shows that they have played a crucial role in placing new issues on the agenda, even when they represent a fundamental challenge to established ways of thought and action.

Sustainable Development

Established institutions and political organisations are usually very slow in addressing new problems, especially if they do not appear to be urgent.[68] In 1979 a report entitled 'The great waste of waste' provided detailed information on the millions of tons of materials that could be recycled and anticipated the electoral backlash that might one day occur against the squandering of valuable resources (16 October 1979: 78). The story did refer to several initiatives that reflected both an increase in awareness and some action by institutions. However, it was only in 1994 that the ALP, which in most respects was ahead of the other major parties in addressing environmental concerns, committed itself to reducing by 50 per cent the amount of wastes to landfill by the year 2000.

The notion of sustainable development was not widely used until the late 1980s. Attempts to combine economic development and conservation have often been clumsy. In a report on ALP policy on Kakadu national park, John Stackhouse argued for the joint development of minerals and the environment. In reality, he was arguing for the former. First, he pointed out that the government's decision not to allow further development in Kakadu meant that between $70 and $100 billion worth of minerals, the equivalent of Australia's international debt, would not be exploited. He argued that: 'The revenue-earning alternatives are tourism (which the service has been embracing recently) or royalties from mining. Mining has got to be the way to go. The potentials of Kakadu's minerals are so great that the mining companies have been remarkably patient' (30 September 1986: 32). However, Stackhouse also suggested that the exploitation of mineral resources would still leave most of the park intact: 'As far as Kakadu is concerned, the physical reality is that it is big enough to allow several uranium or other mining developments to take place within the park and, based on the experience of the Ranger mine, see them go ahead without affecting the big picture of the environment' (30 September 1986: 36).

Until 1989 there had only been four stories in *The Bulletin* that focused on issues like recycling. Between 1989 and 1994 there were twenty-four stories. *The Bulletin*, reflecting the adversarial style of the media, has repeatedly pointed to the tensions that can arise when one attempts to implement sustainable development. In a story about tourism, the Whitsunday Islands are said 'to be identified with colourful entrepreneurs and jet-setting tourists luxuriating in tropical islands with healthy pricetags' (10 May 1994: 38). Another story on ecotourism questions its impact: 'But as developers rush to erect their five-star eco-lodges in native bush and install the natural soaps, recycled paper and solar heating, even mildly sceptical people are entitled to ask if this is really conservation or just con? (7 June 1994: 37). A story on the development of South-East Queensland points out that 'it is being loved to death' by the tens of thousands of people who are moving into the region (24 May 1994: 30).

However, some recent stories have painted a positive picture of the possibilities for successfully combining tourism and conservation (for instance, in an account of an enterprise in the Kimberley region of Western Australia, 22 November 1994: 40–2). Overall, despite the adversarial and critical approach adopted by *The Bulletin*, the focus on combining development and environmental protection reflects a new phase in the perception of environmental issues and in the discarding of some of the old stereotypes.

CHAPTER 15

Public Opinion and Survey Research

The presentation of the arguments in this book so far suggests the following causal chain.[69] Expert communities provide intellectual frameworks. They also play a key role in design, innovation and discovery. Some of these frameworks and discoveries are eventually adopted either by political parties or by social movements. On occasion the social movements are not only quicker off the mark in taking up new ideas, they are themselves innovators. On other occasions political parties pre-empt any initiative being taken up by social movements. In the case of environmental issues, there are situations in which political parties have been so slow in adapting to changes in outlook that new political parties have been formed to articulate some of the concerns of environmentalists, including the so-called 'new politics' parties (Müller-Rommel 1989). Established parties have generally adapted to the new situation and taken on many of the green issues (Papadakis 1989; 1993; McAllister and Studlar 1995). Both political parties and social movements play a crucial role in setting the agenda for politics. The media, though they have their own particular preoccupations (namely, simplifying and selling news), are a significant agency for the agenda-setters. As noted in chapter 13, the media draw on a variety of sources: the expertise of scientists and the arguments of intellectuals as well as information provided by established parties, by governments and by social movements. Information from the media is crucial in framing and forming public opinion. In this sketch public opinion is placed at the end of the causal chain. It is not proactive but rather reactive and manipulable. There is a vast literature on whether or not this is the case.

I would argue that it partly depends on what one means by public opinion. For example, it has been suggested that the analysis of public opinion should differentiate between 'top-of-the-head' responses to opinion polls and opinions that represent thoughtful, considered judgements of policy options (Yankelovich 1991). This would provide us with a better understanding of the connection between policy and opinion, and of the possibilities for democracy based on dialogue and consensus rather than on manipulation and control. The following sketch also raises questions like: What is the role of the mass public in politics in general, and in detailed policy-making? What is the significance of public opinion in securing political legitimacy? Does the formation of public opinion represent the process of citizen involvement in decision-making or the manipulation of perceptions? Still, these questions can only be addressed in detail elsewhere.

The aims of this chapter are to elaborate further on the means by which political parties, the media and social movements frame issues and influence public opinion, and to suggest that, despite all this, public opinion can represent the capacity of citizens to evaluate policies and to influence them. In other words, public opinion can and does influence government. The following chapter will then focus on shifts in opinion ever since polls have been conducted on environmental issues.

The Limits and Possibilities of Survey Research

The following discussion of the limits and possibilities of survey research is organised around two themes: democracy and social control; and ambivalence in public opinion.

Democracy and Social Control

Most theories of democracy are based on understandings of the role and significance of public opinion (in other words, of attitudes, feelings and ideas of a large body of people about important public issues). The most influential modern views follow Madison (in the *Federalist Papers*) and see popular participation as working through a representative system of government – with the result that 'public opinion' is at one remove from the process of government itself.[70]

Theories of democracy tend to divide along the following lines: the democratic idealists, who celebrate popular participation in decisions; and the democratic elitists (like Schumpeter 1994), who are critical of excessive public involvement. Some of the idealists imply that since democracy is good, then more democracy is always better (see Held 1987). Others (like Habermas 1989 and Ginsberg 1986) share this faith in democracy but are alert to some of the difficulties. These different approaches have vital implications for arguments about the relationship between public opinion and popular government in contemporary society.

Though many writers on public opinion have attempted to move away from concerns of political theory to addressing empirical questions about political behaviour (McAllister 1992: 53), their research is (implicitly) framed by enduring normative issues. Debates about whether or not the mass public has any role to play in policy-making tend to be based on views about the sophistication of ordinary citizens, and the volume and complexity of political issues in liberal democracies. Among the most influential studies on the limitations of popular participation in decision-making are those that focus on: the long-term instability of individual policy preferences over most issues (Converse 1964); and the inability of the electorate 'to judge the rationality of government actions' (Campbell et al. 1960: 543; see also Zaller 1992). These claims have been challenged on the grounds that:

- opinion surveys have failed to capture the true state of public opinion (Achen 1975);
- an approach to public opinion that differentiates between poor and high-quality

opinion – in other words, between top-of-the-head, short-term reactions to big issues and more thoughtful and considered judgements – will reveal that citizens can make a decisive contribution to self-governance and consensus building (Yankelovich 1991);
- when citizens are allowed to define politics in terms of their own interests, they demonstrate a high level of political sophistication (Dalton 1988);
- in specific policy areas, public opinion shows structure and coherence (Nie and Rabjohn 1979);
- the rise in educational levels and in time devoted to news, politics and current events by the mass media have contributed to greater sophistication among ordinary citizens in assessing politics (Dalton 1988);
- even if there is instability in beliefs and ideology at the individual level, the opposite is true at the aggregate level of society (Feld and Grofman 1988);
- there is a strong correspondence between detailed policy outcomes and public opinion (Page and Shapiro 1992; Popkin 1991).

Contemporary political science, particularly in the USA, emphasises the notion of an 'attentive public' or, more frequently, an inattentive public. The guiding assumption of this cognitive approach to public opinion is that the public is poorly informed about policies, and not particularly interested in them. This approach is elitist: 'Elites define quality by their own standards of ideological coherence and being well-informed. The concept of the attentive public presupposes the elite definition and seeks to find among the public that minority of people whose thought-processes mirror this model most closely' (Yankelovich 1991: 19).

Yankelovich perceives a gap between the way elites conceptualise public opinion and the way ordinary citizens actually view policies; he sees this as part of a culture that values information at the expense of thoughtful judgement. He characterises the culture that emphasises the importance of specialised knowledge and skills, of experts and of public apathy to issues as part of a 'Culture of Technical Control' (see Yankelovich 1991: 8–9). Here Yankelovich echoes a recurring theme in recent work on elites, namely their relationship to democracy (see Bottomore 1994: 191).

The relationship between public opinion and democracy can also be explored by defining public opinion in terms of whether or not people are engaged in 'manipulation' or 'communication' (Habermas 1989). For Habermas, the public sphere is a domain for communication rather than manipulation. His treatment of the public sphere is therefore close to one of the standard notions of civil society as a source of moral and other standards – in part because it is a sphere of social interaction that is relatively free of state control. Habermas criticises social psychological approaches which rob public opinion of its 'social character'. For him, public opinion represents 'the critical reflections of a public competent to form its own judgements' (1989: 90). Habermas draws on Mills (1956) to provide an empirically useful definition of critical public opinion. Yankelovich, who is also interested in the likelihood of a shift from mass opinion to the development of public judgement, draws on Habermas to explore the possibilities for 'intersubjective understanding', for 'reason' and for 'dialogue' (see also chapter 5 in this book for a discussion of these issues).

Like Habermas, Noelle-Neumann (1984) criticises contemporary studies for ignoring the social character of public opinion. However, she appears to posit the inevitability of public opinion as a form of social control. Public opinion is used as a social sanction. The principal mechanism in the formation of public opinion is the fear of isolation and the pressure to conform. To support her arguments, Noelle-Neumann cites the seminal work by Lippmann (1922) (who argued that public opinion reflects stereotypes and a 'moralized and codified version of facts') and psychology (Asch 1951), anthropology (Mead 1937), sociology (Ross 1901) and political theory (notably, Rousseau and de Tocqueville).[71]

Ambivalence in Public Opinion

Analysis of public opinion data can be used to support a wide range of theories on the public's feelings about certain issues and on the nature and origins of mass opinion. People's attitudes on most issues appear to be ambivalent (see Hochschild 1981; Zaller 1992). However, Yankelovich (1991) has posited a three-stage process to overcome ambivalence in public opinion. The first stage entails 'consciousness raising', in other words, public awareness of an issue (usually generated by media attention to it). In the second phase, the public might 'work through' the issue, in other words, become actively involved or engaged in the issue and experience changes in attitudes. The third stage involves 'resolution' of the issue in three ways: cognitive resolution, resolving inconsistencies; emotional resolution, confronting ambivalent attitudes and reconciling the differences; and moral resolution, placing ethical considerations above narrowly defined self-interest (Yankelovich 1991: 63–5).

Yankelovich acknowledges that most of what is reported as public opinion remains for a long time in the first stage, and that contemporary institutions – including those influenced by expert communities, politicians and the media – hinder rather than facilitate the processes of working through or resolving issues. It is hardly surprising, therefore, that public opinion tends to be characterised as ambivalent.

A further problem with analyses of opinion surveys is that they often fail to recognise that data in themselves do not provide perceptual insights into the world (De Bono 1991) and that data can be used to support a variety of theories (Papadakis 1992). An appreciation of ambivalence or consistency and stability in attitudes, and of the centrality of perceptions to political debates, would improve our understanding of the processes of social control and of democracy. These concerns lead us back to a number of points that arose in the discussion of the relationship between public opinion and politics. Public opinion can be regarded as easily manipulable and open to exploitation. Alternatively, as Yankelovich has argued, there are possibilities for experiencing the beneficial effects of public opinion, of judgements that represent not only an awareness of policy issues but the resolution of conflicting perspectives and of ambivalence.

In so far as public opinion represents public judgement, the possibility emerges for constructive dialogue and for communication in the manner suggested in chapter 5. This path is not an easy one, and some writers have chosen to focus on the barriers to intersubjective understanding and on the difficulties of dialogue. For them, public opinion does not so much breathe life into democracy as sustain self-referential systems of communication. For Luhmann, public opinion is one of the most significant ways in which the political system observes the external environment. It reinforces the self-referential qualities of the political system (Luhmann 1990a: 215–7). Luhmann, in drawing attention to the 'fictional' character of public opinion, rejects the idea that public opinion refers 'to what actually occurs in the consciousness(es) of individual/many/all persons at a particular point in time' (1990a: 205–6). He appears to treat public opinion as mass opinion and as the top-of-the-head reaction to opinion polls.

Public opinion does not accurately represent what people think, since that would amount to 'an indescribable chaos of simultaneous difference' (Luhmann 1990a: 206). For Luhmann, the transformation of public opinion into something that, through the media and the political system, represents 'the continual reproduction of communication by communication' (1990a: 207) and 'the return of politics upon itself' has far-reaching consequences: 'it forces the surely painful renunciation of expectations of rationality and hopes of a revitalization of civil republican "life"' (Luhmann 1990a: 217).[72] This pessimistic conclusion is entirely consistent with an account of public opinion as mass opinion rather than public judgement.

However, the ambivalent or consistent characteristics of public opinion can be exploited or put to good use, and not only by established political organisations. Social movements and the mass media often question the attempts by established political parties to mould public opinion. Drawing on public opinion studies, social movements and 'new politics' parties have challenged conventional political organisations on the grounds that:

- they poorly represent the increasingly diverse aspirations of ordinary citizens (Dalton and Kuechler 1990);
- they are incapable of addressing contemporary problems;
- they exploit public institutions for their own ends (for instance, through the extension of political patronage); and
- they manipulate the legal system to ensure that the state funds many of their activities (Scheuch and Scheuch 1992).

A further criticism is that experts, including political scientists, do little to develop the process of public judgement on policy issues, preferring instead to characterise public opinion as inattentive or uninformed (Yankelovich 1991).

Despite his apparent pessimism, Luhmann does entertain the notion that public opinion influences the process of political reform. First, he acknowledges the decisive role of 'new politics' parties and social movements, and suggests that as they lose their spontaneous character new attempts can be made 'to reintroduce disorder into the system' (Luhmann 1990a: 235). In politics, he adds, 'this process does not proceed any faster than public opinion allows'. Luhmann clearly wants politics to operate in a more genuinely pluralistic fashion and to respond to public judgement. Part of the solution lies in the development of new social movements and of public opinion. Another possibility is the renunciation of the entanglement of government and opposition 'in a moral scheme, in the sense that one side (ours) is the only good and respectable one, while the other acts immorally and reprehensibly' (Luhmann 1990a: 237).[73]

Any attempt to make politics more responsive to new challenges requires an appreciation of the limits and possibilities of public opinion in this process. Much of the contemporary analysis of public opinion either fails to address or replicates the following problems:

- how to convey reality through language;
- how to measure and categorise perceptions, especially over long periods of time;
- the use of absolute categories and rigid dichotomies; and
- the adversarial approach to debating issues and to characterising public opinion.

If these factors are taken into account, we may be in a better position to evaluate the important contributions that can be made by survey research, in providing us with:

- evidence of trends in public opinion over time;
- an understanding of climates of opinion (and how they have been influenced by the mass media, political parties and social movements as well as by intellectual and scientific breakthroughs);
- a guide to some of the major political and social changes that have taken place over several decades;
- an appreciation of the consistency, variability and ambivalence in public opinion;
- insights into the relationship between shifts in opinion and changes in policy; and
- an awareness of changes in focus in electoral surveys (in other words, changes in topics and in how questions are framed).

Having noted some of the limits and possibilities for survey research both in this and in previous chapters, the following chapter is dedicated to analysis of data on patterns of public opinion about environmental issues in Australia.

CHAPTER 16

Mass Opinion on Environmental Issues

The analysis in this chapter concentrates on issues like uranium mining and nuclear energy, forests, conservation and environment, mining, sustainable development, pollution, views on government taxes and spending to promote environmental protection, and views on the pricing of products to reflect the costs to the environment.

The data on public opinion about environmental issues have been arranged under the following headings:

- the relative importance of environmental issues
- the perceived seriousness of environmental problems
- nuclear energy as a threat
- government action
- trust in organisations
- environment, economy and the framing of public opinion
- individual behaviour and the willingness to pay for environmental protection.

The principal sources include surveys conducted since 1945 by Morgan Gallup and other survey research organisations like ANOP, the Australian Election Surveys (AES), the National Social Science Survey, and various studies commissioned by government departments and agencies like the Resource Assessment Commission.

The Relative Importance of Environmental Issues

Data on long-term trends in public opinion about the environment as a major policy issue have been gathered since the early 1970s. Although polling organisations have at times used different questions to measure public opinion, one can draw together these diverse sources in order to form a picture of the overall trends. Another consideration is to relate these trends to political processes. The basis for making this connection has been established in part III, which presented data on the articulation of concerns about the environment in the platforms and policy speeches of political parties. Moreover, other studies have shown how the environment has featured as a significant issue during election campaigns (Papadakis 1990; 1993; 1994).

Table 16.1 presents some of the earliest evidence of trends in public opinion. A significant feature in the design of these questions is that respondents were presented with a list of twelve major policy issues to choose from. The environment is therefore not treated in isolation. The data show that, on average, around one-third of respondents had paid attention to pollution and the environment as an issue. On the more searching question, whether they felt that this was the problem about which they had the *greatest* concern, we find a much smaller percentage.

Table 16.2 presents data on views about government action on the environment. As in the previous table, for most people this issue does not head their list of priorities for government action. The data are especially useful as a measure of public concern since respondents were not offered any prompts. This represents a stringent measure of salience (Dunlap 1989; Dunlap and Scarce 1991). The most significant change in trends occurred in 1989 with a sudden rise, between February and June, in the level of importance of conservation and the environment from 7 to 26 per cent.

Before commenting on this sudden change, I want to focus on the connection between these data and the following: the analysis of party platforms in part III of this book, the discussion about public opinion and survey research in chapter 14, and the framework outlined in chapter 3 (figure 3.1).

First, it is only in the mid-1970s that polling organisations first took seriously the issue of conservation (and environment). As noted in part III, it was only around 1972 that the major parties (for instance, Whitlam in his policy speech) made a significant effort to place the environment on the political agenda.

Second, though public awareness of the environment as an issue was steady (at the aggregate level) throughout the 1970s and 1980s, only a small minority had resolved that this was an issue of the greatest concern. Still, this interest in environmental issues was sufficient to attract the attention of political parties, the mass media and polling organisations.

Third, soon after polling organisations seized on the environment as an issue (in 1975), it became less important as a problem of greatest concern (see table 16.1). It remained at that low level for well over a decade. This coincided with a period of Liberal government and of disquiet about the prospects for the Australian economy.

Fourth, this trend in opinion was matched by the low standing of environmental issues on the agenda of all the major political parties. For example, for much of this time even the ALP focused less on the environment than it had during the early 1970s. However, the new force in Australian politics, the Australian Democrats, immediately articulated many of the concerns of environmental activists.

Table 16.1 Level of public concern about the environment and pollution, 1975–86 (per cent)

Statement	1975	1976	1977	1978	1979	1980	1982	1983	1985	1986
Attention to this problem	39	38	33	36	33	32	30	27	32	25
Problem of greatest concern	7	5	3	4	3	4	4	4	2	4

Respondents were shown a card with 12 items and asked: 'There are many problems facing Australia today. Which of these problems have you been paying attention to these days? Of the problems mentioned, which one have you been most concerned about?'
Source: Roy Morgan Research Centre (compiled by McAllister 1991, figure 1).

Table 16.2 Public opinion on the importance of government action on conservation and the environment, 1982-95 (per cent)

Date	Most important issue
Feb. 1982	2
Feb. 1983	2
Feb. 1984	4
Feb. 1985	2
Feb. 1986	2
Feb. 1987	2
Feb. 1988	4
Feb. 1989	7
June 1989	26
Sept. 1989	19
Feb. 1990	19
Feb. 1991	15
Feb. 1992	11
June 1992	13
July 1994	12
July 1995	15

Respondents were asked (without any prompts) to name the three most important things the federal government should be doing something about.
Source: Roy Morgan Research Centre.

Fifth, the pattern is matched by media coverage of environmental issues. Following the focus on environmental issues between 1970 and 1973 (see chapter 13), there was a decline in interest. The only exception, between 1973 and 1987, was the focus by *The Bulletin* on the preservation of trees and forests.

We can now turn to the sudden shift in public opinion that occurred in 1989. Hitherto, the green movement had campaigned with some success for the preservation of forests and wilderness areas. The ALP had also become sensitive to the importance of electoral support from environmental groups, and eventually took decisive steps to preserve forests and wilderness areas (see Papadakis 1993). The shift in opinion in 1989 marked a new phase both in public awareness of environmental problems and in attempts to resolve the tension between environment and development. This represented one of the most concerted attempts to move rapidly from the phase of public awareness of an issue to working it through and trying to resolve it. If we apply the criteria posited by Yankelovich (as outlined in the previous chapter), we can plausibly argue that the ALP government was successful in raising public awareness of environmental issues and in animating the process of working through the tensions between environment and development. However, there is some way to go before we can be confident of resolving the ambivalence in attitudes to environment and development in many spheres.

The decisive shift in opinion took place between February and June 1989. There appear to be two principal reasons for this. The first was the concentration on the greenhouse effect. The second arises from the political success of the Green Independents in Tasmania.

By the mid-1980s scientists had become increasingly aware of the possibility of the warming of the earth's atmosphere as a result of carbon dioxide emissions. In 1988, at a conference held in Toronto, more than three hundred scientists and policy-makers from about fifty countries and international organisations noted that a 50 per cent reduction in carbon dioxide emissions would have to be achieved in order to stabilise the atmospheric concentration of greenhouse gases. They suggested, as an initial target, a 20 per cent reduction in carbon dioxide emissions by the year 2000. Coincidentally, in 1988 and 1989, many countries experienced exceptionally warm weather. In the USA and Canada there was a severe drought. Though there was no necessary connection between these experiences and the greenhouse effect, some scientists and the media did speculate on the link between the two. Fears about the greenhouse effect also coincided with speculation about the impact of CFCs on the depletion of ozone at high altitudes, and the potential catastrophe that could be unleashed by the hole in the ozone layer.

The second principal reason for a shift in public awareness was the rise of environmental groups in political contests, notably the capture by Green Independents of five out of thirty-five seats in elections to the Tasmanian parliament on 13 May 1989. One of the most contentious issues during this election was the proposal by the Tasmanian government to build a huge pulp mill at Wesley Vale. Tasmania already had a strong tradition of opposition to projects by environmental groups. These groups now held the balance of power in parliament, and the ALP was obliged to share power with them in order to form a government in Tasmania. At the federal level, the ALP realised that the success of Green Independents represented a serious electoral challenge and it reacted swiftly. The federal environment minister, Senator Graham Richardson, argued that the states should yield to the federal government their powers over environmental policy, since they had failed to deal with what was now a national problem of pollution and preservation of nature. He also promised an unprecedented publicity campaign for national standards in water quality:

> I'm going to give them a hell of a lot of publicity and people are going to know then if the water they drink or swim in is safe. And in a lot of places they are going to discover it's not and when they do, they are going to turn around to their governments and say: 'What the hell are you doing about this?' (*The Bulletin* 6 June 1989: 49).

The former ALP minister of the environment, Barry Cohen, noted that the 'stunning success of the Independents in Tasmania, where they gained almost 20% of the vote' had brought the conservation movement to the brink of becoming 'the third force in Australian politics' (*The Bulletin* 6 June 1989: 55). Given these concerns, it is not surprising that in July 1989 the prime minister launched a statement on the environment which included a programme for planting one billion trees by the year 2000. The opening lines of his statement refer to the greenhouse effect and to the depletion of the ozone layer:

> The world's natural environment is under siege. In just over 200 years since the Industrial Revolution, human activity has increased the Earth's temperature, raising the spectre of the greenhouse effect. Massive areas of the world's tree cover have been destroyed and we are obliterating thousands of living species. We have polluted the world's oceans, seas and rivers, degraded the Earth's soils, damaged the fragile Arctic and Antarctic environments. Rainfall in Europe and North America contains industrial acids. We have managed to punch a hole in the ozone layer (Commonwealth of Australia 1989: iv).

The views of environmental groups were now being articulated at the highest levels of government and by the mass media. In 1989 the principal foci of stories in *The Bulletin* were sustainable development, green politics and pollution (including the greenhouse effect). Although the data on trends in public opinion show a gradual decline in concern about the environment as the most important issue after June 1989, there is no sign of a complete reversal to the trends reported in the 1970s through to the late 1980s. As with most political issues, concern about the environment is subject to cycles of attention (see Downs 1972). However, the overall trend over the past two or three decades has been towards a rise in concern (for parallel data, see Dunlap and Scarce 1991: 659, table 1).

Another way of assessing the significance of shifts in opinion about the environment is to place it in the context of electoral contests. Table 16.3 examines data from two sources, namely the AES (conducted by means of a mail questionnaire) and a series of telephone surveys carried out by the Newspoll organisation. The AES shows that in 1987 the environment was very important to 31 per cent of respondents but ranked only ninth in importance on a list of ten issues. In 1990 it rated as important for 52 per cent of respondents and ranked fifth out of ten issues. In 1993, in the midst of a major recession, the environment still rated as extremely important to 41 per cent of respondents. However, its ranking among all issues dropped to ninth position. The results of the Newspoll telephone surveys reflect a steadier pattern of concern about the environment. The differences between the two sets of results may derive from the methods used to gather information, the slight variation in wording of the questions, and the different contexts and timing of the surveys.

For the majority of respondents, economic issues remain at the top of the agenda. However, two trends are worth noting. The first, which I shall address later, arises from the concept of sustainable development and the willingness of many people to accept that the goals of economic development and environmental protection are not always necessarily in conflict. The second trend is the emergence of the environment as a permanent feature on the political agenda, even if there is occasionally a decline in public attention. Another way of testing this argument about future trends is to ask respondents what issues are likely to worry them and their families most in ten years from now. The 1993 AES confirmed that the environment had been demoted as a current political issue. However, when asked about the future, respondents ranked the environment much higher: 10.6 per cent ranked this as the issue likely to be of greatest concern, a figure surpassed only by concerns about unemployment (27.9 per cent) and health (13.7 per cent).

Other surveys, conducted in 1991 and 1993, produced similar results. These surveys located concern about the environment in the context of other issues by asking

Table 16.3 Public opinion on the importance of the environment as an election issue, 1987–94 (per cent)

Opinion			Survey 1		
		1987	1990	1993	
Most/extremely important		31	52	41	
Rank[a] (*n*)		9	5	9	
Of concern to self and family[b]		–	11	4	
			Survey 2		
	1990	1991	1992	1993	1994
Very important	62	59	57	58	62

In the first survey respondents were asked, 'When you were deciding about how to vote, how important was each of these issues to you personally?' In 1987 respondents had a choice of 10 issues; in 1990, 9 issues; in 1993, 14 issues. The percentage refers to responses coded as 'most important' (in 1987) or 'extremely important' (in 1990 and 1993) on a three-point scale (which also included codes for 'quite important' and 'not very important').

The second survey asked, 'How important an issue would you say each of the following was to you on how you would vote in a federal election. Would you say of the issue that it is very important, fairly important, or not important on how you would vote?' The figures represent the percentage of respondents who indicated that the environment was 'very important' as an issue.

[a]The rank is based on the total percentage scores for the question on the importance of the environment compared to the total percentage scores for all other issues. For instance, in 1987 the environment ranked 9th out of 10.

[b]The percentage is based on the follow-up question, 'Which of these issues has worried you and your family most in the last 12 months?' and refers to those who coded the environment as the issue of most concern.

Source: Australian Election Surveys; Newspoll (see Lothian 1994).

respondents in an open-ended question to nominate the most important issue currently facing Australia. Unemployment and the economy were mentioned most often (see table 16.4). In 1991 respondents were three times more likely to be concerned about unemployment than about the environment. Two years later the ratio was closer to 15:1, following a sharp decline in concern about the environment as a most important issue. These figures are not surprising, given the severity of the economic recession – the worst since the Great Depression. Paradoxically, the environment remained an issue of great concern to many people (see Papadakis 1994).

In 1991 respondents were asked to select from a list of thirteen issues which would be the most important in ten years' time. The environment was ranked first (with 24 per cent), followed by unemployment (19 per cent) and pensions and care for the aged (10 per cent) (ANOP 1991: 16). In the 1993 ANOP survey respondents were asked whether they believed unemployment and the environment would become more or less important issues in Australia in ten years' time. Again, the environment ranked higher than unemployment by a significant margin. Whereas 56 per cent agreed that unemployment would become a more important issue in ten years' time, 77 per cent agreed that the environment would. This confirms my

Table 16.4 Public opinion on the environment in the context of other issues, 1991–93 (per cent)

Most important issue	Dec. 1991	Sept. 1993
Unemployment: not enough jobs	38	49
State of the economy: economic management, recession, budget, debt, balance of payments	24	30
Environment: pollution, water and air, ozone layer, land degradation	12	3

Respondents were asked to nominate the most important issue currently facing Australia.
Source: ANOP 1991: 15; 1993: 11.

assumption that we are well into the first of the three stages posited by Yankelovich, the phase of consciousness raising about the environment, and that progress is now being made towards working through the implications of this new awareness.

Perceived Seriousness of Environmental Problems

So far I have reported on surveys that treat public opinion on the environment as a homogeneous issue. Writers like Rohrschneider (1988) and McAllister (1994) have argued that the public conceptualises the environment in a *variety* of dimensions, for instance, a local or national or cosmopolitan dimension. Interestingly enough, the cosmopolitan dimension, the one that reflects national and international concerns, is the most likely to preoccupy the majority of people. Nearly all of the survey questions outlined in this chapter have a national and cosmopolitan (international) rather than a local focus. The focus on cosmopolitanism is the most crucial for the development and impact of green politics, since it 'has its roots in value change, stimulates increased environmental activism, and helps to mobilise support for and against the major political parties' (McAllister 1994: 22). Although some aspects of the following analysis could benefit from greater differentiation between local and national and international concerns, most of the questions clearly fall into the latter category. Moreover, I have gone to some lengths to draw out the *variety* of considerations about the environment. The preceding analysis shows that although other issues, particularly unemployment and the state of the economy, have tended to be matters of urgent concern, the environment is likely to remain an important issue. The following account attempts:

- to demonstrate that since the early 1970s preoccupation with environmental problems has been shared by a majority of the population; and
- to distinguish between the kinds of issues that are seen to require urgent attention.

Data from the USA show that, when asked to consider the future, people have tended more and more to have deep misgivings about the prospects for the environment. For instance, between 1974 and 1988 the proportion of respondents who felt that severe air pollution would be a serious problem in 25 to 50 years from now has risen from 68 to 82 per cent. The same pattern arose when people were asked about severe water pollution. Moreover, between 1984 and 1988 the proportion who felt that the greenhouse effect would be a serious problem in 25 to 50 years from now rose from 37 to 65 per cent (Dunlap and Scarce 1991: 659–60).

In Australia some of the earliest attempts to document concerns about the environment reflect a keen reaction to the kinds of problems identified by Ehrlich in *The Population Bomb* and the predictions of the Club of Rome in *The Limits to Growth.* In polls conducted in 1970 and 1975, most respondents agreed that the world would be unlivable in twenty years unless controls were enforced to deal with pollution and overpopulation. The question ran: 'In your opinion, is the talk of dangerous overpopulation and pollution of our planet simply the talk of cranks; or is the world likely to be unlivable in twenty years, unless controls are enforced quickly?' The surveys were conducted by Morgan Gallup. In 1970 and 1975, 62 and 57 per cent respectively answered that the world would become unlivable, and 22 and 30 per cent respectively were undecided. Like the discussion in the previous section about public opinion and the greenhouse effect, these findings support the claim that intellectual frameworks and scientific breakthroughs play a decisive part in the process of the formation of opinion (see chapter 3, figure 3.1).

Two decades after warnings by Ehrlich and by the Club of Rome about the problem of pollution, the topic remained high on the agenda. However, compared to other environmental issues, overpopulation was not viewed with the same degree of urgency. Data from the 1990 and 1993 AES show that most people regarded pollution, waste disposal, the destruction of wildlife, soil degradation, and the greenhouse effect as very urgent problems (table 16.5). The proportion who regarded overpopulation as 'not urgent' declined between 1990 and 1993 from 54 to 45 per cent. Both in 1990 and in 1993 pollution was mentioned more frequently than all other issues as the most urgent problem.

Table 16.5 also documents perceptions about whether or not these problems will get worse or be resolved. Overall, most respondents felt that things would either get much worse or remain the same. On most issues only about a quarter of the sample felt that the problems would be solved. The degree of pessimism is similar to that noted earlier in data from the USA. In many respects these data reflect the attempts by the public to work through their concerns about the environment. There is a high level of awareness of environmental problems. There is, as yet, no obvious resolution; hence the pessimism about what might be done about them.

Nuclear Energy as a Threat

The potential threat posed by the development of nuclear energy has in many countries been on the agenda for about four decades. During that period this topic has arisen in opinion surveys all over the world and has also been linked, especially in Western Europe, to the rise of green parties in the late 1970s and 1980s. Several points are worth noting about the situation in Australia:

- as in other countries, there has long been a debate about the benefits and threats of nuclear energy;

Table 16.5 Public opinion on the urgency of environmental problems, now and in the future, 1990–93 (per cent)

	Now[a]						Future[b]				
	Very urgent		Fairly urgent		Not urgent		Get much worse	Remain the same	Be solved	Most urgent problem[c]	
Problem	1990	1993	1990	1993	1990	1993	1990	1990	1990	1990	1993
Pollution	76	73	20	23	4	5	58	20	22	40	38
Overpopulation	26	34	19	22	54	45	37	47	16	5	9
Waste disposal	73	68	22	27	5	5	52	22	26	10	9
Uranium mining	39	30	28	28	34	44	25	55	20	2	2
Logging of forests	49	51	31	25	24	20	26	38	36	10	12
Destruction of wildlife	68	68	21	20	11	9	39	31	31	5	6
Soil degradation	74	73	19	20	8	8	47	28	25	9	7
Greenhouse effect	71	66	17	21	12	13	53	28	19	19	16

[a]Respondents were asked, 'How urgent are each of the following environmental concerns in this country?' Responses were located on a five-point scale ranging from 'very urgent' to 'not urgent', with 'fairly urgent' as the middle category. In this table the first two points on the scale have been recoded into a single category, the mid-point has remained the same ('fairly urgent') and the last two points have also been recoded into one.
[b]Respondents were asked, 'In the next ten years do you believe these environmental problems will get worse or be solved in this country?' Responses were located on a five-point scale ranging from 'get much worse' to 'be solved', with 'remain the same' as the middle category. In this table the first two points on the scale have been recoded into one, the middle point has been retained ('Remain the same') and the last two points have also been recoded into one.
[c]Respondents were asked, 'Which two of these environmental issues has worried you personally the most in the last 12 months? Which is the most urgent? And which is the second most urgent?' (Only replies to the 'most urgent' issue are given in this table.)
Source: Australian Election Surveys.

- unlike many other industrialised countries, Australia has not developed a programme for the generation of nuclear power;
- opinion surveys in Australia have focused not only on the issue of nuclear energy production but also on uranium mining since this is one of the few countries with large deposits of this resource; and
- surveys of opinion about nuclear energy can be traced back to the 1940s, thereby demonstrating a long history of concern with certain environmental problems.

Table 16.6 shows that, as far as opinion pollsters are concerned, the issue has been on the agenda in two main cycles: between the 1940s and early 1950s, and again from the 1970s onwards. Overall, opinion has been fairly evenly divided between advocates and opponents of nuclear energy. A substantial proportion of respondents have remained undecided. During the earlier phase, opponents outnumbered proponents only in 1948. Since 1977 those in favour of nuclear energy have tended to outnumber the opponents, though in 1993 the opponents (38 per cent) outnumbered the proponents (32 per cent). This decline in support for nuclear energy since the late 1970s is consistent with trends in many other industrialised countries where powerful social movements resisted the development of this resource (see, for example, Papadakis 1984). However, there has been no resolution of this issue. The dependence of complex modern societies on fossil fuels has ensured that until we discover or invest in a form of energy that causes minimal pollution and is available in abundance, the development of nuclear energy will remain controversial. Paradoxically, some of the greatest impediments to the development of nuclear energy in Australia may be economic rather than political.

By contrast to the development of nuclear energy, Australia has been effective in exploiting uranium as a resource since the 1940s. Yet it was only in the 1970s, coinciding with powerful social movements opposed to nuclear energy, that uranium mining became a divisive issue. Opposition to uranium mining emanated not only from social movements but also from among members of the ALP who had misgivings that uranium mining would be linked to and encourage the development of nuclear energy and nuclear weapons (Lowe 1989).

In June 1975 Morgan Gallup asked people: 'Should Australia develop its uranium resources for use as nuclear power – or leave the uranium in the ground?' Sixty-two per cent were in favour of Australia developing its uranium resources for use as nuclear power and 25 per cent favoured leaving the uranium in the ground. However, over the next two years support for such development declined steadily to 58 per cent in 1976 and 50 per cent in 1977.

As noted in the previous chapter, the way in which a question is framed can have a decisive influence on the distribution of responses. Whereas in 1977 only 50 per cent of respondents were in favour of developing uranium for use as nuclear power, another question, framed differently, showed that 59 per cent were in favour of uranium mining (table 16.7). Support for developing and exporting uranium for

Table 16.6 Public opinion on nuclear energy, 1947–93 (per cent)

Opinion	1947	1948	1950	1952	1977	1979	1983	1990	1993
Favour	38	33	44	47	53	52	47	38	32
Oppose	38	41	37	30	34	35	46	35	38
Don't know	24	26	19	23	—	13	—	—	28

There was some variation in the wording of the questions:

- 'In the long run, do you think atomic energy will be a benefit or a curse, to the human race?' (1947 and 1952)
- 'In the long run, do you think atomic energy will do more harm than good, or more good than harm?' (1948 and 1950)
- 'Do you think Australia should or should not be developing nuclear power for peaceful purposes?' (1977)
- 'Do you think Australia should or should not develop nuclear power generation?' (1979)
- 'Now a question about nuclear energy. Looking at the top of the next yellow card, which one statement best describes your own opinion? A: nuclear energy is an essential source of fuel and will have to be used despite its risks. B: there is too great a risk involved in nuclear energy and we should not use it,' (1983)
- 'Here are some statements about some environmental issues. Please say whether you strongly agree, agree, neither agree nor disagree, disagree or strongly disagree with each statement . . . Nuclear energy is a real necessity for the future'. (1990 and 1993)

Source: Morgan Gallup Polls; 1990 and 1993 Australian Election Surveys (and McAllister and Studlar 1993: 357).

'peaceful purposes' rose from 59 per cent in 1977 to 66 per cent in 1983. A similar level of support was recorded in 1987. In 1990 and 1993, however, questions framed in a slightly different way showed an apparent decline in support. None the less, the decrease in support recorded between 1990 and 1993, from 56 to 41 per cent, was based on identical questions. A striking feature of the responses in 1993 is the large number who were undecided. This category of undecided respondents is significant, because they may be rejecting the manner in which questions are framed or be opting for an alternative which has not been articulated by political or intellectual leaders. Again, we face a situation in which the issue of uranium mining, because it is closely tied to development and the economy and to a range of strongly conflicting interests, remains far from resolved.

The hypothesised decline in support for uranium mining is also supported by two other pieces of evidence. In 1986 and 1987 people interviewed by Morgan Gallup were asked: 'Do you think Australia should or should not export uranium to France?' There was a 10 per cent increase in opposition to such exports (from 51 to 61 per cent). The main reasons were that France was conducting nuclear tests in the Pacific, that there were no guarantees that the uranium would be used only for peaceful purposes, and that the French were perceived as untrustworthy. In 1985 two French agents were responsible for sinking the *Rainbow Warrior* (owned by Greenpeace) when it was moored in New Zealand. A Greenpeace photographer was drowned as a result of this incident. Another Morgan Gallup survey, not directly related to the question of trust in France, showed that most people (56 per cent) were not in favour of new mines being opened. The respondents were asked: 'As you may know at present *two* uranium mines are *now operating* in Australia, and present Government policy does *not allow* any new mines to be opened. Some people believe that because uranium is of great potential benefit to the Australian economy, more mines should be allowed to be opened. Others believe there is too great a risk involved and no new mines should be allowed. Do you think *new* uranium mines *should* or *should not* be allowed?'

Finally, on the same issue and on the problem of wording questions, table 16.8 should be compared to table 16.7. Table 16.7 included data for 1990 and 1993 which showed a decline in support for the development and export of uranium for peaceful

Table 16.7 Public opinion on the development of uranium, 1977–93 (per cent)

Opinion	1977	1978	1979	1982	1983	1984	1986	1987	1990	1993
Yes	59	59	54	66	66	65	63	64	56	41
No	28	27	32	25	26	29	31	29	31	29
Uncertain	13	14	14	9	8	6	6	7	13	31

Between 1977 and 1987 the question was: 'About developing and exporting uranium for peaceful purposes. Do you think Australia should, or should not, develop and export uranium for peaceful purposes?' In 1990 and 1993, the question was 'Here are some statements about some environmental issues. Please say whether you strongly agree, agree, neither agree nor disagree, disagree or strongly disagree with each statement . . . Australia should mine its uranium.' The figures in 1990 and 1993 combine strongly agree and agree, and strongly disagree and disagree.
Source: Morgan Gallup Polls; Australian Election Surveys, 1990 and 1993.

purposes between 1990 and 1993; and appeared to show that there may have also been a reduction in support between 1987 and 1990. By contrast, table 16.8 frames the question in a different way and takes us through to 1991; it shows that support for uranium mining appeared to remain steady between 1984 and 1991, at 62 and 61 per cent respectively. The data verify the hypothesis that support for uranium mining has remained fairly strong over an extended period of time. Still, many people have misgivings about developing more uranium mines and about the final destination of the product. In examining data on public opinion, it is therefore useful to be aware that:

- some issues, in this case uranium mining and nuclear energy, can be on the agenda for many decades without any strong resolution of the conflicting arguments;
- perceptions are fluid and can be framed in different ways; and
- it can be useful to examine an issue from a variety of perspectives in order to obtain a clearer picture of trends in public opinion or the ambivalent character of public awareness.

Government Action

This section deals with perceptions of the government's role in dealing with environmental issues. The significance of the following analysis is that it focuses less on awareness of issues and more on the working through and resolution of difficult questions. The contribution by governments is, or has the potential to be, crucial in the resolution of conflicts.

We begin by looking at trends of opinion about government spending and regulation to tackle environmental problems. Unfortunately there are no long-term trend data on these questions in Australia. However, data from the USA show that since the mid-1970s a growing proportion of the population has felt that the government is spending too little on improving and protecting the environment, and that environmental protection laws and regulations have not gone far enough (see Dunlap and Scarce 1991: 664, tables 16–19).

Where data are available for Australia, for instance in the 1990 and 1993 AES, they show strong support for government action. In both 1990 and 1993, 67 per cent of respondents indicated that governments should do more to protect the environment, even if this sometimes led to higher taxes (see Papadakis 1993: 146, table 5.4). In

Table 16.8 Public opinion on uranium mining, 1977–91 (per cent)

Opinion	1977	1978	1979	1982	1983	1984	1991
Yes	57	58	52	62	64	62	61
No	30	28	33	27	26	31	30
Uncertain	13	14	15	11	10	7	9

Respondents were asked, 'As you probably know, some of Australia's uranium deposits are now being mined. Do you agree or disagree—with mining Australia's uranium?'
Source: Morgan Gallup Polls.

1993, 65 per cent of respondents strongly agreed or agreed with the statement 'Increase government spending to protect the environment' (26 per cent neither agreed nor disagreed and only 10 per cent disagreed or strongly disagreed). However, caution is required in interpreting these findings: respondents may say that they are willing to pay higher taxes in order to protect the environment, but the actual introduction of those taxes may create a backlash among voters.

Turning to the issue of government responsibilities in a federal structure, qualitative research by ANOP found that, although respondents had little knowledge about the limits of the powers of the federal government in the area of environmental policy, they were prepared to assign far greater powers to it:

> There is strong in-principle support for the Federal government's having more extensive powers in respect of the environment, including powers to set national standards and develop national guidelines for the environment. The environment is seen as a serious long-term issue requiring the commitment and attention of the national government as both standard-setter and arbiter. Australians are often loath to give more power to Canberra but the environment is seen as a special case and the Federal government is seen to require additional powers (ANOP 1991: 61).

The quantitative survey supports this conclusion (table 16.9). Most people were in favour of federal government intervention in setting standards and taking action in the areas of air and water quality, preventing land degradation, protecting plant and animal species, and reducing levels of lead in petrol.

These findings need to be placed in the context of the earlier discussion on the

Table 16.9 Public opinion on national standards and national action by the federal government, 1991–93 (per cent)

Opinion	1991	1993	1991	1993
	National standards			
	Reduce lead level in petrol		Air and water quality	
Should be federal government responsibility	n.a.	73	73	63
Should be state government responsibility	n.a.	20	25	31
Both/Unsure	n.a.	7	2	6
	National action			
	Protect plants and animals		Land degradation	
Should be federal government responsibility	68	59	62	50
Should be state government responsibility	29	35	35	43
Both/Unsure	3	6	3	7

Respondents were asked whether the federal government should be able to set uniform standards for all states on air and water quality and lead levels in petrol, or whether these should be left to state governments. They were also asked whether there should be a national approach, with the federal government taking the main responsibility for land degradation and the protection of plant and animal species, or whether these should be left to state governments.

Source: ANOP 1993: 22, table 10.

relative importance of environmental issues and on the willingness of some groups and individuals within the government to place the environment high on the political agenda. The strong support for federal intervention reflects the much greater emphasis in recent years by the major parties, particularly the ALP, on environmental protection in policy speeches and electoral platforms (see part III).[74] The ALP federal government has made a significant contribution in creating new institutional mechanisms over the past decade (see Papadakis 1993: chapter 4). There has been a strong emphasis on the second and third of Yankelovich's three stages: working through and resolving environmental issues.

Trust in Organisations

The issues of trust and competence are central to discussions about working through and resolving issues as well as to questions about support for, and the legitimacy of, government. As noted in part I, without trust and goodwill between groups emerging from different sub-systems, the possibilities for constructive dialogue and for resolving controversial issues are slim. On the issue of competence we find that, despite the important contribution by government in raising awareness about environmental issues, opinion about who contributes most to environmental protection is more likely than not to rate the government much lower than other groups (table 16.10). For instance, the federal government trailed a long way behind environmental groups and green organisations, and ranked below the media, farmers, local councils (in 1993), and the general public. The element which experienced the sharpest decline in favourable evaluations of perceived contribution was the media. The elements that ranked lowest on both occasions were large companies and industry.

On the question of trust in groups to solve environmental problems, industry also rates lower than all other groups (apart from trade unions) (table 16.11). The forces

Table 16.10 Perceived contribution to environmental protection by different organisations, 1991–93 (per cent)

	A great deal		Quite a lot		A little bit		Not much at all		Unsure	
Organisation	1991	1993	1991	1993	1991	1993	1991	1993	1991	1993
Environmental groups and green organisations	31	24	42	49	18	17	7	8	2	2
Media	7	4	33	26	39	38	19	30	2	2
Farmers	6	8	33	34	37	38	16	14	8	6
Local council	—	6	—	32	—	35	—	23	—	4
General public	4	4	23	25	47	46	24	24	2	1
Federal government	2	3	18	21	50	46	27	26	3	4
State government	2	3	17	22	47	46	31	26	3	3
Large companies and industry	1	1	12	10	41	42	43	44	3	3
Personal contribution	4	8	20	30	55	47	21	14	—	1

Respondents were asked to rate how much various organisations and people are doing to help protect and conserve the environment, and then to rate their own contribution.
Source: ANOP 1991: 32, table 18; and 1993: 26 table 13.

closely associated with the industrial and political revolutions of the nineteenth century are seen as the least responsive to demands for environmental protection. These findings are supported by surveys in the USA which even show a decline in confidence that business and industry will take the initiative to protect the environment and will comply with regulations (see Dunlap and Scarce, 1991: 667, tables 24 and 26).

Environmental groups (and scientists and technologists) are, by contrast, ranked very high (table 16.11). Many people expressed 'some' or 'great' trust in federal and state governments to solve problems. By contrast, political parties have a poor reputation. A plausible explanation for this apparent contradiction (between the rating for parties and for governments) is that people associate political parties with political rhetoric and government with political action (the enactment and implementation of legislation). There is of course a great deal of overlap, for instance, the widespread belief that political parties make promises which governments then go on to break. Not surprisingly perhaps, people tended to rate their own contributions and those of the general public fairly high.

Turning to the credibility of many of these organisations in statements they make about the environment, table 16.12 shows that organisations like the CSIRO and educational institutions rated high consistently. The media tended to fare less well, though it is important to distinguish between their different components. As in table 16.10, the ranking of the media in general has declined significantly. The media component labelled TV science and nature programs retained a high credibility rating. The component labelled TV news and current affairs declined from 50 to 35 per cent, and the credibility rating of newspaper articles dropped from 35 to 26 per cent. By contrast, there was a slight increase in the rating for environmental groups.

It is difficult to arrive at a judgement of the ratings for federal and state governments because of a significant change in the phrasing of the question, which in 1993 referred to a specific government department rather than the government as a whole. One would expect a higher rating for the Department of the Environment than for the government as a whole. The gap between the two is none the less interesting,

Table 16.11 Public trust in groups to solve environmental problems, 1990 (per cent)

Group	No trust	Some trust	Great trust
Scientists and technologists	11	30	59
Environmental groups	15	31	54
The general public	25	43	32
Federal governments	30	53	17
State governments	36	49	15
Political parties	49	43	8
Industry	68	25	7
Trade unions	68	26	5

Respondents were asked, 'How much would you trust each of the following groups to solve environmental problems? No trust? Some trust? Great trust?' Replies were on a five-point scale ranging from 'no trust' to 'some trust' to 'great trust'. The two categories at either end of the scale were recoded into one. The 'some trust' column represents the middle category.
Source: Australian Election Survey 1990.

and it draws attention to the potentially conflicting demands on government, including those by business and economic interests. The ratings for industry groups and large companies remain consistently low.

In sum, this section shows a striking variation in levels of trust in government and non-government organisations to address environmental issues. If, as predicted, environmental issues remain high on the political agenda, certain groups and organisations both within and outside government will need to adapt considerably in order to retain their legitimacy (in so far as this is affected by public opinion). Also, the lack of credibility of many organisations will make it difficult for issues to be worked through, let alone resolved.

Environment, Economy and the Framing of Public Opinion

The data from the previous section cast doubt on the possibilities of constructive dialogue and on whether policy initiatives can be rendered more effective. Nevertheless there is evidence to support the claim that both government and non-government organisations have been able to adapt to changing perceptions. Moreover, they also can play a significant role in influencing perceptions. This takes us back to our initial consideration about the role of political organisations in shaping policy and public opinion (see chapter 3, figure 3.1). In other words, climates of opinion have been influenced by intellectual frameworks that have been taken up by political parties, social movements and interest groups, and articulated by the media. This influence is reflected in the changes of wording in survey questions and in the

Table 16.12 Credibility rating of various groups and organisations, 1991–93 (per cent)

Group	Nearly always 1991	Nearly always 1993	Usually 1991	Usually 1993	Only sometimes 1991	Only sometimes 1993	Usually not 1991	Usually not 1993	Depends/ unsure 1991	Depends/ unsure 1993
Clean up Australia	—	41	—	34	—	14	—	3	—	8
TV science and nature programmes	41	29	45	45	10	21	2	2	2	3
CSIRO	34	36	42	36	15	17	3	3	6	8
Educational institutions (schools, universities)	25	22	42	40	23	29	5	5	5	4
TV news and current affairs	14	9	36	26	40	48	7	16	3	1
Environmental groups	19	19	29	33	34	34	15	13	3	1
Radio news and comment	10	—	35	—	44	—	6	—	5	—
Newspaper articles	8	4	27	22	50	52	11	20	4	2
State government[a]	3	7	11	26	45	42	37	15	4	10
Federal government[a]	2	7	12	24	50	43	33	16	3	10
Large companies and industry groups	1	2	8	8	41	38	46	50	4	2

Respondents were asked to rate how much they believe and take notice of ten different groups and organisations when they say something about the environment.
[a]In 1993 respondents were asked about the state or federal 'department of the environment'. This may account for the much higher credibility rating.
Source: ANOP 1991: 31, table 17; and 1993: 23; table 11.

framing of questions. None of this is to say that public opinion reflects the uncritical acceptance of the frameworks advanced by those who attempt to influence opinions. Still, as suggested in chapter 15, it does demonstrate the possibilities for manipulating public opinion or for delaying the working through and resolution of highly controversial issues. Political parties, social movements and the media all contribute to the formation of public opinion. All these organisations were quick, in the 1970s, to latch on to the notion of *The Limits to Growth* and to articulate the hypothesised conflict between economic growth and environmental protection. This conflict had become so acute in the 1990s that the federal government created new mechanisms for consultation in order to move from an adversarial to a more cooperative framework for dealing with environmental issues (Papadakis 1993: chapter 3).

Political organisations, established institutions and the media have all tended to adopt an adversarial approach in dealing with new challenges. The media have often seized on the character of the relationship between the proponents of economic growth and of environmentalism. It is therefore hardly surprising that since the 1970s opinion polls both in Australia and in other countries have framed questions in a way that reflects this potential conflict rather than the possible compatability of development and environment. The following examples distinguish between an approach that focuses on the potential for conflict (Option 1) and an approach that offers the possibility of a resolution (Option 2):

Option 1

Do you think Australians should concentrate on economic growth even if it means some damage to the environment, or concentrate on protecting the environment even if means some reduction in economic growth? (Saulwick Poll *Sydney Morning Herald* 12 April 1994).

Option 2

A. Australians will increasingly have to make hard choices between economic growth and protection of the environment.
B. It is quite possible to have both a prosperous economy and a healthy environment.
[Respondents are then asked if they] agree strongly with A, agree more with A than B, [find it] hard to say, agree more with B than A, agree strongly with B (Keys Young 1994).

Neither of these questions is 'correct' or 'incorrect'. The answers to both can be useful in examining patterns of opinion, though Option 1 excludes the choices available in Option 2.

In answer to Option 1, the majority support environmental protection rather than economic growth. In 1990, 62 per cent supported environmental protection and 26 per cent economic growth. In 1994 the figures were 57 and 33 per cent respectively (*Sydney Morning Herald* 12 April 1994).[75] The data, despite any arguments about how the question has been framed, show that there was a slight decline in support for environmental protection relative to concerns about economic growth. None the less, they further support the argument that in the midst of a major recession support for environmental protection remained very high (Papadakis 1994).

There are some parallels with data from the USA which show trends over two decades. Table 16.13 reveals that in 1990, 64 per cent of respondents expressed a willingness to sacrifice economic growth in order to protect and preserve the environment. From the mid-1980s there appears to be a majority for this view in the USA. However, an interesting aspect of table 16.13 is the proportion of respondents who 'don't know' or who are unwilling to commit themselves to either of these standpoints. The data can be used to support a number of arguments. The large percentage of 'don't know' responses and the fact that the majority which favours sacrificing economic growth is not an overwhelming one suggest that, as in Australia, it will be some time before there is any resolution of this controversial issue. Another conclusion we might draw from the large number of 'don't know' responses is that for many people this category offers an escape from the rigid framework set by the survey question. This point is emphasised by Dunlap and Scarce (1991: 656), who refer to a study by Ladd (1982) on the same issue. Also, they draw attention to recent studies in which a growing number of people feel we can have both economic growth and environmental protection (see Environment Opinion Study 1990; and Opinion Dynamics Corporation 1990).

When respondents are provided with the opportunity to consider whether or not development and the environment are compatible, as in Option 2, we find that more than half the sample (55 per cent) agree that they are compatible. Only 37 per cent think that they are not and 7 per cent are unsure (Keys Young 1994: 50, table 5.10). Qualitative research shows that the definitions of economic and environmental goals in structured surveys are problematic on two counts: they give the impression that the two goals are necessarily in conflict; and the data suggest that, overall, people are in favour of environmental protection rather than development. The ANOP study shows that respondents tended to be in favour of a '*balance* between achieving economic recovery, increasing employment opportunities and protecting the environment' (ANOP 1991: 53). The respondents anticipated conflict 'because of the perceived differences in the agenda and motives of developers and "greenies"' (ANOP 1991: 54).

Unlike some of the polls cited above, the ANOP qualitative study found that there was not a simple preference for environmental protection rather than economic growth among the majority. Rather, the qualitative research supported the view that most people took the short-term perspective that 'the balance between environment and economy requires more emphasis on the economy and on unemployment at the present time than on the environment'. Only a minority took the longer-term view which emphasised the inter-dependence of economy and environment in the future and saw 'a healthy environment as a necessary precondition to a healthy economy' (ANOP 1991: 55). Still, in a similar study carried out two years later, ANOP concluded that people no longer thought in terms of 'jobs versus the environment', that it was now a question of 'both jobs and the environment': 'While some job losses are considered inevitable, protecting the environment is also perceived to result in a creation of jobs' (ANOP 1993: 6–7).

Table 16.13 Public opinion on the environment versus the economy, 1976–90 (per cent)

Statement	1976	1977	1978	1979	1981	1982	1983	1984	1985	1986	1987	1988	1989	1990
We must sacrifice economic growth in order to preserve and protect the environment.	38	39	37	37	41	41	42	42	53	58	57	52	52	64
We must be prepared to sacifice environmental quality for economic growth.	21	26	23	32	26	31	16	27	23	19	23	19	21	15
Don't know.	41	35	39	32	33	28	42	31	24	23	20	29	27	21

Respondents were asked, 'Which of these two statements is closer to your opinion?'
Source: Dunlap and Scarce 1991: 668, table 28.

There is a close correspondence between these findings from September 1993 and the approach by parties like the ALP and by environmental organisations like the ACF during the March 1993 election campaign (Papadakis 1994). Another indicator of the weakening of old ways of thinking about environment and development was the approach by the federal government to reconciling potential conflicts, for instance, through the establishment of ESD working groups. Respondents to the ANOP survey in 1991 and 1993 were asked whether they were aware of the notion of ESD. In 1991, 20 per cent were aware of ESD and able to define it, 5 per cent were aware but unable to define it, and the remainder were either not aware or unsure.[76] The figures for 1993 were almost identical. Though only a minority understood ESD, this none the less represents a substantial proportion of respondents. Among certain groups a high proportion were aware of the concept: 53 per cent of those with tertiary education, 45 per cent of members of environmental groups (ANOP 1991: 99, table 9.2) and 33 per cent of white-collar workers (ANOP 1993: 102, table 7.1). As stated earlier, public opinion about environmental issues often reflects significant political and social changes. In this case it reflected changes in the approach by the ALP as the party in government, as well as shifts in values among different social groups.

This section has drawn attention to the framing of survey questions in dichotomous terms. The effect of this framework can, however, be modified through various techniques, for instance by using a scale for responses and providing the option of remaining undecided. Table 16.14, for instance, illustrates a range of responses to statements about environment and development. On all but one item (item 3), only a minority are at either extreme. On three items, between 20 and 30 per cent neither agree nor disagree. Even more would probably fall into this category if they were provided with alternatives to the implicitly dichotomous framework that underlies these questions. The data are still interesting because they show that large proportions of the sample have reservations about using arguments about employment and financial benefits in deciding how best to use natural resources.

Dichotomous framing of questions can result in misleading impressions about the willingness of people to pursue a particular course of action or behaviour. Data from the AES (1990 and 1993) show that around 80 per cent of respondents feel that 'industry should be prevented from causing damage to the environment, even if this sometimes leads to higher prices'. This finding is significant. However, it does not mean that voters will immediately support a political party that forces industry to raise its prices in order to protect the environment. The question reflects a climate of opinion. It suggests that 'in public' most people are willing to say that they are for the environment and are prepared to make financial sacrifices. How far this is reflected in their actual behaviour is a different matter. Yet the data show that there is widespread moral support for consideration of the environment to an extent that was perhaps difficult to contemplate two or three decades ago. On this and related issues, public opinion does appear to be moving towards the resolution that there is a price to be paid for development and that everyone will have to share the cost.

Table 16.14 Public opinion on environment and development, 1991 (per cent)

Statement	Strongly agree	Agree	Neither	Disagree	Strongly disagree
1. Jobs are the most important thing in deciding how to best use our natural resources such as mineral deposits and forests.	12	11	26	25	26
2. Development should be allowed to proceed where environmental damage from activities such as mining is possible but very unlikely.	15	18	20	20	26
3. In deciding how to use our natural resources, it is more important to consider the needs of future generations than our own.	65	22	9	2	2
4. In deciding how to use our natural resources such as mineral deposits and forests, the most important thing is the financial benefits for Australia.	17	14	27	21	20
5. If areas within national parks are set aside for development projects such as mining, the value of the parks is greatly reduced.	38	23	17	13	10

Source: Imber et al. (1991, table 5.10).

Individual Behaviour, and Willingness to Pay for Environmental Protection

Much of the data has so far concentrated on general views and attitudes about environmental issues. These data may provide policy-makers with crucial information about the effectiveness of their efforts to influence public opinion and about changing perceptions that may need to be incorporated in policy shifts. Policy-makers also want to bring about changes in behaviour. Questions that focus on behaviour can provide another useful indicator of whether or not we are any closer to a resolution of some issues. The following account, though it does not actually demonstrate whether or not behaviour has changed, centres on the willingness of people to contribute to environmental protection in a practical manner.

For instance, survey researchers have attempted to estimate how willing people are to pay for improvements in the environment and how they themselves behave on a day-to-day basis. Studies, both in Australia and in other countries, have attempted to estimate the willingness of respondents to pay particular amounts for an increase in environmental protection. In the USA respondents were asked: 'How much per month would you personally be willing to pay for all the goods and services you use as a consumer, if you knew that as a result of your paying higher prices business and industry would be able to operate in a way that did not harm the environment?' (see Dunlap and Scarce 1991: 669–70). Between 1984 and 1987 the median amount remained stable at around eight to nine dollars. In 1990 it leapt to thirty-seven dollars. Other surveys in the USA showed a similar sudden shift in willingness to pay for environmental protection between 1989 and 1990 (see Dunlap and Scarce 1991: table 36). In Australia a survey conducted by the Morgan Gallup Research Centre on behalf of the Electricity Commission of New South Wales showed that, in response to the newly perceived threat of a greenhouse effect, many respondents were prepared to contemplate increases to their quarterly electricity bills (*Sydney Morning Herald* 18 September 1989).

Even if we argue that the actual figures cannot be used as a precise measure of the dollar amounts that people would be ready to pay, trend data show a drastic shift in both concern and issues that would lead to changes in behaviour and willingness to pay.[77] The shift appears to occur at around the same time as noted in table 16.2 on trends in perceived importance of the environment as an issue relative to other issues. The explanations offered for the shifts in opinion noted in table 16.2 may equally apply here.

One of the most ambitious efforts to document the readiness by Australians to pay for environmental protection was a survey conducted on behalf of the Resource Assessment Commission. It focused on the willingness to pay for the preservation of the Kakadu Conservation Zone. It adopted a technique known as contingent evaluation in attempting to place dollar values on aspects of the natural environment (for a full explanation of the technique see Imber, Stevenson and Wilks 1991). The survey was conducted in September 1990, a time when the environment had reached an all-time high on the political agenda.

Expression of a willingness to pay *some* dollar amount (leaving aside the precise figure) can be taken as a general indicator of support for environmental preservation. There is no need, in these circumstances, to judge the validity of the particular dollar estimates. Rather, willingness to pay becomes an expression of a general sentiment. The question was asked in relation to a specific, well-defined issue. The responses to the question can be compared to responses to questions from other attitudinal surveys and to other questions from the RAC survey.

Respondents were presented either with a 'major' or a 'minor' scenario of the damage that might be caused by the exploitation of the mine at Coronation Hill. They were told that adding this zone to the Kakadu national park would cost them money in two ways. The government would forgo revenue from the mining company if the mine did not proceed, and funds would be needed to establish the zone as part of the park and to manage it each year. Respondents were told that this would mean a reduction in their income by various amounts: 'So you can see that adding this zone to the Park would affect your take-home pay or the income that you personally have to live on. Would you be willing to have your income reduced by about $2 (or $5 or $1) a week, that's $100 (or $250 or $50) per year, for the next ten years to add this area to Kakadu national park rather than use it for mining?' Overall 2034 respondents were asked one of these questions: 1322 replied 'yes' and 712 replied 'no', representing a division of 66 and 34 per cent. These results are consistent with replies to similar questions used in the AES (Papadakis 1993: 146, table 5.4).

The RAC survey also asked people about whether or not they recycled things like paper and glass. Seventy per cent of the sample answered in the affirmative. Although these figures provide no indication of how often people undertake these tasks, they are supported by the data in table 16.15 which show for the period 1991 to 1993 an increase, on most dimensions, in the effort by individuals to do something for the environment.[78] Data from other countries also suggest significant changes in behaviour over the past two decades (see Dunlap and Scarce 1991: 671, table 44). In Western democracies like Australia these changes have arisen not only as a result of educational campaigns and measures adopted by established political organisations, but also through the actions of environmental groups in highlighting the problems, in suggesting some solutions, and in motivating people both to reconsider their priorities and to behave in a different manner. Support for environmental groups has remained high in the 1990s. The 1990 and 1993 AES showed that around 75 per cent of respondents either 'approved' or 'strongly approved' of environmental groups, and that 26 per cent of respondents had either joined or considered joining such a group (Papadakis 1994: 70, table 1; Papadakis 1993: 148–53).

The analysis of the rise of social movements, of party platforms and policy speeches and of the mass media has shown that concern about the environment as a major policy issue can be traced back several decades. How does this relate to public opinion? Opinion polling organisations have, since the 1940s, responded to concern about the environment. However, the focus has, until recently, been highly selective. The earliest surveys concentrated on nuclear energy, including atomic weapons. By the late 1960s and early 1970s, reflecting scientific breakthroughs and the influence of new intellectual frameworks, pollution and uranium mining became issues of widespread public concern. On all these topics there remained significant divisions both between experts and between policy-makers and political parties. Hence, we are some way from achieving a resolution. Perhaps more than many other issues the outcome of the conflict over environmental protection is perceived to have profound

Table 16.15 Individual action on environmental problems, 1991–93 (per cent)

Individual action	Dec. 1991	Sept. 1993
'A great deal', 'quite a lot' or 'a little bit'	79	85
The main action is:		
1. Recycling (put out papers, bottles for collection)	52	67
Followed by:		
2. Composting (compost scraps; compost bin)	12	21
3. Planting trees (native plants; Landcare)	9	16
4. Buying environmentally friendly products	18	11
5. Litter control (clean-ups; pick up rubbish)	8	11
6. Conserving water (don't waste water)	8	8
7. Reducing water pollution (sinks; drains)	4	7
8. Reducing use of chemicals (less fertilisers)	5	5
9. Driving car less (bike; public transport)	5	5
10. Not buying aerosols with CFCs	7	5
11. Conserving energy (saving power)	9	5

Source: ANOP 1993: 29, table 15.

implications for the national economy and for its development in the context of global competition. This means that resolution of some issues will require agreements to be struck not only within but between nation-states. The strongest arguments, for instance, against introducing high standards for pollution control are that competitors in other countries will immediately take advantage of this and that investors will flee Australia. As I suggested earlier, many of these arguments are being challenged at both the conceptual and the practical level. Moreover, there has been more activity than ever before by national governments towards reaching transnational agreements on environmental issues (see, for example, Porter and Brown 1991; von Weizsäcker 1994).

Securing a place for the environment on the national political agenda has been a slow process. Campaigns for conservation and preservation can be traced back to the nineteenth century (Papadakis 1993). They all achieved significant breakthroughs in the creation of national parks and areas reserved for wilderness. Yet, it was only in the late 1960s and early 1970s, notably with campaigns to save Lake Pedder in Tasmania and with world-wide attention on the harmful effects of pollution, that the environment began to be taken seriously as a national political issue. Ironically, just when polling organisations began to include the environment in a systematic way in polls about key policy issues, there was a temporary decline in public attention (see table 16.1).

Campaigns for the preservation of forests can be traced to the early years of this century. Yet, it was only in the late 1970s and early 1980s that political parties and the mass media took the issue seriously and contributed to raising public awareness. Futhermore, despite vigorous campaigns (like the ones against the construction of the Franklin Dam or for the preservation of tropical rainforests), it was only in the late 1980s that there was a significant shift in public opinion towards placing the environment high on the national political agenda and in the breadth of issues addressed by opinion polls. Again, as in the early 1970s, the principal reasons appear to be the influence at an international level of scientific breakthroughs and intellectual paradigms, and the move by established political parties to adopt significant aspects of a green agenda.

In the 1980s the pressure from environmental groups and their influence in marginal electorates helped to develop dialogue between interest groups and the established political organisations, and to accelerate adaptation to many demands by environmentalists. Much of this dialogue was driven by fear rather than a desire to address new challenges in a constructive manner. None the less, at the broader societal level, awareness of environmental issues has grown significantly over the past seven years. Some of the issues still represent a fundamental challenge to past practices and we are still a long way from achieving a resolution of conflicts between interest groups. The most significant changes take place when new concepts are developed, which then gain widespread acceptance within the electorate, and governments attempt to foster collaboration in implementing reforms across the boundaries of nation-states.

As I suggested in chapter 5, a key element in this process is the success or failure of political systems in promoting constructive dialogue between sub-systems of society. Attempts to influence and monitor public opinion can either degenerate into various forms of manipulation or reflect ambivalence and the failure to resolve conflicts. A more difficult but worthwhile option is to treat the formation of public opinion as a process in which policy-makers can benefit from the judgement of many people on important issues. It may also be a process in which policy-makers play an active role in offering the benefits of expert advice to citizens who remain interested in politics (despite its many negative connotations) and who want to have a say in how they are governed.[79] Public judgement and the social movements that influence and articulate public opinion both play a key role in disrupting the circularity of political communication and in revitalising political institutions. In some instances social movements have mobilised enough support to compel established political organisations to respond to changes in public opinion. In others, social movements have been formed because of the failure by government to heed public opinion. This chapter has shown the possiblilities for public opinion to assist social movements and other political organisations to reshape the agenda for environmental politics.

PART V

Conclusion

CHAPTER 17

Possibilities for Constructive Dialogue

The Importance of Perceptions

In politics, as in all other areas of social life, perceptions are more powerful than logic. De Bono recounts the apocryphal story from the Cold War of the race between an American ambassador and a Russian ambassador: 'The American ambassador won. The race was reported in the local press to the effect that there had been a race and the Russian ambassador had come second and the American ambassador had come just one before the last person in the race. There was no mention that this was a two-person race' (De Bono 1991: 46). De Bono then emphasises that there can be no truth in perception: 'It is always from a point of view. It is never complete.'

This fundamental point arises in portrayals of environmenmental politics and institutional change. Anyone wanting to influence perceptions about the failure by government to address environmental issues needs to look no further than the useful study by Philip Toyne, the former director of the ACF. Toyne reflects that Australia, both as a nation and a continent, leads the world in the rate of mammal extinction; that, since European settlement, we have wiped out eighteen species of mammals, a hundred species of higher plants, three species of birds, one species of reptile, and two species of freshwater fish; and that four hundred terrestrial and marine invertebrates and three thousand plants are at risk (Toyne 1994: 3–4).

By contrast, if you want to create the impression that the government has been successful in tackling environmental issues, you could focus, as did the ALP in the 1993 election campaign, on actions which prevented the construction of the Franklin Dam in 1983, the creation of a huge World Heritage area in Tasmania, the tripling in size of the Kakadu national park and its inscription on the World Heritage List, and the protection of Uluru national park, the Queensland Wet Tropics, Fraser Island and Shark Bay (see part III of this book for other illustrations).

If this account engenders complacency, you can always emphasise the challenges we face, like soil erosion, the destruction of rainforests, the depletion of the ozone layer, the increase in greenhouse gases, acid pollution, and the exhaustion of natural resources.

Perceptions, as De Bono has argued, are always from a point of view. This means that there is vast potential for misunderstanding and manipulation. I have already noted that survey questions framed in slightly different ways can lead to a radically changed distribution of responses. A great deal hinges on perceptions, which are based on particular experiences and values. The ambiguity surrounding language and communication can be exploited in numerous ways, some of which are peculiar to an adversarial system (see chapter 1). Often there is a genuine breakdown in communication. These two factors, the ambiguity surrounding communication and the breakdown in communication, provide politicians and the media with infinite opportunities for presenting issues from different points of view (as shown for instance in chapter 14 on media stereotypes). However, there are sometimes limits to the success of politicians in influencing our perceptions. A telephone survey of 531 electors carried out by Morgan Research in 1995 revealed that 84 per cent of respondents believed that 'federal politicians lie at election time in order to win votes' (*The Bulletin* 12 September 1995: 14–17). Only 24 per cent agreed that 'federal politicians usually tell the truth' – 67 per cent disagreed with the statement. Above all, 91 per cent agreed 'that federal politicians twist the truth to suit their own arguments'.

These findings raise some interesting questions about the role and character of public opinion in a democracy. These include the possibilities for shaping opinion and the opportunities for it to form an important part of a process of judgement of issues, of constructive dialogue and of communication (see chapter 15). The findings also imply a lack of confidence in the effectiveness of established political organisations to deal with new challenges, though, as we saw in chapter 16, the level of trust in different organisations to address environmental issues does vary considerably.

The Possibilities for Environmental Politics and Institutional Change

These considerations bring us back to the central questions, namely:

- What are the possibilities for established political organisations and institutions to adapt to new challenges (parts I and II)?
- How are new ideas and discoveries taken up by political parties, social movements and interest groups (part III)?
- How do these organisations influence the media, or how are they used by the media to articulate political issues (parts III and IV)?
- What is the likelihood of a shift from public awareness of various environmental issues to their resolution (part IV)?

A key concern in this book has therefore been the effectiveness of political organisations and the possibilities for a constructive dialogue both between political organisations and between political and other sub-systems (as defined by Luhmann). One way of ensuring that government and other political organisations address new challenges in an effective manner is through constructive dialogue. Dialogue is constructive when both parties are looking for solutions that will benefit both sides, where parties attempt to develop an empathetic understanding of divergent viewpoints and of divergent goals. If, as I pointed out earlier, a political or bureaucratic system is not open to dialogue and to exploration of new ideas, it is likely to be characterised by arrogance or complacency or both.

One of the aims in this chapter is to revisit the arguments developed at the beginning of the book, and particularly in chapter 4, about whether our political structures have been rendered otiose and whether our political institutions can address new challenges. These speculations are not as far-fetched as they might at first appear. Even those who have studied formal government processes from the insider's point of view have noted the factors that restrict, redirect and reshape government. The conventional view posits, for instance, that 'Cabinet is the heart of government' and that Cabinet 'determines strategy' for the government; 'decides what legislation is to be introduced'; 'arbitrates between ministers and departments'; controls parliament; and ensures 'the government's electoral survival' (Weller 1990: 28). Yet, the same writer also looks at the restrictions imposed on government, like the pressure of time, masses of information, factional disputes, and 'great difficulty in maintaining any broad perspective into which it can fit its different proposals'. He concludes that Cabinet 'is seldom master of its own agenda, as it has to react to crises that force items on it', and that Cabinet is really like any other indecisive committee, whose capacity is 'more limited than legend asserts' (Weller 1990: 28–9).

Although there has been a resurgence in the study of institutions and a shift in focus towards the enduring regularities governed by rules, norms and strategies (see Crawford and Ostrom 1995), it is widely recognised that to concentrate on the established rules and procedures arising from political institutions can take us only so far. One is reminded of the crucial distinction between established political organisations and the developments that occur outside them. This also recalls the importance of observing both tradition (and established rules and procedures) and innovation (as articulated by new political movements and other social forces).

The question still lingers whether or not government has been rendered less effective than is hypothesised by political theory. Take the recent efforts to gain greater control over the bureaucracy. Thompson has argued that bids by Australian governments 'to exert more control over the bureaucracy, to assert supremacy over policy direction and to create a responsive, accountable public service' have all but failed (Thompson 1990: 43). This is in contrast to the perspective adopted by Keating (1993) and Weller (1993).

In order to grasp these issues, in the context of environmental politics and institutional change, this book has explored both the obstacles that prevent effective policy-making and the possibilities for overcoming them. For instance, after identifying some of the obstacles, I have maintained that it is possible (though difficult) for political and other institutions to engage in constructive dialogue and for effective policies to emerge out of this process.

In this chapter, table 17.1 summarises some of the reasons for being both pessimistic and optimistic about the possibilities for politics to respond to challenges and for the political system to be effective. The left-hand column is labelled obstacles, the right-hand column outlines some of the possibilities for overcoming these impediments.

The first distinction in table 17.1 is between the tendency for established political organisations to adopt the conventional institutional practice of responding to crisis

Table 17.1 Government response to new challenges: obstacles and possibilities

	Obstacles	Possibilities
1	Response is mainly to crises	Response is based on principles for long-term action Focus on consequences and on stewardship
2	Inertia (tradition)	Adaptation (innovation)
3	Binary codes	Options and alternatives
4	Path dependence Evolution Circles of history	Design New concepts
5	Excessive analysis Focus on what is and on behaviour	Design and vision Focus on potential
6	Self-referential system Circularity of political communication The relative autonomy of politics Agenda-setting by elites	Dialogue between systems (trust, goodwill, competence) social communication Expert communities Social movements/public opinion
7	Public opinion • top-of-the-head response • possibilities for manipulation	Public opinion • considered judgements • possibilities for communication

situations rather than developing principles and perspectives for long-term action, in other words, for dealing with the long-term consequences of prevailing institutional practices. In the area of environmental policy, a key principle would be the one of stewardship and consideration of the needs of future generations. Before commenting on the other obstacles and possibilities, I want to focus on the relevance of the distinction between the response to urgent problems and the lack of emphasis on important but 'non-urgent' issues. To do this, I refer to the framework for analysis presented in chapter 3 (see figure 3.1). This is replicated in figure 17.1 (first column) along with two examples of how this model might be applied to the issues of DDT and the destruction of forests.

For the moment I want to focus on the second row in the first column of figure 17.1, in other words on political organisations (like parties, interest groups and social movements) as the key mechanism for taking up new ideas and for attaching value to these ideas. As North (1990) has argued, although institutions represent the 'rules of the game' or 'the humanly devised constraints that shape human interaction', political organisations, including political parties and regulatory agencies, can influence the institutional framework. I would maintain that one of the principal means of realising this goal is constructive dialogue. Still, the process of dialogue and of changes in policy, let alone of change in institutional practices, can be either slow or rapid. This depends on the issue and on whether or not it is perceived as urgent and requiring immediate attention, or important but not necessarily urgent. This distinction between urgent issues and important but non-urgent issues underlies some of the discussions in the literature on social problems (see Spector and Kitsuse 1987). The focus on important but non-urgent problems also corresponds to the radical reformist approach championed by writers like Jänicke (1990), who suggests that established institutions and organisations have failed to take preventative measures and to address important issues because they have focused on crises and on symptoms rather than on the underlying causes (see chapter 4 in this book).[80]

The second and third columns of figure 17.1 attempt to summarise some of the findings from two of the case studies reported in previous chapters. The first arises

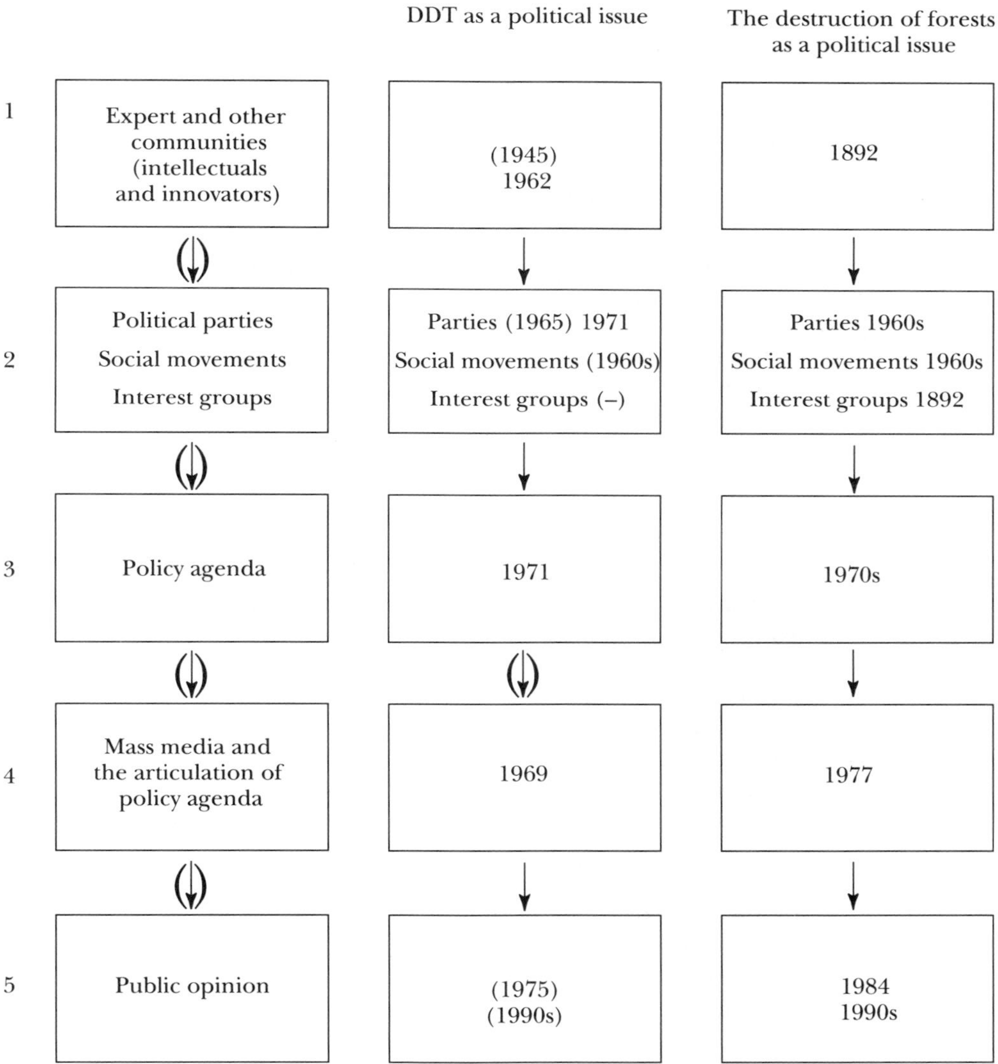

Figure 17.1 Hypothetical sequence of the shaping of the policy agenda and public opinion on two political issues

from the perceived threat posed by pesticides like DDT. Figure 17.1 (column 2) shows that the issue first reached the headlines in the 1940s. However, the real breakthrough was in 1962 when Rachel Carson published *Silent Spring*. The survey of *The Bulletin* showed that it took seven years after the publication of *Silent Spring* for the first news story on DDT to appear. *The Bulletin* reported that restrictions on DDT were introduced as early as 1964. Yet, in the five-year period up to 1969, there was a fourfold increase in the use of DDT, to about two million pounds a year.

Apart from demonstrating the inertia of institutions, the history of the use of DDT in Australia shows how difficult it can be for communication to take place between self-referential systems. As noted in chapter 8, knowledge about the impact of DDT on the environment did not immediately result in effective legislation. Restrictions were introduced only when environmental concerns were translated into the language of economics, when the government feared the loss of a lucrative trade in the export of meat.

Turning to party platforms, we find that the ALP did mention the use of pesticides in 1965. However, it was only in 1971 (nearly a decade after the publication of *Silent Spring*) that the ALP and the Liberals referred categorically to DDT and the need to find alternatives. Still, one could maintain that the response by elites to the issue of DDT was fairly rapid. Some support for this argument arises from the fact that DDT did not appear to feature in studies carried out by polling organisations. This is not to suggest that pollution of air, water and land did not become an issue. As noted in figure 17.1 (column 2), in the mid-1970s polling organisations did take up the issue of the environment in a systematic way (see also chapter 16). Also, in the 1990s there has been a revival of interest in the damage caused by pollution. The main argument here is that, compared to issues like the destruction of forests or oil pollution, political organisations did respond to what appeared to be a crisis situation.

This claim is backed by the contrasting experience of the destruction of forests (figure 17.1, third column). In Australia, modern organisations concerned about environmental protection can be traced to the Royal Societies which were formed in Tasmania in 1842 and in Victoria in 1859. The focus on forests can be traced to the late nineteenth century, for instance to 1892, when conservation groups campaigned for the first national park in South Australia. These groups were successful in 1919 in preserving the Flinders Chase.

Who would have anticipated the long-term impact of the earliest environmental groups in Australia like the Wild Life Preservation Society and the Mountain Trails Club or of the National Parks and Primitive Areas Council in challenging the predominant approach to land use which attached little value to the preservation of forests? Through lobbying by such groups, between 1932 and 1962 Australian governments dedicated fourteen national parks and other schemes. Yet, it took several decades for governments to set up appropriate structures for managing national parks and to incorporate these ideas into party platforms. Campaigners like Myles Dunphy, with their proposals in the 1930s for statutory intervention to perserve wilderness areas, were certainly 'decades ahead' of their time (Thompson 1986). From the 1940s through to the 1970s the focus by the major parties was almost exclusively on development (chapters 9 to 12). This is reflected in the analysis of media accounts (chapter 13). With respect to polling organisations, the main interest in forests arose, in 1984, from the dispute over the proposal to construct the Franklin Dam. Following that, the campaigns to preserve rainforests as well as other native forests have gained considerable momentum and become linked with the recent focus on soil erosion and on the greenhouse effect.

I have used these two examples of political responses to concerns about DDT and about forests to illustrate some of the differences in the response by governments to issues that are perceived either as urgent, or as important but not in need of urgent attention. In some cases, there has been a huge effort by government to take drastic action and to shift public opinion. In other cases, changes have been slow despite the obviousness of the problem.

This distinction arises in many other cases, for instance, if we compare the responses to oil pollution of the oceans and to the destruction of the ozone layer. Whereas responses to the problem of oil pollution have been slow and ineffective (see chapter 8), reaction to the depletion of the ozone layer has been swift. In 1974 two American scientists, F. Sherwood Rowland and Mario Molina, discovered that the release of CFCs into the atmosphere would destroy a significant proportion of the ozone layer. Their findings were upheld by the National Academy of Sciences, and in 1978 the American government prohibited the use of CFCs in nearly all aerosols. The discovery of a thinning of the ozone layer in the 1980s prompted further action. By 1990 eighty countries had agreed to phase out CFCs by the year 2000. There is now a strong prospect that by 1998 the current trend towards the depletion of the ozone layer will cease and that over time the amount of ozone will be restored to previous levels.

These case studies and the data presented in part III on the response by political parties serve to highlight the capacity of the political system to deal with crises. Political capacity is enhanced if the crises are articulated by works like *Silent Spring* and by the media; if they are adopted by social movements, interest groups and new political parties (like the Australian Democrats); and if they form the basis for challenges by newly constituted groups often emerging within the prevailing structure of political elites (see Papadakis 1993, particularly chapter 1 on accounts of political change arising from challenges like environmentalism). The case studies also show that political elites can become locked into certain ways of seeing things. In relation to the forests, it took them a long time to realise that environmental concerns might reflect changes in values. For decades the initiatives originated outside government. There were no votes to be won from protecting trees, even though there was considerable knowledge about some of the consequences of destroying forests (like the problem of soil erosion).

The political system did not address a long-term and important issue that did not require urgent attention. In the case of DDT the government did respond to a crisis, namely pressure by a foreign government to improve environmental standards. The distinction therefore is between issues that have to be acted on urgently and issues that are important but do not necessarily qualify for urgent action. Established political organisations are beginning to question the concentration on urgent issues, as we saw in the chapters on policy speeches and electoral platforms. For instance, the ALP, in 1994, committed itself to a 'precautionary approach' in dealing with the important but 'non-urgent' issues of the impact of greenhouse gases. Again, and this mirrors the propositions by writers like Jänicke, the Democrats in their policy speeches and statements ever since the 1970s have argued for long-term policies to deal with the issue of energy supplies. In addition, the Liberals, the ALP and the Democrats have begun to articulate the principle of caring for future generations as an integral part of their environmental policies. The notion of stewardship has made its mark on the political agenda.

Turning back to table 17.1, I will begin by focusing on the obstacles that may reduce the effectiveness of governments seeking to carry out reforms, and then discuss some of the possibilities for overcoming these barriers. The second item in table 17.1 recalls the proposition made in chapter 1: that our political system can be first-rate in its capacity for adaptation and its stubborn attachment to ways of thinking (like adversarialism) that may prevent us from exploring new ways of seeing and doing things. In table 17.1 inertia and tradition are portrayed as impediments to effective policy-making, though this is not always necessarily the case. As Putnam has observed, institutional history can supply a strong foundation for adaptation to new challenges. Also, as noted in chapter 12, environmentalism, by successfully challenging established practices and becoming partly institutionalised, can benefit from the slow movement of institutional history. On the question of adaptation, I have shown that policies and structures that formed a key part of the foundations of the Australian polity in the early part of this century have come under severe challenge or become redundant, increasing the capacity of established political parties to adopt concerns about the environment (part III), and changing perceptions about the possibilities and character of economic development (part IV).

Another obstruction to tackling problems is the use of binary codes (discussed at some length in chapters 4 and 5). An important consideration is that binary coding, by definition, makes it difficult to conceive of alternative ways of perceiving situations and of processing information. The problem of binary coding arises in political argument between established organisations, in the media reporting of these debates, and in the formulation of the questions utilised in survey research.

The next obstacle has been conceptualised as path dependence. We have noted the arguments by North and Putnam about how the performance of institutions is, or can be, reinforced by history. The value of the work of these writers, as well as Luhmann and Jänicke, has been to highlight structural or systemic impediments to political action. The focus on path dependence and evolution, as well as on the 'virtuous circles of history', emphasises what is and what has been (see De Bono 1994). Its stress is on analysing past trends in order to solve problems or to predict the future. As De Bono has suggested, this kind of approach can take us only so far in trying to deal with new challenges. There is a need for more emphasis on designing alternatives and on developing new concepts which assist in this process.

Item 5 in table 17.1 serves as a reminder that some of the approaches we have so far considered appear to rely heavily on the analysis of particular practices. Attempts to observe what *is* (rather than what *can be*) can take us only so far. For any kind of progress, both in politics and in the study of politics, we still need to infer from the general to the particular, to make certain assumptions in order to make some sense of the vast amount of information on political life (Papadakis 1995). As Mayntz

(1984) has argued, we will often be confronted by the lack of knowledge about a social system.

Another obstacle, which is related to the previous ones, is the development of self-referential systems and the circularity of political communication (see the discussion about the work by Luhmann in chapters 4 and 5). Again, there are powerful echoes of the notion of institutional inertia. There are also strong links with arguments about the relative autonomy of politics and of agenda-setting by political actors (see chapter 8 on inertia and adaptation by political parties).

Although, as I have mentioned above, all these concepts are useful in identifying some of the potential impediments that weaken the responsiveness by government to new challenges, they represent only the obstacles. If we devise different concepts and different ways of perceiving the challenges to government, we may create the possibilities for overcoming some of the obstacles posited above and in previous chapters. It is important to note that some of the obstacles outlined in table 17.1 sit easily with an adversarial approach to politics. For instance, adversarialism thrives on the use of the distinct categories characteristic of binary codes. Adversarialism also tends to enhance rather than diminish the circularity of political communication. Adversarialism usually aggravates rather than diminishes conflicts. A different approach is required from the one that concentrates almost exclusively on exposing the faulty logic of opponents. One option is to try to design solutions, ideally in collaboration with those representing a different standpoint – hence the emphasis on constructive dialogue.

Jackson (1995) has suggested that we may need to reconsider the fundamental concepts used to characterise our political system because they are often wide of the mark or too abstract, and because we may have become too complacent about existing concepts to the detriment of developing new ideas. Marsh (1995) has argued for sketching out a possible future for politics that looks beyond the current party system and enables us to meet new challenges. This is not to argue for abstract thinking for its own sake or for ideas that bear no relationship at all to current or past practices. Rather, it is to point to the possibility of devising new ways of seeing things and thereby presenting alternatives to prevailing practices.

In this book I have already touched on some of these alternatives and shown how they arise from the deliberation by intellectuals, scientists and innovators, and from the programmes and policies developed by social movements as well as new and established political parties. The second column of table 17.1 summarises some of the concepts that form the basis for these alternatives.

I have already touched on the significance of principles for long-term action and for dealing with important but 'non-urgent' issues. I have also drawn attention to the capability demonstrated by the political system for adaptation. The adaptation can also take the form of new initiatives by the state. Data on these kinds of initiatives can be found in part III of this book (see also Papadakis 1993; Jänicke and Weidner 1995). Another useful source is von Weizsäcker (1994), who provides a comprehensive account of both the possibilities for, and actual innovations by, the state. For instance, he points out that environmental policy has, in many countries, led to the growth of environmental technology and industries. In the Federal Republic of Germany it has been estimated that 700 000 jobs may 'relate directly to environmental protection, and the number is growing' (von Weizsäcker 1994: 204). The Rhine now leaves North Rhine Westphalia, the most heavily industrialised state in Germany, in a cleaner condition than it enters. There have been similar improvements to the River Thames in England and the Ohio River in the USA (von Weizsäcker 1994: 177).

The state and industry are considering 'new models of wealth' (in other words, models which include the notion of sustainability) which take into account that across the world we are losing some 3000 square metres of forest and 1000 tonnes of topsoil every second (von Weizsäcker 1994: 205). These models of wealth enable us to perceive pollution and waste as an immediate cost to society. Environmental protection could be transformed from an economic cost to an economic benefit as perceptions change and as people purchase goods for their durability, for ease in recycling and repair (von Weizsäcker 1994: 207). In some countries the state and industry are already applying new concepts like energy productivity (which entails a reduction in the consumption of energy, coupled with the maintenance of prosperity): 'Between 1973 and 1985, for instance, Japan achieved a reduction in energy use, not least because of high energy prices, of 31 per cent, from 19 to 13 megajoules per constant dollar of GNP, while in Canada, with low energy prices, the best that could be managed was a reduction from 38.3 to 36' (von Weizsäcker 1994: 178). Other areas of innovation include the introduction of 'tradeable permits' for emissions, as well as other economic instruments including emission charges, user charges, product charges, administrative charges, extended environmental liability, and tax breaks (von Weizsäcker 1994: 124–5).

It is interesting that Jänicke et al. (1989) have found that a non-adversarial approach to addressing new challenges has, in the long run, shown a higher level of correspondence with environmental protection than a conflictual one (cited in von Weizsäcker 1994: 142). This lends further support to the emphasis in this study on the application of constructive dialogue.

One is reminded of the perceptions of politics and the political system promoted by writers like Luhmann. His approach, despite its 'realism', can be challenged by exploring the possibilities for dialogue: dialogue between social systems, and social communication. As indicated in chapter 5, although political and other systems are often self-referential, they also try to cooperate in solving problems. Besides the examples in that chapter, it is also useful to consider initiatives at three levels: local, like the Landcare groups in Australia and the Citizens' Initiative and many other groups in Germany (see Papadakis 1984); national, like the ESD working groups in Australia; and international, like the UN conferences in Stockholm in 1972 and in Rio de Janeiro in 1992. Just as significant are the intergovernmental agreements on greenhouse gases, oil pollution and biodiversity, and the work by non-governmental organisations like Greenpeace, the World Wide Fund for Nature and the Business Council for Sustainable Development (see Schmidheiny 1992).

Although they do not represent the central focus of this study, the rise of social movements (see chapter 6) draws attention to the possibilities for adaptation by the political system and changes in the institutional practices of political organisations. In the 1950s membership of the Sierra Club, one of the leading conservation organisations in the USA, stood at around 7000. By the mid-1960s it had risen to

70 000, and by 1984 the club had 350 000 members. In Britain membership of the National Trust rose from 170 000 in 1968 to 1.5 million in 1984 (McCormick 1989). In 1984, within six months of its formation, the Nuclear Disarmament Party in Australia received 640 000 first-preference votes in elections to the Senate. According to recent estimates, between 300 000 and 500 000 people are members of conservation and environmental groups in Australia (Papadakis 1993; 1994).

The green movement represents an important source of political change in Western democracies. Paradoxically, many of its supporters and sympathisers expect established political organisations to become even more involved in regulating behaviour. The green movement also reflects the effort by many people to alter institutional practices, to promote education about the environment, to set standards, and to encourage industries to protect the environment. The green movement has therefore become part of a process in which we may come to reformulate policies in many areas: economic growth; the measurement of wealth and of GNP; relations between wealthy and poor countries; energy and material resources; transport; agriculture; biodiversity; making polluters and consumers pay more realistic costs for environmental damage; taxation; and international relations.

Many of these changes are the result of new ideas on methods to address intractable problems or to improve on current ways of doing things. At times, this has meant that people have had to detach themselves from traditional ways of conceptualising social systems and from traditional ways of tackling issues (notably the adversarial approach and the adoption of rigid dichotomies and categories). To move away from the use of binary codes means to consider new possibilities like sustainable development, energy productivity and biodiversity. It means full consideration of the possibility of achieving both a reduction in factors that cause environmental damage and a rise in prosperity. The overall direction is therefore to explore the significance of discoveries and conceptual innovations which have broken the virtuous circles of history. These innovations do not arise only in the field of technology. They pertain to the awareness of different lifestyles, the adaptation of models for preserving nature, and the invention of new forms of lobbying and political action. Provided new concepts can be formulated and opportunities to promote these concepts are seized by a political organisation, an issue that has smouldered in the background of political debate for long periods of time can rapidly become politically significant.

In considering the nature and character of political action, the concept of public opinion is crucial (item 7 in table 17.1). As noted in chapter 15, there is an abiding debate over whether public opinion is proactive or reactive and manipulable. The distinction by Yankelovich between 'top-of-the-head' responses to opinion polls and considered judgements of policy options is useful inasmuch as it raises the possibility of a democracy based on dialogue and consensus rather than on manipulation and control. It creates the possibility for resolution of certain issues. This cannot occur, unless expert communities, the media and political organisations adopt a constuctive approach and take the path of facilitating rather than hindering the processes of working through or resolving issues (Yankelovich 1991).

The focus in this book on the obstacles and possibilities for change represents an attempt to understand both the context for political change and the apparent limitations imposed by institutional practices, and to suggest how we can transcend them. Arguments about institutional inertia, self-referential systems and binary coding should not be used to pour cold water over efforts to reform the political system. Rather, they can be turned into both challenges and opportunities. To do this, we must question our reliance on binary codes, modify the focus on absolute truths, explore opportunities for institutional innovation, draw selectively on aspects of the political culture, and develop flexible expectations. Examples of the latter are the recognition that the state may not always be the guiding centre, and the exploration of market and price mechanisms as part of a strategy for changing institutional practices. If we reduce the traditional emphasis on absolute truths and on fundamental conflicts between environment and development, more opportunities may arise for the state to deal in a constructive way with conflicts between the values we attach to the environment and to development. We may also revive the chances for politics to remain relevant and to make a difference.

Appendix
Codes used in Tables 9.1 to 12.1

Environmental issues addressed in party platforms and policy speeches by the Liberal and National Parties, the Australian Labor Party and the Australian Democrats are listed here.

The items marked 'd' refer to proposals for development; the items marked 'e' refer to proposals for environmental protection. The items marked 'd*' or 'd/e' refer to proposals that pertain both to environmental protection and to development. Some of the proposals under 'sustainable development' are marked 'e' though they pertain to both development and environmental protection.

Antarctica

d claims to Antarctica
d1 research into Antarctica
e general statement(s) on preservation
e1 conservation of flora and fauna
e2 prevent mining
e3 place on World Heritage List
e4 repudiate claims of sovereignty; turn into an internationally administered area
e5 Antarctica as a world park

Atomic energy

d general statement(s) in support of development
d1 research and development
d2 Atomic Energy Commission
d3 atomic plant at Jervis Bay
d4 research into nuclear waste disposal (SYNROC)
d5 critique of ALP policy on nuclear-free zone (see also d3 under 'Uranium mining')
d6 build a nuclear power station
e general statement(s) in support of environmental protection
e1 suspend nuclear testing; nuclear-free zone in southern hemisphere
e2 opposition to nuclear power
e3 world-wide nuclear freeze
e4 close down Lucas Heights nuclear reactor

Environment (general)

e general statement(s) in support of environmental protection
e1 Commonwealth Office of the Environment under Prime Minister's Department
e2 National Advisory Council for Commonwealth and states
e3 support World Conservation Strategy
e4 support National Conservation Strategy
e5 application of Environment (Impact of Proposals) Act
e6 support Australian Heritage Commission
e7 support National Trust
e8 examine environmental impact of development projects undertaken with Australian aid

e9 ensure that environmental impact studies are completed before undertaking Commonwealth development projects
e10 apply conditions to mining operations relating to environmental disturbance and the rights of land users
e11 assessment of environmental considerations prior to initiation of new transport systems
e12 conservation of marine resources
e13 'polluter pays' principle
e14 Australian Environmental Corps for unemployed (volunteers)
e15 develop national environmental data bank
e16 support in principle for World Heritage listing
e17 support for Australian heritage and national estate listing
e18 examine environmental impact of development projects and apply controls
e19 quality of life
e20 cooperate with international agencies (including UN,OECD, IUCN) to ensure environmental protection
e21 support basic research (in natural sciences, humanities and social sciences)
e22 controls on advertising
e23 consideration of price and regulatory mechanisms
e24 a department responsible for environment and conservation
e25 annual State of the Environment Report
e26 discourage tourist development in conservation areas
e27 tax incentives for owners of heritage area or item
e28 Environmental Protection Agency
e29 set national environmental standards
e30 develop an Environmental Survey of Australia in collaboration with states and territories, CSIRO and other agencies
e31 implement 1992 Rio Summit Agenda 21

Forests

d develop afforestation
d1 Forest Industry Research Fund
d2 remove quotas on woodchipping
d3 private forestry projects
d4 tax deductions (for buildings, housing for employees in logging areas, or other aspects of business)
d5 government funds for forest industry
d6 state forestry agencies to operate on a fully commercial basis
d* conservation of forests
e/d national forest strategy
e/d1 self-sustaining forestry industry
e/d2 integration of ecological, economic and recreational values
e preservation of existing forests
e1 buy back land for national parks and reserves
e2 protect or enlarge parklands or national parks
e3 declare Alligator Rivers Region national park, NT
e4 protect Alligator Rivers Region from effects of uranium mining
e5 support National Parks and Wildlife Service
e6 nominate Kakadu National Park for World Heritage listing
e7 proposal for a major national park in South-West Tasmania
e8 youth project in reafforestation
e9 National Tree Programme (for Greening Australia by 1988)
e10 protect Northern Australia (e.g. Kakadu, Kimberleys, Cape York Peninsula)
e11 National Parks and Wildlife Conservation Bill
e12 save Daintree rainforests
e13 nominate Uluru National Park for World Heritage listing
e14 protect rainforests
e15 Grasslands Ecology Unit within National Parks and Wildlife Service
e16 introduce national system of parks and reserves
e17 no woodchipping licences except for sawmill waste
e18 protect forests in Pacific Basin countries
e19 tax incentives for landowners to retain forests
e20 no grazing or mining or forestry practices in any national park or reserve
e21 restrictions on pulp mills
e22 ban imports of rainforest timbers from Malaysia
e23 ban rainforest logging

e24 more trainee jobs in the Australian National Parks and Wildlife Service
e25 ban clearing of native forests for softwood plantations
e26 environmental impact planning for proposals to export woodchips
e27 conserve tropical rainforests in ASEAN and South Pacific regions
e28 environmental impact studies of development in forests
e29 restrictions in woodchip licences
e30 National Forest Inventory and National Wilderness Inventory
e31 restrictions on import of tropical rainforest timbers
e32 implement 1992 Rio Summit Statement of Forest Principles

Franklin Dam

e1 offer Tasmanian government $500 million (or other support)
e2 oppose Franklin Dam

Great Barrier Reef (GBR)

d1 viewed as 'living marine resources' within a fishing exclusion zone
e1 no drilling or mining
e2 declaration or extension of GBR Marine Park
e3 nominate GBR for World Heritage listing
e4 support GBR Marine Park Authority
e5 protect GBR

Green groups

e1 support foundation of World Wide Fund for Nature in Australia
e2 support voluntary organisations
e3 cooperate with environmental groups
e4 finance and legal access for conservation groups

Land resources

d general statement(s) in support of development
d1 cash advances for agricultural and pastoral leases in Northern Territory
d2 tax allowances and credits
d3 Australia Rural Bank
d4 encourage agro-forestry
d5 encourage land settlement
d6 capital for the Development Bank
d/e sustainable agriculture
d/e1 tree farming for windbreaks
e1 soil conservation
e2 National Soil Conservation Programme
e3 national land use inventory
e4 Landcare programme
e5 tax allowances and credits
e6 on-farm conservation (assistance)
e7 plant one billion trees
e8 legislation against grazing and cropping in marginal land
e9 initiatives against desertification
e10 limit and control all mining and quarrying in coastal regions

Natural resources

d general statement(s) in support of development
d1 expenditure on research for development of natural resources
d2 Ministry of Development or of Northern Development or of Economic Development
d3 National Development Commission
d4 subsidies for mineral prospecting
d5 minerals in Northern Territory
d6 Development Bank
d7 develop mineral resources
d8 Commonwealth Development Bank
d9 develop Northern Australia/NT
d10 develop port of Darwin
d11 foreign investment
d12 export natural resources
d13 Australian Overseas Projects Corporation (for Australian firms to compete for development projects)
d14 mining at Coronation Hill
d15 abolish Resource Assessment Commission
d16 National Council of Development
d17 subsidy for chemical fertilisers (including superphosphates)
d18 Australian Rural Bank
d19 North Australia Development Commission
d* concept of conservation
e consider environmental factors in exploration of mineral resources
e2 monitor environment and restore areas affected by mining

Other energy

d full development of power resources
d1 develop coal mining
d2 search for oil reserves (with government subsidies)
d3 National Energy Advisory Council
d4 gas exploration
d5 develop synthetic fuels
d6 develop hydro-electricity (see also Snowy Mountains scheme under 'Water resources')
d7 National Fuel and Energy Board/ Commission
e1 restrain growth of energy consumption, conserve fuel
e2 solar energy
e3 renewable energy sources
e4 tax incentives for developing renewable energy sources

Pollution

e general statement(s) in support of environmental protection
e1 urban waterways, sewerage and beach pollution
e2 reduce greenhouse gas emissions
e3 identify and reduce sources of acid rain
e4 Coordinating Committee on Climate Change
e5 protect ozone layer
e6 expert working party on air and water pollution
e7 address problem of visual pollution
e8 restrictions on motor vehicles in major business districts
e9 encourage use of unleaded petrol
e10 ban backyard burning in urban areas
e11 studies into health problems of those living near oil refineries, oil smelters, coal loaders etc.
e12 establish pollution control commissions
e13 ban billboards
e14 reduce unnecessary street lighting
e15 retain airport curfews
e16 monitoring system for air and water quality
e17 noise abatement
e18 create car-free zones/encourage use of bicycles
e19 research into greenhouse effect
e20 implement 1992 Rio Summit Convention on Climate Change
e21 national strategy for reduction in vehicle emissions
e22 national strategy for lead abatement
e23 phase out ozone-depleting substances
e24 encourage innovation to find safe substitutes for ozone-depleting substances
e25 transfer 'ozone-benign' technologies to developing countries
e26 develop natonal greenhouse response strategy
e27 evaluate urban development in the context of need to reduce greenhouse gas emissions
e/d consider national interests in global fora on Climate Change

Public education

e1 educate public on interdependence of resource conservation and sustainable development
e2 public awareness of environment and conservation (through media and schools and other institutions)

Sand mining

e1 prohibit or phase out mineral sand exports
e2 prohibit sand mining on Moreton and/or Fraser Islands
e3 prohibit sand mining in national parks

Species diversity

d eradication of pests (rabbits, dingoes, ticks, noxious weeds)
d1 'responsible policy' on marketing and export of kangaroo hides, meat and wildlife, such as birds
d2 national Kangaroo Monitoring Study (for planning commercial exploitation)
d3 develop resource accounting techniques and assessments for industries interested in biological resources
d/e control of feral animals
e protect flora and fauna
e1 survey of flora and fauna

e2 fund conservation groups engaged in protecting species diversity
e3 legislation to control trade in endangered species
e4 protect natural habitat through soil conservation
e5 protect endangered species
d/e6 code of practice for humane treatment of animals/animal welfare standards
e7 protect plant genetic resources
e8 ratify/'implement' Convention on Biodiversity signed at Rio Summit in 1992
e9 survey and protect sea mammals and birds
e10 animal rights
e11 ban export of live fauna
e12 ban import of all seal products
e13 inquiry into death of penguins
e14 total ban on killing indigenous species
e15 Royal Commission into kangaroo industry
e16 total ban on export of indigenous species
e17 ban on imports of furs, ivory etc.
e18 oppose genetic engineering
e19 prevent export of live native freshwater fish
e20 National Commission for Animals
e21 conservation of kangaroos
e22 national strategy for maintaining biological diversity
e23 develop international convention for maintaining biological diversity

Sustainable development

e/d 'sustained environmentally sound development'
e/d1 ecologically sustainable cities
e/d2 support for environmental industry products
e1 balance between development and conservation, economy and environment
e2 balance between present and future requirements in use of natural resources
e3 Department of Sustainable Development
e4 sustainable management of fish or timber or other resources
e5 ecologically sustainable development
e6 sustainable agriculture

Uranium mining

d1 develop and export uranium for civilian purposes
d2 develop and export uranium for defence purposes
d3 critique of ALP policy on nuclear-free zone (see also d5 under 'Atomic energy')
d4 assess feasibility of uranium enrichment industry
d5 develop and export uranium from restricted number of mines
e1 Ranger Uranium Inquiry on environmental protection
e2 oppose uranium mining
e3 ban exports of uranium
e4 moratorium on mining
e5 oppose dumping of nuclear waste in oceans

Waste management

e1 promote recycling
e2 control hazardous chemicals and waste
e3 ban the use of CFCs
e4 apply Basel Convention (1992) on movement of waste between countries
e5 use 'non-polluting' methods of sewage disposal (methane generation or composting)
e6 controls on crop spraying and pest control machines
e7 controls on herbicides, pesticides
e8 resiting of chemical industries to industrial areas
e9 total ban of CFCs for export
e10 no burning or high-temperature incineration of intractable wastes
e11 Recycled Products Development and Marketing Corporation
e12 bio-gas extraction from landfills
e13 Environmental Contamination Authority
e14 system for identifying dangerous chemicals
e15 public information on contaminants
e16 waste furnace for safe combustion of contaminants
e17 monitor origins, movement and disposal of hazardous wastes

e18 reverse wasteful industrial processes
e19 50 per cent reduction of wastes to landfill
e20 national facilities for storage of hazardous waste
e21 national inventory of pollutants

Water resources

d general statement(s) in support of development
d1 Snowy Mountains scheme
d2 CSIRO research into rain-making
d3 establish Water Resources Council
d4 fishing exclusion zones
d5 National Water Resources Programme or National Water Conservation Authority
d6 support or expand Water Resources Programme
d7 Bicentennial Water Resources Programme
d8 National Water Conservation Strategy
d9 support for acquaculture industry
d* conserve water for development purposes
d/e coastal management strategy
d/e1 Institute of Oceanography or promote marine science
d/e2 ecologically manageable harvesting rates for coastal fisheries
d/e3 Institute of Fresh Water Studies
e1 ban on driftnet fishing
e2 clean up major waterways
e3 coast protection strategy
e4 non-chemical control of exotic aquatic weeds
e5 inventory of all Australian rivers
e6 user-pays principle for anyone using water from or into river systems
e7 protection of mangroves
e8 worldwide ban on driftnets
e9 national system of marine and estuary reserves
e10 inventory of wetlands
e11 monitor impact of irrigation from ground water and surface water
e12 preservation of wetlands
e13 national marine conservation strategy

Whaling

e1 public inquiry
e2 work towards world-wide ban on commercial whaling
e3 promote conservation of whales
e4 Australian Whaling Commission
e5 circumpolar whale sanctuary extending south of 40°S
e6 200-mile offshore sanctuary for whales
e7 ban on import of whale products

Notes

1 For a fuller discussion of the notions of trust and goodwill see Handler (1988). The relevance of these notions is explored in chapter 5 of this book.

2 In a discussion of interests Hindess notes the distinction between individual and collective interests and suggests: 'The attribution of interests may serve normative or explanatory purposes: in the one case it is used to recommend action or to justify action taken on behalf of others, for example by governments, parents or social workers: in the other it is used to explain or to predict behaviour' (Hindess 1994b: 293).

3 Of course how one arrives at consensus is a matter for debate and is a recurring theme in the remainder of the book.

4 Again, the relevance of these notions is discussed in chapter 5.

5 A summary of the recent literature in this field can be found in Crawford and Ostrom (1995).

6 The notion of the quality of life associated with postmaterialist values is discussed more fully in chapter 2.

7 The limitations of these traditions have been identified by sociologists (Luhmann 1990a), by political scientists (Holmes 1979) and by critics of social and political theory (Hindess 1991; 1993; 1994). Some of the most persuasive suggestions for 'going beyond' these traditions and developing creative and constructive systems of thought can be found in De Bono (1994; 1991).

8 I am grateful to Peter Corrigan for drawing my attention to this view of adversarialism as a mechanism that promotes the 'embodiment' of particular values. He goes on to suggest that pragmatism may involve 'the capacity to "dis-embody" concepts or ideas from the self or the party or the group'. This is compatible with the argument at the end of this chapter that principles and pragmatism are not dissimilar in so far as they are concerned about the consequences of human action.

9 Chapter 5 links these arguments to an account of the political system that focuses on the problem of coordination between politics and economics, politics and concern about the environment and so on. I will also explore the paradox whereby, despite the general use of adversarial approaches and the problems of coordination, a pragmatic approach to politics is practised widely.

10 For evidence of focus on quality of life issues see the survey conducted by the ANOP (1991: 37).

11 In the specific sense, a concept represents 'a way of doing something which achieves a purpose and provides values' (De Bono 1992a: 195).

12 There is some disagreement over whether or not March and Olsen provide a strict or consistent enough definition of institutions. Sjöblom cautions against the 'wide' definition of institutions because it then becomes 'more difficult to say anything precise about the

ways in which they matter' (1993: 401). Sjöblom also provides a detailed list of the kinds of issues that need to be taken into account in trying to construct a definition.

13 Another account which argues for the centrality of political institutions in addressing the issues of democracy and economic success is the one by Marsh (1995).

14 Although the data used by Jänicke are drawn primarily from the Federal Republic of Germany, his conclusions are relevant to other advanced industrial societies. This work was originally published in German in 1986. The translation into English provides some recognition that the arguments are applicable to other countries.

15 'In the 1980s rightwing politicians succeeded in winning elections, but lost the battle of the budget. After a decade in which politicians such as Margaret Thatcher and Ronald Reagan have scored great electoral success, government remains big' (Rose 1989a: 12; see also De Swaan 1988: 228–9).

16 Davis et al. (1993) also refer to the 'autonomy' of the bureaucracy, the problems in achieving any central political coordination of the increasingly fragmented public sector, and the scope for 'administrative discretion'.

17 Jänicke was a parliamentary delegate for the Green Party in the Federal Republic of Germany in the 1980s. His concern about the impotence of politics is based both on these experiences and on his academic expertise in political economy.

18 They prefer to regard sociology as 'the analysis of the social, which can be treated at any level (for example, dyadic interaction, social groups, large organizations or whole societies)' (Abercrombie et al. 1988: 231).

19 Instead, Mann investigates the complex networks of power that emerge in social relationships. Though this represents an improvement on the restrictive metaphors of functionalist sociology (as articulated by Parsons and by aspects of Marxist accounts), Mann still uses the term *society* to address the problem of studying societies in isolation from one another.

20 He argues that we need first of all to find a theoretical basis for comparing different countries and 'then to find differences in real life situations' like the impact of hunger and violence (Luhmann in Sciulli 1994: 66). Interestingly, Mann (1986), who has made an important contribution by drawing us away from narrow understandings of society (based on the boundaries of a nation-state), retains the traditional meaning of society as a 'social community' or an 'association of persons' when analysing the sources of power.

21 This is not dissimilar to the recognition by Mann (1986) that each source of power, be it religious, economic or military, can exist *independently of other sources.*

22 The term *environment* is here used to refer to the distinction between a system and its environment posited by Luhmann, and not to the issue of environmental protection.

23 Luhmann makes three points. The Marxist approach simply measures the achievements of the modern state against an ideal or utopia. The issue of ownership of the means of production is seen as the central one. The Marxist critique may be 'politically' radical, but in conceptual and theoretical terms is somewhat antiquated (1990a: 28–9).

24 This theme arises in the work of writers like Schmitt (1985), Foucault (1977) and Habermas (1981a) (see Van Krieken 1991: 2–3).

25 Similar arguments could be mounted about the systems theory developed by Talcott Parsons – for instance, that it could only emerge and have some plausibility in the context of the United States in the mid-twentieth century. Again, I shall maintain that the adaptation of these ideas by Luhmann as well as a selective approach to his ideas yields concepts which are useful to understanding and contributing to changes in a variety of social, historical and geographical settings.

26 As before, the term *environmental* is used to refer to Luhmann's distinction between a system and its environment.

27 Although Luhmann has something in common with Talcott Parsons, the latter had no interest in self-referential systems: 'Parsons, after all, found no place for himself in any of the more tiny boxes of his system. Because it excludes its author (and its reader?), his theory can claim to be general but not universal' (Luhmann in Sciulli 1994: 39). Luhmann goes far beyond Parsons by trying to understand how systems reproduce themselves through their own internal dynamics. Luhmann also addresses some of the shortcomings of

Parsons's approach through a more persuasive account of how systems reproduce themselves: 'For example in Parsons's functional differentiation of society into four subsystems and each of these into four sub-subsystems, etc., the substantive analytical categorizing always is theoretically motivated by an observer who remains external to the system being analysed. Parsons's functionalism is unable to appreciate how a system could constitute itself through its own autopoietic processes' (Krippendorff 1991: 139).

28 The issue of communication arises in Habermas, from his earliest work on communication in the bourgeois public sphere (1989, first published 1962) to his theory of communicative action (1981a). There are also significant differences between the two writers. Habermas, in a critique of Luhmann, assumes that communicative rationality is possible within social sub-systems. Luhmann, on the other hand, rejects Habermas's notion of communicative rationality as inadequate for complex social systems (see Miller 1994: 110–11).

29 Though he uses the term *legitimation crisis*, Luhmann criticises writers like Jänicke who use this term without having developed a broader theory of society. He suggests that these theorists 'complain before understanding' and that 'if one wanted to be consistent', one would have to acknowledge similar shortcomings in the fields of science, education, economy, religion, law and family life: 'failure everywhere because no system can control the interdependencies of its environment adequately (law of requisite variety)' (Luhmann 1990a: 58).

30 Luhmann draws an interesting analogy to the brain: 'Just as in the brain, there are no direct stimulus/response relations for such systems. Instead, everything that the system is able to do is determined with regard to what takes place within it' (Luhmann 1990a: 40).

31 Luhmann describes the legal system as 'normatively closed' but 'cognitively open'. The two conditions are seen as reciprocal: 'The openness of a system bases itself upon self-referential closure, and closed "autopoietic" reproduction refers to the environment. To paraphrase the famous definition of cybernetics by Ashby: the legal system is open to cognitive information but closed to normative control' (Luhmann 1990b: 229).

32 Luhmann refers to Bachrach and Baratz (1970) and their notion of 'non-decisions' in politics and to Scharpf (1971) and his notion of 'negative co-ordination' in administration. His own formulation of the problem reads: 'If the new paradox is that solutions create problems because problems create solutions; time becomes the critical variable, which can also mean that "saving" (i.e. gaining) time and avoiding decisions for the time being becomes the core virtue of politics. And consequently, it is not he who has the competence and power of final decisions who is sovereign, but he who has the possibility of avoiding situations in which he has no further alternative than to make a certain decision and to use his power' (Luhmann 1990b: 171).

33 Apart from public opinion, Luhmann regards social movements as a relevant (though inadequate) mechanism for the self-observation of society (see the discussion in the chapter on social movements).

34 This is not to say that members of social movements do not question tendencies towards their institutionalisation for fear of losing their edge and becoming just another political party.

35 The apparent lack of coordination between function systems may also have less to do with modern society's differentiation into different sub-systems than with the fear by individual social actors of having to engage in 'a painful learning process' which would force them to justify more adequately their own position, or with reference to politicians, their legitimacy: 'Hence, the impression of an "organized irresponsibilty" that one gets every day by reading the newspaper is not a reflex of modern society's differentiation into different functional systems; it rather seems to be a consequence of the fact that modern society's democratic institutions for public decision-making cannot yet keep pace with society's evolutionary process of differentiation and its underlying logic of dissent' (Miller 1994: 120).

36 However, Luhmann argues that new social movements have little to offer in the way of a theory of society. Modern society, he suggests, may be 'too dependent for self-description on the entirely inadequate basis of social movements' (Luhmann 1989: 126). It would be more accurate to state that many movements do not have an *explicit* theory of society. Most,

if not all, movements are bound to have an implicit theory of society, even if it appears to be contradictory or confused.

37 However, he is less preoccupied than Luhmann with the contribution by social movements to an adequate theory of society.

38 The process of self-description through social movements is described in the following manner by Luhmann: 'Fortunately, there is an essential connection between modern society's (semantic) deficits of self-description and the (structural) system-form "social movement". As a position for the description of society within society the movement places itself in difference to society. It seeks to affect society from within society as if it occurred from outside. This paradox creates the instability of the observation position and the dynamics of the social movement makes allowances for this without realizing it. This may very well lead to changes, to semantic or structural results that in one way or another come to terms with the facts' (Luhmann 1989: 126).

39 Rather than recount in detail the critiques of these accounts, I want to concentrate on their relevance to arguments about innovation and institutional change. For more detailed consideration of these approaches see Papadakis (1988; 1993) and Scott (1990).

40 It is possible of course to find illustrations to support both accounts (see Papadakis 1984; 1988; and 1993).

41 Luhmann not only describes the fundamentalist approach as morally self-righteous but as concealing a profound problem faced by many 'revolutionary' movements as 'critical' observers of society: 'The problem seems to be that one has to recognize the dominant social structure – whether seen as "capitalism" or "functional differentiation" – to assume a position against it. Today this is not as easy as in the nineteenth century because the hope for a historical resolution of the difference, i.e., the hope for revolution, no longer obtains. A functional equivalent for the theoretical construct "dialectics/revolution" is not in sight and therefore it is not clear what function a critical self-observation of society within society could fulfill' (Luhmann 1989: 126).

42 This idea and the following arguments are based on the critique of Western thinking by De Bono (1991).

43 De Bono suggests that one of the greatest threats to the development of new ideas is the phrase 'the same as . . .': 'If we go to a sufficiently general level, many ideas can be said to be the same as other ideas. After all, both a horse and an airplane are just ways of getting from point A to point B. Should we have dismissed the concept of an airplane because we had the horse? The answer is that we probably would have done so. In fact, the British admiralty dismissed the idea of the wireless telegraph because they already had a way of signalling with flags' (De Bono 1992a: 101–2).

44 There is nothing essentially right or wrong about this step-wise process, since we need to incorporate new ideas into our existing value system: 'We would have no way of telling whether the idea was truly crazy or simply unrecognizable in our present state (patterns) of knowledge. So we can only recognize ideas that have a logical link-back. It therefore follows that all valuable creative ideas must be logical in hindsight. To put it more simply: the word "valuable" automatically means logical in hindsight' (De Bono 1992b: 15).

45 Much of the information in this and the next two sections is drawn primarily from Papadakis (1993).

46 The settlement by Aboriginals also reminds us of the ambivalent character of the relationship between humans and nature. Contrary to what is often assumed, the relationship was far from straightforward (see Papadakis 1993: 47–9).

47 Legislation was later introduced for the broader protection of both these and many more animals (Native Animals Protection Act, 1903; Birds and Animals Protection Act, 1918). At the state level, bird species like black swans, wild duck and plovers were protected during a closed season from 1860 onwards in Tasmania, and several other Acts extended this protection to include more bird species in 1868 and brush and forest kangaroos in 1874.

48 The main differences between the early campaigns and successes and the influence of environmentalism today lie in the number of people who have been mobilised and the influence of environmental concerns on the political agenda as whole.

49 This is not to suggest that established political organisations acted with undue haste!

50 Although the origins of many of these movements can be traced back even further, I am focusing on the period after the Second World War. In Germany, for instance, the rise of environmentalist citizens' initiatives and their demands for involvement in policy decision-making in the 1970s was facilitated by the student and anti-authoritarian movements of the 1960s (Papadakis 1984: 8–13). Similar connections were made in the United States and Britain: 'Environmentalism in the United States finally matured when it intersected with the heterogeneous social movements of the day. Reaching its crest at the end of a decade of social activism, the environmental revolution, argues Fox [1981], borrowed from all the major movements, the primary link being chronological, in that activists turned to the environment at the end of the 1960s as the civil rights and antiwar movements lost momentum. In both Britain and the United States, many of the young supporters of the environmental movement had been introduced to activism through the experiences of other protest campaigns' (McCormick 1989: 64).

51 The focus by environmentalists on catastrophes had earned them the title 'doomsday brigade'.

52 As I shall show later, the trust in scientists, technologists and expert communities arises in many other areas of concern. The more unusual phenomenon is the trust in an interest group. In this case the interest group (namely, the environmental movement) is regarded differently to other more 'selfish' interest groups.

53 Greenpeace, like many successful enterprises, was able to maintain interest in its activities by diversifying and focusing on numerous other issues. Between 1981 and 1991 Greenpeace increased its world-wide revenue, which was entirely from non-government sources, from $1.2 million to $100 million.

54 Societies may, for instance, possess the technological know-how but be unable to use it. As De Bono points out, the ancient Egyptians, Greeks and Romans had all the required technology to measure time (including water clocks and hour glasses) but lacked the concept for doing this in an effective manner. Their efforts to divide the day and night into two separate parts of twelve hours each were hampered by the fact that in the Mediterranean the length of the day and the night varied throughout the year: 'Trying to divide varying quantities into equal amounts is not easy. It was only in the thirteenth century that Arabian mathematician Abu L'Hassan came up with the idea of measuring a day from the sun's peak on one day to its peak (midday) on the next day, and then dividing this into twenty-four hours. It was not until 1863 that the Japanese realised the value of this new concept. Concepts are extremely important, but very difficult to generate. In hindsight, of course, almost all successful concepts seem easy and obvious' (De Bono 1992a: 69–70).

55 The following account is based on Nicholson (1987: 44–6) and McCormick (1989: 57–8).

56 Rose draws on the work by Hobsbawm and Ranger (1983) on this topic.

57 Throughout this chapter I will refer to 'the National Party' even though it has changed its name on several occasions. The party was originally called the Country Party of Australia (1921 to May 1975) and the National Country Party of Australia (May 1975 to October 1982). Since then, it has been called the National Party of Australia.

58 The copy of the speech analysed here is the booklet issued by the party after the 20 November 1972 policy speech. As with most policy addresses, the actual speech did not cover all the points outlined in more detail in the booklet.

59 The following account is drawn largely from Papadakis (1994).

60 All the references in this chapter relate to the policy documents listed in the References under Australian Democrats.

61 These five points are made by Page et al., (1987: 24).

62 'The causal status of this finding, however, is uncertain. Commentary may be an indicator of broader influences, such as media bias in the selection and presentation of other news, of consensus among the U.S. media or elites generally, or of a perceived public consensus' (Page et al. 1987: 39).

63 It could be argued that 'objectivity' may not be the point here, that the actual concern by Iyengar and others is about the removal of the context in which events take place, and that

the real issue may be the disappearance of complexity rather than objectivity. It could therefore be argued that the enforced simplicity of media presentations weakens their validity or helpfulness as an account of what is actually going on. The lack of other relevant information may mean that 'the facts' are presented in a misleading manner. However, I would suggest that in most situations it is difficult for the media to present us with all the facts or, at the very least, the facts are likely to be presented from a point of view. I am grateful to Peter Corrigan for raising this issue.

64 'The difficulty is that . . . message intensity involves more than just the number and salience of stories that are carried in the media. It also involves characteristics of a mass audience that does or does not find a story interesting. In the long run, it will be desirable to distinguish sharply the separate contributions of media attention and mass receptivity to the penetrating power of a given message, which is how I defined message intensity. Progress on this problem will involve more than better story-counting techniques. It will likely involve the union of a more refined theory of the "message receiver" with a closely allied theory of media content analysis' (Zaller 1992: 294–5).

65 The exceptionally high figure for 1977 is largely accounted for by a series of stories featuring all the major national parks in Australia.

66 The coding of these stories was carried out by a research assistant, who was asked to keep a detailed record of all comments that could be construed as pro-development and pro-environment. She then counted up the number of lines dedicated to each direction and then made a judgement about the direction of the story. If there was any doubt about the direction of the story, it was coded as neutral. The author carried out independent and similar analyses on a sample of the stories to ensure consistency and to provide a further judgement on the stories. In all cases he reached the same conclusion as the research assistant.

67 This is not meant to imply that *The Bulletin* or, indeed, any other sector of the mass media paid any less attention to the economy, to economic growth and to development over this period. As with government departments that become the spokespersons for particular points of view (the Ministry of Defence for the arms industry and so on), journalists covering particular fields are likely to report on the opinions of particular lobby groups or expert communities. The key aspect of these data is how they demonstrate that the mass media was making a growing and significant contribution to influencing public opinion and political debate on environmental issues – issues which until the 1970s barely rated a mention.

68 In the 1990s, the government is still struggling with the problem of recovering waste (see Industry Commission 1991).

69 See also chapter 3 and figure 3.1 in that chapter.

70 Some of the connections between classical thinkers and contemporary ideas are explored by Hindess (1991; 1993); Dunn (1992) and Held (1987).

71 The theme of the social character and the manipulation or framing of public opinion (by elites and the mass media) is also taken up by Ginsberg (1986), Edelman (1988), Iyengar (1991), Zaller (1992) and Pratkanis and Aronson (1991).

72 See also the conclusion by Samuel Beer on how public opinion, can, in certain situations, appear to be the product of ignorance, confusion and manipulation or, alternatively, to be 'creative, consecutive and democratic' (Beer 1974: 178).

73 Luhmann illustrates the dangers of such entanglement between politics and morality by referring to the campaign by Senator Joe McCarthy in the United States in the 1950s: 'As soon as he accused the Democratic Party of communist sympathies and undercurrents his career was over. For in a democracy one cannot treat one's opponent as if he or she were not capable (worthy) of being elected. But this is precisely what one does when one makes the political scheme coincide with the moral one' (Luhmann 1990a: 238).

74 Many environmental groups have also been strongly in favour of federal intervention and some leading figures have argued that this is one of the key issues in trying to introduce effective reforms of environmental policy (see Toyne 1994).

75 These polls were conducted by telephone.

76 Respondents were asked if they had seen, heard or read anything about ecologically sustainable development and, if so, what they understood it to mean. Respondents defined ESD as development without harming the environment, a balance between development and the environment, preservation and regeneration of resources, saving the environment, and preserving forests and reafforestation.

77 As numerous studies have shown, confronted by an ethical issue of this sort (rather than a precise measure of their readiness to pay for the implementation of particular policies) people are likely to adopt a benign attitude which reflects their political beliefs and preferences (see Goodin and Roberts 1975; Brennan 1989). Symbolic values and ethical concerns often overshadow egoistic interests in shaping opinions about collective decision-making (Lowery and Sigelman 1981; Citrin 1979).

78 The decline in effort to buy environmentally friendly products may be linked to two issues: first, the problem of cost; second, and perhaps more importantly, controversies over the labelling of such products and the need for more consistent standards and regulations.

79 This argument is supported by anecdotal evidence. A feature article in *The Bulletin* (12 September 1995: 14–17) on 'Dirty Politics' suggested that voters were cynical about politics (for some of the findings from this report see chapter 17 in this book). However, a 'community phone-in' organised by the Australian Democrats after the publication of this poll elicited a strong response among voters, who, far from being resigned about 'dirty politics', appealed to politicians to take action to ensure that there was greater honesty, integrity and accountability in the political process (*The Bulletin* 26 September 1995: 26).

80 The distinction between urgent and important but non-urgent issues is now commonly used in the literature on time management (see, for example, Covey et al. 1994).

References

Abercrombie, N., Hill, S. and Turner, B. 1988. *The Penguin Dictionary of Sociology*. London: Penguin Books (2nd edition).

Achen, C. H. 1975. 'Mass Political Attitudes and the Survey Response', *American Political Science Review*, 69, 1218–31.

AES: see McAllister et al. 1990; Jones et al. 1993.

Aitkin, D. 1973. 'The Australian Country Party' in H. Mayer and H. Nelson (eds), *Australian Politics*. Melbourne: Cheshire, pp. 415–26.

ANOP Research Services. 1991. *The Environment and the ESD Process: An Attitude Research Analysis*. Vol. 1, Sydney: ANOP.

ANOP Research Services. 1993. *Community Attitudes to Environmental Issues*. Prepared for the Department of the Environment, Sport and Territories.

Asch, S. E. 1951. 'Effects of Group Pressure upon the Modification and Distortion of Judgements' in H. Guetzkow (ed.), *Groups, Leadership and Men*. Pittsburgh: Carnegie.

Australian Democrats. 1977a. *Policy Speech*. Don Chipp, 23 November 1977.

Australian Democrats. 1977b. *Principles and Provisional Policies*. 1977 Federal Election.

Australian Democrats. 1979. *Policy Papers*. Part 2 (March).

Australian Democrats. 1983. *Policy Speech*. Don Chipp, 1983 Federal Election.

Australian Democrats. 1984. *Uranium*. Official Policy (October).

Australian Democrats. 1986. *Antarctica* (August) (as amended July 1990).

Australian Democrats. 1987. *Election Platform. We've made 252 firm decisions to give you a peaceful prosperous future, You can depend on us.*

Australian Democrats. 1988a. *Sustainability, Conservation and Development* (January).

Australian Democrats. 1988b. *Environmental Proposals* (January).

Australian Democrats. 1988c. *Fishing Resources*.

Australian Democrats. 1988d. *Water – Rivers, Wetlands and Catchments* (January).

Australian Democrats. 1988e. *The Coastal Zone* (January).

Australian Democrats. 1988f. *Soil Conservation* (January).

Australian Democrats. 1988g. *Forest Conservation and Mangement* (January).

Australian Democrats. 1988h. *Wildlife* (January).

Australian Democrats. 1988i. *Environmenal Education and Participation* (January) (as amended June 1989).

Australian Democrats. 1989. *Pollution, Toxic Wastes and Recycling* (October).

Australian Democrats. 1990. *Election Platform Statement for the 90s. Give A Damn-Vote Democrat.*

Australian Democrats. 1991. *Genetic Engineering and Animal and Plant Patenting* (March).

Australian Democrats. 1993a. *Forests. 1993 Federal Election Action Plan.*

Australian Democrats. 1993b. *Wildlife Protection. 1993 Federal Election Action Plan.*

Australian Democrats. 1993c. *Protection of Animals. 1993 Federal Election Action Plan.*

Australian Democrats. 1993d. *Energy and Greenhouse. 1993 Federal Election Action Plan.*

Australian Election Survey: *see* McAllister et al. 1990; Jones et al. 1993.

Australian Labor Party, 1945–94. Party Platforms.

Australian Labor Party, 1946–93. Policy Speeches.

Bachrach, P. and Baratz, M. S. 1962. 'The Two Faces of Power', *American Political Science Review*, 56, 947–52.

Bachrach, P. and Baratz, M. S. 1963. 'Decisions and Nondecisions: An Analytical Framework', *American Political Science Review*, 57, 632–42.

Bachrach, P. and Baratz, M. S. 1970. *Power and Poverty: Theory and Practice.* New York: Oxford University Press.

Banks, J. A. 1972. *The Sociology of Social Movements.* London: Macmillan.

Barwick, G. 1974. 'Environmental Conservation. A Prerequisite for Sustained Productivity' in R. Dempsey (ed.), *The Politics of Finding Out: Environmental Problems in Australia.* Melbourne: Cheshire.

Bean, C. and Papadakis, E. 1994. 'Polarized Priorities or Flexible Alternatives?', *International Journal of Public Opinion Research*, 6, 264–88.

Bean, C. and Papadakis, E. 1995. 'Minor Parties and Independents: Electoral Bases and Future Prospects' in I. Marsh and J. Uhr (eds), *Party Systems, Representation and Policy Making: Australian Trends in Comparative Perspective. Australian Journal of Political Science*, special issue 30, 111–26.

Beer, S. 1974. 'Two Models of Public Opinion: Bacon's "New Logic" and Diotima's "Tale of Love"', *Political Theory*, 2, 163–80.

Beilharz, P. 1994. *Transforming Labor: Labor Tradition and the Labor Decade in Australia.* Melbourne: Cambridge University Press.

Bennett, L. 1990. 'Toward a Theory of Press-State Relations in the U.S.', *Journal of Communication*, 40, 103–25.

Bernstein, R. 1983. *Beyond Objectivism and Relativism: Science, Hermeneutics and Practice.* Oxford: Basil Blackwell.

Bottomore, T. 1994. 'Elite Theory' in W. Outhwaite and T. Bottomore (eds), *The Blackwell Dictionary of Twentieth Century Social Thought.* Oxford: Basil Blackwell, pp. 190–2.

Brand, K. W. 1982. *Neue Soziale Bewegungen: Entstehung, Funktion und Perspektive neuer Protestpotentiale.* Opladen: Westdeutscher Verlag.

Brand, K. W., Büser, D. and Rucht, D. 1986. *Aufbruch in eine neue Gesellschaft: Neue soziale Bewegungen in der Bundesrepublik Deutschland.* Campus: Frankfurt and New York.

Brennan, G. 1989. 'Politics *with* Romance: Towards a Theory of Democratic Socialism' in P. Pettit and A. Hamlin (eds), *The Good Polity.* Oxford: Basil Blackwell, pp. 49–66.

Brennan, G. and Buchanan, J. M. 1985. *The Reason of Rules: Constitutional Political Economy.* New York: Cambridge University Press.

Breyer, S. 1982. *Regulation and its Reform.* Cambridge, Mass.: Harvard University Press.

Bride, T. F. (ed.) 1898. *Letters from Victorian Pioneers.* Melbourne: Government Printer.

Brittan, S. 1975. 'The Economic Contradictions of Democracy', *British Journal of Political Science*, 5, 129–59.

Buchholz, R. A., Marcus, A. A. and Post, J. E. 1992. *Managing Environmental Issues: A Casebook.* Englewood Cliffs, N.J.: Prentice-Hall.

Bulletin, The, 1960–94.

Burgmann, V. 1993. *Power and Protest.* Sydney: Allen and Unwin.

Burkhart, J. A. and Kendrick, F. J. (eds) 1971. *The New Politics: Mood or Movement?* Englewood Cliffs, N.J.: Prentice-Hall.

Buttel, F. 1992. 'Environmentalization: Origins, Processes, and Implications for Rural Social Change', *Rural Sociology*, 57, 1–27.

Campbell, A., Converse, P., Miller, W. and Stokes, D. 1960. *The American Voter.* New York: Wiley and Sons.

Carson, R. 1962. *Silent Spring.* Boston: Houghton Mifflin.

Citrin, J. 1979. 'Do People Want Something for Nothing: Public Opinion on Taxes and Government Spending', *National Tax Journal*, Supplement, 32, 13–29.

Cohen, B. 1963. *The Press and Foreign Policy.* Princeton, N.J.: Princeton University Press.

Cohen, J. L. 1985. 'Strategy or Identity: New Theoretical Paradigms and Contemporary Social Movements', *Social Research,* 52, 663–716.

Cole, H. S. D., Freeman, C., Hohoda, M. and Pavitt, K. L. R. 1973. *Thinking About the Future: A Critique of the Limits to Growth.* London: Chatto and Windus.

Commoner, B. 1971. *The Closing Circle: Nature, Man and Technology.* New York: Knopf.

Commonwealth of Australia. 1989. *Our Country. Our Future.* Canberra: Australian Government Publishing Service.

Converse, P. 1964. 'The Nature of Belief Systems in Mass Publics' in D. E. Apter (ed.), *Ideology and Discontent.* New York: Free Press, pp. 219–27.

Cook, F. L., et al. 1983. 'Media and Agenda Setting: Effects on the Public, Interest Group Leaders, Policy Makers, and Policy', *Public Opinion Quarterly,* 47, 16–35.

Costar, B. and Woodward, D. (eds) 1985. *Country to National: Australian Rural Politics and Beyond.* Sydney: Allen and Unwin.

Covey, S., Merrill, A. R. and Merrill, R. R. 1994. *First Things First.* New York: Simon and Schuster.

Crawford, S. E. and Ostrom, E. 1995. 'A Grammar of Institutions', *American Political Science Review,* 89, 582–600.

Crick, B. 1993. *In Defence of Politics.* London: Penguin Books (4th edition).

Crouch, C. 1983. 'New Thinking on Pluralism', *Political Quarterly,* 54, 363–74.

Crozier, M. J., Huntington, S. P. and Watanuki, J. 1975. *The Crisis of Democracy.* New York: Trilateral Commission.

Curtice, J. 1989. 'The 1989 European Election: Protest or Green Tide?', *Electoral Studies,* 8, 217–30.

Dalton, R. 1988. *Citizen Politics in Western Democracies.* New Jersey: Chatham House.

Dalton, R., Flanagan, S. and Beck, P. (eds) 1984. *Electoral Change in Advanced Industrial Democracies,* Princeton, N.J.: Princeton University Press.

Dalton, R. and Kuechler, M. (eds) 1990. *Challenging the Political Order: New Social Movements in Western Democracies.* Cambridge: Polity Press.

Davis, G., Wanna, J., Warhurst, J. and Weller, P. 1993. *Public Policy in Australia.* Sydney: Allen and Unwin (2nd edition).

De Bono, E. 1991. *I Am Right. You Are Wrong.* London: Penguin Books.

De Bono, E. 1992a. *Sur-Petition.* London: Fontana.

De Bono, E. 1992b. *Serious Creativity.* London: Fontana.

De Bono, E. 1993. *Water Logic.* London: Viking.

De Bono, E. 1994. *Parallel Thinking.* London: Viking.

De Swaan, A. 1988. *In Care of the State.* Cambridge: Polity Press.

Downs, A. 1972. 'Up and Down with Ecology – the "Issue-Attention Cycle"', *Public Interest,* 28, 38–50.

Dunlap, R. E. 1989. 'Public Opinion and Environmental Policy', in J. P. Lester (ed.), *Environmental Politics and Policy.* Durham, N.C.: Duke University Press.

Dunlap, R. E. and Scarce, R. 1991. 'The Polls – Poll Trends. Environmental Problems and Protection', *Public Opinion Quarterly,* 55, 651–72.

Dunn, J. (ed.) 1992. *Democracy: The Unfinished Journey. 508 BC to AD 1993.* Oxford: Oxford University Press.

Ecologist, The. 1972. *Blueprint for Survival.* Penguin: Harmondsworth.

Edelman, M. 1988. *Constructing the Political Spectacle.* Chicago: University of Chicago Press.

Ehrlich, P. R. 1968. *The Population Bomb.* New York: Ballantine Books.

Elkington, J. and Burke, T. 1987. *The Green Capitalists.* London: Victor Gollancz.

Environment Opinion Study. 1990. *A Survey of American Voters: Attitudes toward the Environment.* Wahington D.C.: Environment Opinion Study.

Erbring, L., Goldenberg, E. N. and Miller, A. H. 1980. 'Front Page News and Real World Cues: A New Look at Agenda-Setting by the Media', *American Journal of Political Science,* 24, 16–49.

Evans, P. B., Rueschemeyer, D. and Skocpol, T. (eds) 1985. *Bringing the State Back In.* New York: Cambridge University Press.

Feld, S. L. and Grofman, B. 1988. 'Ideological Consistency as a Collective Phenomenon', *American Political Science Review*, 82, 773–88.

Foucault, M. 1977. *Discipline and Punish.* London: Allan Lane.

Fox, S. 1981. *John Muir and His Legacy: The American Conservation Movement.* Boston: Little, Brown and Co.

Fuchs, S. 1990. '*Ecological Communication.* By Niklas Luhmann' (book review), *American Journal of Sociology*, 96, 747–8.

Gans, H. 1980. *Deciding What's News.* New York: Vintage.

Giddens, A. 1987. *Social Theory and Modern Sociology.* Cambridge: Polity Press.

Ginsberg, B. 1986. *The Captive Public: How Mass Opinion Promotes State Power.* New York: Basic Books.

Goodin, R. and Roberts, K. 1975. 'The Ethical Voter', *American Political Science Review*, 69, 926–8.

Goodin, R.E. 1992. *Green Political Theory.* Cambridge: Polity Press.

Habermas, J. 1976. *Legitimation Crisis.* London: Heinemann.

Habermas, J. 1981a. *Theorie des Kommunikativen Handelns.* Vols 1 and 2, Frankfurt: Suhrkamp.

Habermas, J. 1981b. 'New Social Movements', *Telos*, 49, 33–7.

Habermas, J. 1989. *The Structural Transformation of the Public Sphere.* Cambridge: Polity Press.

Halberstram, D. 1979. *The Powers That Be.* New York: Dell.

Hall, P. 1986. *Governing the Economy: The Politics of State Intervention in Britain and France.* New York: Oxford University Press.

Hancock, I. 1995. 'The Liberal Party Organisation' in S. Prasser, J. R. Nethercote and J. Warhurst (eds), *The Menzies Era: A Reappraisal of Government, Politics and Policy.* Sydney: Hale and Iremonger, pp. 80–92.

Handler, J. 1988. 'Dependent People, the State, and the Modern/Postmodern Search for the Dialogic Community', *UCLA Law Review*, 35, 999–1113.

Hawkins, D. J., Coney, K. A. and Best, R. J. 1980. *Consumer Behaviour.* Dallas: Business Publications Inc.

Heathcote, R. L. 1972. 'The Visions of Australia, 1770–1970' in A. Rapoport (ed.), *Australia as Human Setting.* Sydney: Angus and Robertson, pp. 77–98.

Held, D. 1987. *Models of Democracy.* Cambridge: Polity Press.

Hindess, B. 1987. *Freedom, Equality and the Market.* London: Tavistock.

Hindess, B. 1991. 'Imaginary Presuppositions of Democracy', *Economy and Society*, 20, 173–95.

Hindess, B. 1993. '"The Greeks Had a Word for It": The *Polis* as a Political Metaphor', Conference of the Australian Political Studies Association, Monash University.

Hindess, B. 1994a. 'Citizenship in the Modern West' in B. Turner (ed.), *Citizenship and Social Theory.* London: Sage, pp. 19–35.

Hindess, B. 1994b. 'Interests' in W. Outhwaite and T. Bottomore (eds), *The Blackwell Dictionary of Twentieth Century Social Thought.* Oxford: Basil Blackwell, pp. 293–4.

Hoad, B. 1969. 'The Much Makers. Where Does Pollution Stop?' *The Bulletin*, 26 April, 25–9.

Hobsbawn, E. and Ranger, T. (eds) 1983. *The Invention of Tradition.* Cambridge: Cambridge University Press.

Hochschild, J. 1981. *What's Fair?* Princeton, N.J.: Princeton University Press.

Holmes, S. T. 1979. 'Aristippus in and out of Athens', *American Political Science Review*, 73, 111–28.

Imber, D., Stevenson, G. and Wilks, L. 1991. *A Contingent Valuation Survey of the Kakadu Conservation Zone.* Resource Assessment Commission, Research Paper 3, Vol. 2, Canberra: Australian Government Publishing Service.

Industry Commission. 1991. *Recycling.* Vols I and II, Report No. 6, Canberra: Australian Government Publishing Service.

Inglehart, R. 1990. *Culture Shift in Advanced Industrial Society.* Princeton, N.J.: Princeton University Press.

Israel, A. 1987. *Institutional Development: Incentive to Performance.* Baltimore: Johns Hopkins University Press.

Iyengar, S. 1991. *Is Anyone Responsible?* Chicago: Chicago University Press.

Iyengar, S., Peters, M. D. and Kinder, D. R. 1982. 'Experimental Demonstrations of the "Not-So-Minimal" Consequences of Television News Programs', *American Political Science Review*, 76, 848–58.

Jackson, R. J. 1995. 'Foreign Models and Aussie Rules: Executive–Legislative Relations in Australia', *Political Theory Newsletter*, 7, 1–18.

Jaensch, D. 1983. *The Australian Party System.* Sydney: George Allen and Unwin.

Jaensch, D. 1992. *The Politics of Australia.* Melbourne: Macmillan.

Jänicke, M. 1990. *State Failure: The Impotence of Politics in Industrial Society.* Cambridge: Polity Press.

Jänicke, M. and Weidner, H. 1995. *Successful Environmental Policy.* Berlin: edition sigma.

Jänicke, M. et al. 1989. 'Structural Change and Environmental Impact: Empirical Evidence on 31 Countries in East and West', *Intereconomics*, 24, 24–34.

Johnson, C. 1989. *The Labor Legacy: Curtin, Chifley, Whitlam and Hawke.* Sydney: Allen and Unwin.

Jones, R. et al. 1993. *Australian Election Study 1993: User's Guide for the Machine-Readable Data File.* Canberra: Social Science Data Archives, Research School of Social Sciences, Australian National University.

Jupp, J. 1982. *Party Politics: Australia, 1966–81.* Sydney: George Allen and Unwin.

Keating, M. 1993. 'Mega-departments: The Theory, Objectives and Outcomes of the 1987 Reforms' in P. Weller, J. Forster and G. Davis (eds), *Reforming the Public Service.* Melbourne: Macmillan, pp. 1–15.

Kelly, P. 1994. *The End of Certainty.* Sydney: Allen and Unwin (2nd edition).

Keys Young. 1994. *Benchmark Study on Environmental Knowledge, Attitudes, Skills and Behaviour in New South Wales.* Vols 1 and 2, prepared for the Environment Protection Authority, New South Wales.

Kirchheimer, O. 1956. 'The Transformation of the Western European Party Systems' in J. La Palombara and M. Weiner (eds), *Political Parties and Political Development.* Princeton, N.J.: Princeton University Press, pp. 177–200.

Kitschelt, H. 1986. 'Political Opportunity Structures and Political Protest: Anti-Nuclear Movement in Four Democracies', *British Journal of Political Science*, 16, 57–85.

Kornhauser, W. 1959. *The Politics of Mass Society.* Glencoe, Ill.: Free Press.

Krippendorff, K. 1991. 'Society as Self-Referential: *Ecological Communication* by Niklas Luhmann' (book review), *Journal of Communication*, 41, 136–40.

Kuhn, R. 1989. 'What a Labor Government Is', *Politics*, 24, 147–53.

Ladd, C. E. 1982. 'Cleaning the Air: Public Opinion and Public Policy on the Environment', *Public Opinion*, 5, 16–20.

Lempert, R. 1988. 'The Autonomy of Law: Two Visions Compared' in G. Teubner (ed.), *Autopoietic Law: A New Approach to Law and Society.* Berlin: De Gruyter and European University Institute.

Liberal Party, 1948–82. Party Platforms.

Liberal Party, 1946–93. Policy Speeches.

Lindblom, C. E. 1977. *Politics and Markets.* New York: Basic Books.

Lippmann, W. 1922. *Public Opinion.* New York: Macmillan.

Lothian, J. A. 1994. 'Attitudes of Australians Towards the Environment: 1975 to 1994', *Australian Journal of Environmental Management*, 1, 78–99.

Lowe, I. 1989. 'Minerals and Energy' in B. W. Head and A. Patience (eds), *From Fraser to Hawke.* Melbourne: Longman Cheshire, pp. 110–31.

Lowery, D. and Sigelman, L. 1981. 'Understanding the Tax Revolt: Eight Explanations', *American Political Science Review*, 75, 963–74.

Luhmann, N. 1975 *Macht.* Stuttgart.

Luhmann, N. 1982. *The Differentiation of Society.* New York: Columbia University Press.

Luhmann, N. 1989. *Ecological Communication.* Cambridge: Polity Press.

Luhmann, N. 1990a. *Political Theory and the Welfare State.* Berlin: De Gruyter.

Luhmann, N. 1990b. *Essays on Self-Reference.* New York: Columbia University Press.

MacKuen, M. B. 1984. 'Exposure to Information, Belief Integration, and Individual Responsiveness to Agenda Change', *American Political Science Review*, 78, 372–91.

Maddox, G. 1989. *The Hawke Government and Labor Tradition*. Melbourne: Penguin Books.

Maddox, G. and Battin, T. 1991. 'Australian Labor and the Socialist Tradition', *Australian Journal of Political Science*, 26, 181–96.

Mair, P. 1983. 'Adaptation and Control: Towards an Understanding of Party and Party System Change' in H. Daalder and P. Mair (eds), *Western European Party Systems*. London: Sage, pp. 405–29.

Mair, P. 1989. *The Changing Irish Party System: Organisation, Ideology and Electoral Competition*. London: Frances Pinter.

Mann, M. 1986. *The Sources of Social Power*. Vol. 1, Cambridge: Cambridge University Press.

March, J. G. and Olsen, J. P. 1984. 'The New Institutionalism: Organizational Factors in Political Life', *American Political Science Review*, 78, 734–49.

March, J. G. and Olsen, J. P. 1989. *Rediscovering Institutions: The Organizational Basis of Politics*. New York: Free Press.

Marsh, I. 1995. *Beyond the Two-Party System*. Melbourne: Cambridge University Press.

Martinez-Alier, J. 1990. *Ecological Economics*. Oxford: Basil Blackwell.

Mayntz, R. 1984. *Implementation politischer Programme II*. Opladen: Westdeutscher Verlag.

McAllister, I. 1991. 'Community Attitudes to the Environment, Forests and Forest Management in Australia', Resource Assessment Commission, Forest and Timber Inquiry, Consultancy Series, Number FTC91/09.

McAllister, I. 1992. *Political Behaviour*. Melbourne: Longman Cheshire.

McAllister, I. 1994. 'Dimensions of Environmentalism: Public Opinion, Political Activism and Party Support in Australia', *Environmental Politics* 3, 22–42.

McAllister, I. and Moore, R. (eds) 1991. *Party Strategy and Change: Australian Political Leaders' Policy Speeches since 1946*. Melbourne: Longman Cheshire.

McAllister, I. and Studlar, D. 1993. 'Trends in Public Opinion on the Environment in Australia', *International Journal of Public Opinion Research*, 5, 353–61.

McAllister, I. and Studlar, D. 1995. 'New Politics and Partisan Alignment', *Party Politics*, 1, 197–220.

McAllister, I. et al. 1990. *Australian Election Study 1990: User's Guide for the Machine-Readable Data File*. Canberra: Social Science Data Archives, Research School of Social Sciences, Australian National University.

McCombs, M. and Shaw, D. L. 1972. 'The Agenda-setting Functions of the Mass Media', *Public Opinion Quarterly*, 36, 176–87.

McCormick, J. 1989. *The Global Environmental Movement*. London: Belhaven Press.

McEachern, D. 1991. *Business Mates: The Power and Politics of the Hawke Era*. New York: Prentice Hall.

Mead, M. 1937. 'Public Opinion Mechanisms among Primitive Peoples', *Public Opinion Quarterly* 1, 5–16.

Meadows, D. H., Meadows, J., Randers, J. and Behrens III, W. W. 1974. *The Limits to Growth*. London: Pan Books (originally published in 1972).

Michels, R. 1962. *Political Parties: A Sociological Study of the Oligarchical Tendencies of Modern Democracy*. New York: Free Press (originally published in German in 1911).

Miller, M. 1994. 'Intersystemic Discourse and Co-ordinated Dissent: A Critique of Luhmann's Concept of Ecological Communication', *Theory, Culture and Society*, 11: 101–21.

Mills, C. W. 1956. *The Power Elite*. New York.

Mitnick, B. 1980. *The Political Economy of Regulation*. New York: Columbia University Press.

Müller-Rommel, F. 1989. 'The German Greens in the 1980s: Short-term Cyclical Protest or Indicator of Transformation?', *Political Studies*, 37, 114–22.

Myrdal, G. 1944. *An American Dilemma*. New York: Harper and Row.

National Party of Australia, 1921–91. Party Platforms.

National Party of Australia, 1946–93. Policy Speeches.

Neckel, S. and Wolf, J. 1994. 'The Fascination of Amorality: Luhmann's Theory of Morality and its Resonances among German Intellectuals', *Theory, Culture and Society*, 11, 69–99.

Nicholson, M. 1987. *The New Environmental Age.* Cambridge: Cambridge University Press.

Nie, N. and Rabjohn, J. 1979. 'Revisiting Mass Belief Systems Revisited', *American Journal of Political Science,* 23, 139–75.

Noelle-Neumann, E. 1984. *The Spiral of Silence.* Chicago: Chicago University Press.

North, D. 1990. *Institutions, Institutional Change and Economic Performance.* New York: Cambridge University Press.

North, D. C. 1990. 'Institutions and a Transaction Costs Theory of Exchange' in J. Alt and K. Shepsle (eds), *Perspectives on Positive Political Economy.* New York: Cambridge University Press.

O'Connor, J. 1973. *The Fiscal Crisis of the State.* New York: St. Martin's.

Offe, C. 1976. 'Crisis of Crisis Management: Elements of a Political Crisis Theory', *International Journal of Politics,* 6, 28–67.

Olson, M. 1983. *The Rise and Decline of Nations.* New Haven: Yale University Press.

Opinion Dynamics Corporation. 1990. *Energy and the Environment: The New Landscape of Public Opinion.* Cambridge, Mass.: Cambridge Energy Research Associates.

Ostrom, E. 1990. *Governing the Commons: The Evolution of Institutions for Collective Action.* New York: Cambridge University Press.

Page, B., Shapiro, R. and Dempsey, G. 1987. 'What Moves Public Opinion?' *American Political Science Review,* 81, 23–43.

Page, B. I. and Shapiro, R. Y. 1983. 'Effects of Public Opinion on Policy', *American Political Science Review,* 77, 175–90.

Page, B. I. and Shapiro, R. Y. 1992. *The Rational Public: Fifty Years of Trends in Americans' Policy Preferences.* Chicago: University of Chicago Press.

Pakulski, J. 1991. *Social Movements: The Politics of Moral Protest.* Melbourne: Cheshire.

Papadakis, E. 1984. *The Green Movement in West Germany,* London: Croom Helm.

Papadakis, E. 1988. 'Social Movements, Self-limiting Radicalism and the Green Party in West Germany', *Sociology,* 22, 433–54.

Papadakis, E. 1989. 'Green Issues and Other Parties: *Themenklau* or New Flexibility?' in E. Kolinsky (ed.), *Policy Making in the West German Green Party.* Berg Publishers, pp. 61–85.

Papadakis, E. 1990. 'Minor Parties, the Environment and the New Politics' in C. Bean, I. McAllister and J. Warhurst (eds), *The Greening of Australian Politics.* Melbourne: Longman Cheshire, pp. 33–53.

Papadakis, E. 1992. 'Public Opinion, Public Policy and the Welfare State', *Political Studies,* 40, 21–37.

Papadakis, E. 1993. *Politics and the Environment: The Australian Experience.* Sydney: Allen and Unwin.

Papadakis, E. 1994. 'Development and the Environment' in C. Bean (ed.), *The 1993 Federal Election. Australian Journal of Political Science,* special issue 29, 66–80.

Papadakis, E. 1995. 'Comments on R. J. Jackson "Foreign Models and Aussie Rules: Executive–Legislative Relations in Australia"', *Political Theory Newsletter,* 7, 28–33.

Papadakis, E. and Bean, C. 1995. 'Minor Parties and Independents: The Electoral System' in I. Marsh and J. Uhr (eds) *Party Systems, Representation and Policy Making: Australian Trends in Comparative Perspective. Australian Journal of Political Science,* special issue 30, 97–110.

Papadakis, E. and Taylor-Gooby, P. 1987. *The Private Provision of Public Welfare.* Brighton: Wheatsheaf.

Parker, P. 1991. 'The Advance of the Green Guards', *New Scientist,* 3 August: 44.

Parkin, F. 1968. *Middle Class Radicalism.* New York: Praeger.

Poguntke, T. 1989. 'The "New Politics Dimension" in European Green Parties' in F. Müller-Rommel (ed.), *New Politics in Western Europe: The Rise and Success of Green Parties and Alternative Lists.* Boulder: Westview Press, pp. 175–94.

Popkin, S. L. 1991. *The Reasoning Voter: Communication and Persuasion in Presidential Campaigns.* Chicago: University of Chicago Press.

Porter, G. and Brown, J. W. 1991. *Global Environmental Politics.* Boulder: Westview Press.

Powell, J. M. 1976. *Environmental Management in Australia, 1788–1914.* Melbourne: Oxford University Press.

Pratkanis, A. R. and Aronson, E. 1991. *Age of Propaganda: The Everyday Use and Abuse of Persuasion.* New York: W. H. Freeman and Company.

Pusey, M. 1991. *Economic Rationalism in Canberra: A Nation-Building State Changes Its Mind.* Cambridge: Cambridge University Press.

Putnam, R.D. 1993. *Making Democracy Work: Civic Traditions in Modern Italy.* Princeton, N.J.: Princeton University Press.

Rawson, D. 1991. 'How Labor Governs: Labor in Vain?' in B. Galligan and G. Singleton (eds), *Business and Government under Labour.* Melbourne: Longman Cheshire, pp. 189–200.

Redclift, M. 1987. *Sustainable Development.* London: Methuen.

Renon, K. D. 1994. 'Social Movement' in W. Outhwaite and T. Bottomore (eds), *The Blackwell Dictionary of Twentieth Century Social Thought.* Oxford: Basil Blackwell, pp. 597–600.

Richardson, D. and Rootes, C. (eds) 1995. *The Green Challenge: The Development of Green Parties in Europe.* London: Routledge.

Robertson, T. S. 1967. 'The Process of Innovation and the Diffusion of Innovation', *Journal of Marketing,* 14–19 (January).

Rohrschneider, R. 1988. 'Citizens' Attitudes Towards Environmental Issues: Selfish or Selfless?', *Comparative Political Studies,* 21, 347–67.

Rose, R. (ed.) 1980. *Challenge to Governance.* Beverly Hills: Sage.

Rose, R. 1989a. *Ordinary People in Public Policy.* London: Sage.

Rose, R. 1989b. *Politics in England: Change and Persistence.* Glenview, Ill.: Scott, Foresman (5th edition) .

Rosengren, K. 1981. 'Mass Media and Social Change: Some Current Approaches' in E. Katz and T. Szecsko (eds), *Mass Media and Social Change.* Beverly Hills: Sage, pp. 247–63.

Ross, Edward, A. [1901] 1969. *Social Control: A Survey of the Foundations of Order.* Cleveland and London: The Press of Case Western Reserve University.

Rubin, C. T. 1994. *The Green Crusade: Rethinking the Roots of Environmentalism.* New York: Free Press.

Rush, M. 1992. *Politics and Society: An Introduction to Political Sociology.* London: Harvester Wheatsheaf.

Sartori, G. 1973. 'What is Politics?', *Political Theory,* 1, 5–26.

Sartori, G. 1976. *Parties and Party Systems.* Cambridge: Cambridge University Press.

Scharpf, F. 1971. 'Planung als politischer Prozeβ', *Die Verwaltung,* 4, 1–30.

Schattschneider, E. E. 1960. *The Semi-Sovereign People: A Realist's View of Democracy in America.* New York: Holt Rinehart and Winston.

Scheuch, E. K. and Scheuch, U. 1992. *Cliquen, Klüngel und Karrieren.* Hamburg: Rowohlt.

Schmidheiny, S. 1992. *Changing Course: A Global Business Perspective on Development and the Environment.* Cambridge, Mass.: MIT Press.

Schmitt, C. 1985. *The Crisis of Parliamentary Democracy.* Cambridge, Mass.: MIT Press.

Schumacher, E. F. 1973. *Small is Beautiful: Economics as If People Mattered.* London: Blond and Briggs.

Schumpeter, J. A. [1942] 1994. *Capitalism, Socialism and Democracy.* London: Routledge.

Sciulli, D. 1994. 'An Interview with Niklas Luhmann', *Theory, Culture and Society,* 11, 37–68.

Scott, A. 1990. *Ideology and the New Social Movements.* London: Unwin Hyman.

Shamshullah, A. 1990. 'The Australian Democrats' in J. Summers, D. Woodward and A. Parkin (eds), *Government, Politics and Power in Australia.* Melbourne: Longman Cheshire (4th edition),pp. 166–77.

Shepsle, K. A. 1989. 'Studying Institutions: Some Lessons from the Rational Choice Approach,' *Journal of Theoretical Politics,* 1, 131–47.

Sigal, L. 1973. *Reporters and Officials.* Lexington, Mass.: D. C. Health.

Simonis, U. E. 1989. 'Ecological Modernization of Industrial Society: Three Strategic Elements', *International Social Science Journal,* 121, 347–61.

Sjöblom, G. 1993. 'Some Critical Remarks on March and Olsen's *Rediscovering Institutions*', *Journal of Theoretical Politics,* 5, 397–407.

Sklair, L. 1994a. 'Global Sociology and Environmental Change' in M. Redclift and T. Benton (eds), *Social Theory and the Environment.* London: Routledge.

Sklair, L. 1994b. 'Global System, Local Problems: Environmental Impacts of Transnational Corporations along Mexico's Northern Border', in H. Mair and W. Williams (eds), *Environment and Housing in Third World Cities*. Chichester: Wiley, pp. 85–105.

Smelser, N. 1962. *Theory of Collective Behaviour*. London: Routledge and Kegan Paul.

Smith, Z. A. 1992. *The Environmental Policy Paradox*. Englewood Cliffs, N.J.: Prentice-Hall.

Spector, M. and Kitsuse, J. I. 1987. *Constructing Social Problems*. New York: Aldine de Gruyter.

Stretton, H. 1992. 'Barry Hindess, *Choice, Rationality and Social Theory*, and *Reactions to the Right*', (book review), *Australian and New Zealand Journal of Sociology*, 28, 122–5.

Strom, A. 1979. 'Some Events in Nature Conservation Over the Last Forty Years' in W. Goldstein (ed.), *Australia's 100 Years of National Parks*. Sydney: National Parks and Wildlife Service, pp. 65–73.

Sylow, K. 1994. 'The Tasmanian Conservation Movement and the Press', *Australian and New Zealand Journal of Sociology*, 30: 203–10.

Teubner, G. 1983. 'Substantive and Reflexive Elements in Law', *Law and Society Review*, 17, 239–85.

Teubner, G. 1986. 'After Legal Instrumentalism?' in G. Teubner (ed.), *Dilemmas of the Welfare State*. Berlin: De Gruyter, pp. 299–325.

Thompson, E. 1990. 'Ministers, Bureaucrats and Policy-making' in J. Summers, D. Woodward and A. Parkin (eds), *Government, Politics and Power in Australia*. Melbourne: Longman Cheshire (4th edition), pp. 43–55.

Thompson, P. 1986. *Myles Dunphy: Selected Writings*. Sydney: Ballagirin.

Tiver, P. G. 1978. *The Liberal Party: Principles and Performance*. Milton, Qld: Jacaranda.

Tolba, M. K. 1989. 'Engagement und Sensibilität' in G. Brundtland, P. Ehrlich, A. Schreiber and H. Schreiber (eds), *Die Umwelt bewahren*. Saarbrücken: Breitenbach, pp. 11–19.

Touraine, A. 1974. *The Post-Industrial Society*. London: Wildwood House.

Touraine, A. 1981. *The Voice and The Eye*. Cambridge: Cambridge University Press.

Toyne, P. 1994. *The Reluctant Nation*. Sydney: ABC Books.

Turner, J. H. 1986. *The Structure of Sociological Theory*. Chicago: The Dorsey Press (4th edition).

Valder, J. 1983. *Liberal Party of Australia. Report of the Committee of Review. Facing the Facts*. Canberra: Liberal Party of Australia.

Van Krieken, R. 1991. 'The Poverty of Social Control: Explaining Power in the Historical Sociology of the Welfare State', *Sociological Review*, 39, 1–25.

Ward, I. 1991. 'The Changing Organisational Structure of Australia's Political Parties', *Journal of Commonwealth and Comparative Politics*, 29, 153–74.

Warhurst, J. 1990. 'The National Campaign' in C. Bean, I. McAllister and J. Warhurst (eds), *The Greening of Australian Politics: The 1990 Federal Election*. Melbourne: Longman Cheshire, pp. 17–32.

Warhurst, J. 1994a. 'The Australian Conservation Foundation: The Development of a Modern Environmental Interest Group', *Environmental Politics*, 3, 68–90.

Warhurst, J. 1994b. 'The Labor Party' in A. Parkin, J. Summers and D. Woodward (eds), *Government, Politics, Power and Politics in Australia*. Melbourne: Longman Cheshire (5th edition), pp. 139–59.

Weber, M. 1904 (1949). '"Objectivity" in Social Science and Social Policy', in *The Methodology of the Social Sciences*. Glencoe, Ill.: Free Press.

Weissberg, R. 1976. *Public Opinion and Popular Government*. Englewood Cliffs, N.J.: Prentice-Hall.

Weizsäcker, E. U. von. 1994. *Earth Politics*. London: Zed Books.

Weller, P. 1990. 'Cabinet and the Prime Minister' in J. Summers, D. Woodward and A. Parkin (eds), *Government, Politics and Power in Australia*. Melbourne: Longman Cheshire (4th edition), pp. 28–42.

Weller, P. 1993. 'Reforming the Public Service: What Has Been Achieved and How Can It Be Evaluated?' in P. Weller, J. Forster and G. Davis (eds), *Reforming the Public Service*. Melbourne: Macmillan, pp. 222–36.

Whitelock, D. 1985. *Conquest to Conservation: History of Human Impact on the South Australian Environment*. Cowandilla: Wakefield Press.

Wilson, J. Q. (ed.) 1980. *The Politics of Regulation*. New York: Basic Books.

Woodward, D. 1985. 'The Federal National Party' in Costar and Woodward (eds), 1985, pp. 54–67.

Woodward, D. 1990. 'The Australian Labor Party', in J. Summers, D. Woodward and A. Parkin (eds), *Government, Politics and Power in Australia.* Melbourne: Longman Cheshire (4th edition), pp. 156–65.

World Commission on Environment and Development. 1990. *Our Common Future.* Melbourne: Oxford University Press.

Yankelovich, D. 1991. *Coming to Public Judgement.* Syracuse: Syracuse University Press.

Zaller, J. 1992. *The Nature and Origins of Mass Opinion.* Cambridge: Cambridge University Press.

Index